Lesbian Realities/
Lesbian Fictions
in Contemporary Spain

Lesbian Realities/ Lesbian Fictions in Contemporary Spain

Edited by Nancy Vosburg and Jacky Collins

Lewisburg
BUCKNELL UNIVERSITY PRESS

Published by Bucknell University Press
Co-published with The Rowman & Littlefield Publishing Group, Inc.
4501 Forbes Boulevard, Suite 200, Lanham, Maryland 20706
www.rlpgbooks.com

Estover Road, Plymouth PL6 7PY, United Kingdom

British Library Cataloguing in Publication Information Available

Library of Congress Cataloging-in-Publication Data Available

ISBN: 978-1-61148-020-7 (cloth : alk. paper)
ISBN: 978-1-61148-021-4 (electronic)

♾ ™ The paper used in this publication meets the minimum requirements of
American National Standard for Information Sciences—Permanence of Paper
for Printed Library Materials, ANSI/NISO Z39.48-1992.

Printed in the United States of America

Contents

Lesbian Realities/
Lesbian Fictions
in Contemporary Spain

Introduction
Nancy Vosburg and Jacky Collins

Lesbian Identity in Spain

On july 3, 2005, during the administration of the socialist party (PSOE) under the leadership of Socialist Prime Minister Luis Zapatero Rodríguez, the Spanish parliament passed legislation entitling same-sex couples to marry and to receive all the attendant benefits previously afforded only heterosexual married couples. In doing so, Spain became only the fourth country in Europe to legislate same-sex marriage rights to date, the others being the Netherlands, Belgium, and Norway. This was a turn of events which no doubt left the demised dictator Francisco Franco, who had ruled Spain with an iron fist during his almost forty years as head of state (1937–75) and had subjected gays and lesbians to homophobic laws proclaiming them "dangerous," spinning in his grave. The end of the dictatorship had brought about a surge of vindications, with gay rights groups emerging from the underground, organizing and demonstrating until the social and political pressure engendered culminated in the passing of the current marriage law. Notwithstanding these momentous developments, impacting the lives of both gays and lesbians, at the turn of the millennium, little information was available outside Spain, or in English, on lesbian culture within the Iberian peninsula.

One of the principal obstacles to tracing the development of lesbian identities has been the invisibility of women's relationships, both heterosexual and homosexual, throughout history. This has been particularly evident in contemporary Spain, where, as Annie Brooksbank Jones has commented, "lesbians and lesbian feminists have had a low profile."[1] Chris Perriam has observed that in Spain, as in many European countries, lesbians—in contrast to gay men—have lacked a public voice or space where they are able to express themselves as lesbians.[2] Indeed, until recently much about this sector of society has remained veiled; at the beginning of the 1990s, in an article on the lesbian

9

community in Spain in the mainstream national newspaper *El País*, Rosa Montero described lesbianism as "una homosexualidad oculta" [a hidden homosexuality].[3] It is important to distinguish between the experiences of gay men and lesbians, since as Montero explains "[m]ientras los *gay* han normalizado considerablemente su situación y su presencia, las lesbianas continúan de algún modo en la clandestinidad" [19; while gay men have normalized considerably their situation and presence, lesbians continue in some way in secret]. Further, as Carmen G. Hernández reveals, gay men have fought publicly for their rights for many years, while lesbians, although actively supportive of gay men and feminist organizations in their political activism, have until recently lacked their own voice and space in Spanish society.[4] Paradoxically, lesbian involvement in these two movements during the decades following the end of the dictatorship can be seen to have contributed to the problem of lesbian invisibility, since despite lesbian support, the gay and feminist movements in fact did little to represent or foreground lesbian identity and sexuality.

Nevertheless, as Mili Hernandez has commented, towards the end of the 1990s, advances were beginning to be made as gay and lesbian organizations acknowledged the need to bring the issue of lesbian visibility to the forefront of public debate as part of their social and political agendas.[5] A decade on from the Montero article, evidence of an emerging lesbian identity can be gleaned from a subsequent article in *El País* on lesbian visibility in contemporary Spanish society.[6] However, reference is also made to the limited and limiting essentialist notions of lesbian identity and the need to deconstruct this identity through the application of queer theory. Further observations point to the reluctance of many women, in particular those in the public eye, to own their identity openly and the need for lesbians in Spain to voice their demands for equal citizenship rights and civil liberties (46).

Diane Richardson has identified a number of specific conditions necessary for the emergence of specific sexual/social movements: a decline in the influence of the family and religious institutions in defining and determining people's lives; the emergence of a community that supports this sense of self; a measure of economic prosperity that allows some degree of independence and social mobility and a level of social tolerance of difference and pluralism.[7] As a result of the transformation that Spanish society underwent with the restoration of democracy, such conditions could be said to have been established, thus fostering the emergence of a lesbian and gay movement that has advanced, gained momentum and transformed over the last three decades. It is within the context of this movement, and the societal and legislative changes it has given rise to, that it has since become possible to map the development of a lesbian identity in Spain.

The groups which organize around sexual identities in Spain remain predominantly of mixed gender, meaning they tend to join together under the "GLTB" categorization. However, the lesbian membership frequently constitutes a minority element within larger groups. This gender imbalance is further highlighted by the fact that, since the decriminalization of lesbian and gay organizations in 1981, although the Spanish gay male identity has progressed from an initial position of being stereotyped to enjoying greater acceptance and diversification, it is only during the last fifteen years that it has been possible to refer to the emergence of a specific lesbian identity.

Although the notion of queer identities was first mooted in Spain a decade ago, the adoption of the term "queer," or the Spanish equivalent "bollo/marica," has been problematic, as demonstrated by the limited number of groups that have taken on this label. A key aim of most GLTB activist groups is to work toward "normalization" and integration into mainstream society, an approach which runs contrary to queer politics' resistance to such notions. Nevertheless, the majority of such groups do seem willing to adopt certain queer concepts, such as plurality and diversity, which has led to the process of deconstructing gay and (to a lesser extent) lesbian identities.[8] Indeed, among younger Spanish lesbians there is a growing tendency to reject the former stereotypical butch or masculine appearance traditionally associated with lesbian identity, and with it the term "camionera" [diesel dyke].

Moreover, as a result of the feeling of discontent that grew among lesbian groups in reaction to Montero's article in *El País*, during the mid-1990s such groups, in particular in Barcelona and Madrid, carried out various campaigns which took up the issue of lesbian visibility within Spanish society seeking to "romper con los estereotipos que envuelven a la homosexualidad femenina dando a conocer [. . .] *la diversidad del mundo lésbico; y reivindicar los mismos derechos y una plena aceptación social*" [break with the stereotypes that encompass female homosexuality to reveal . . . the diversity of the lesbian world; and claim equal rights and complete social acceptance].[9] As part of these campaigns, El Grupo Lesbos [The Lesbos Group]—one of the three main lesbian groups in Barcelona at the time—celebrated the Jornadas de Visibilidad del Lesbianismo [Lesbianism Visibility Conference] on March 25–26, 1995. This gathering, as did similar groups at the time, rejected the notion of a homogeneous lesbian identity, preferring to acknowledge a spectrum of identities around the construct of lesbian. Further, until the end of the decade, these debates often failed to examine the question of lesbian sexuality; and even when addressed, it was often concluded that sexual practices were a matter of personal choice rather than being open to public debate, neither the feminist nor the lesbian movements in Spain having at that time developed a politics of desire. As Viñuales has argued, Spanish radical feminism still perceives female identity as homogeneous in order to maintain its ideology of being the voice of every woman, thus negating the existence of diversity among women (80). Against this background, the concept and diversity of Spanish lesbian identity warrants a more in-depth treatment, and it is the aim of this anthology to provide a significant and coherent contribution to the body of knowledge within an evolving subject area that has heretofore been relatively underresearched.

THE DEVELOPMENT OF A LESBIAN LITERARY TRADITION

The representation of lesbians in Spanish literature in the second half of the twentieth-century can be divided into three different periods: the years 1964–75, the last decade of the dictatorship of Francisco Franco; the years of the "transition" from dictatorship to democracy, 1975–85; and the mid-1980s to the present.

The first period was characterized by the emergence of lesbian figures that represented a morally censurable and prohibited world and were generally cast under a veil of disapproval. In essence, these lesbian characters echoed the social situation confronted by women who opted to make public their sexual orientation. In Ana María Matute's 1964 novel, *Los soldados lloran de noche* [The Soldiers Cry at Night], for example, Marta recalls the relationship between her mother, Elena, and Dionisia, a woman who because of her suspicious social activities breaks with the "decent woman" image (perfect wife/ideal mother) imposed by the Francoist morality. When Dionisia attempts to seduce the eighteen-year-old Marta, she becomes a morally reprehensible and perverse figure who ruptures the socially dominant "order" of the period.

In Teresa Barbero's *El último verano en el espejo* [The Last Summer in the Mirror], a finalist for the 1967 Premio Nadal, the word "lesbian" is used for the first time in the post-war period. While the protagonist recounts her own initial sexual awakening with another student in a religious school for girls, it is clear that societal pressure to conform to the Francoist morality is still problematic, as the two students are seen by other characters as "mujeres malas" [bad women]. Ana María Moix's 1969 novel, *Julia*, also depicts the isolation and marginalization of the eponymous narrator, whose lesbian desires, first for her aunt and later for her professor, must be coaxed out of the silences of the text.

Other novels from this morally constrained period include María Luz Malecón's *Celia muerde la manzana* [Celia Bites the Apple] from 1972, in which lesbian characters are depicted as products of traumatic experiences or bad influences, and Montserrat Roig's 1976 novel, *Tiempo de cerezas* [Time of the Cherries], which recuperates Teresa Barbero's cliché of sexual encounters between students in the religious schools.

With Franco's death in 1975, the beginning of the political transition to democracy in Spain, and the first Jornadas de la Liberación de la Mujer [Women's Liberation Conference] in Madrid, the development of a feminist consciousness and the backlash against the sexual repression of the dictatorship resulted in new narratives that presented more complex lesbian characters, opening the way to what may be considered a true lesbian literature. No longer are lesbians depicted as innocent school girls or as ostracized, traumatized, marginalized, or perverse figures. On the contrary, lesbian characters created during this second period emerge from ignominy and infamy to become fully developed women who are conscious of their sexual desires and who fight to consummate them. While they are not always successful in achieving their desires, they at least represent and anticipate a new universe of possibilities for the lesbian subject.

Within this framework of new possibilities, Carme Riera's two epistolary short stories, "Te dejo, amor, en prenda la mar" [I Leave You, My Love, the Sea as a Token] (1975) and "Pongo por testigo a las gaviotas" [The Seagulls as My Witnesses] (1977), evoke the lesbian relationship that existed some years before between a professor and her student. While the social and moral constraints of the late 1960s still prevail, and despite the ambiguity created by Riera in her use of pronouns and proper names in the original Catalan texts, the stories present us with characters who are fully integrated social subjects. Their relationship is sensual, erotic, and suggestive of new possibilities in the complex of human relationships.

Perhaps the most significant novel during the second period identified is Esther Tusquets's *El mismo mar de todos los veranos* [The Same Sea as Every Summer] (1978). Until this moment, no author in Spain had represented lesbian sexuality in such an explicit manner. A complex novel characterized by an almost baroque style, the text presents us with a mature woman who, because of her privileged economic and social status, has the liberty to engage in a relationship with a much younger woman as a means of rebelling against the stunted and rigid social taboos of the Catalan aristocracy. After living a passionate amorous adventure with her young Colombian student, however, the narrator is forced to return to her fold, not because of her fear of social marginalization, but rather because of the weight of the same socioeconomic ties that allowed her to rebel in the first place.

Although Tusquets wrote two additional novels exploring female sexuality that form a trilogy with the aforementioned novel, she does not return to an explicitly lesbian character until her 1981 collection, *Siete miradas en un mismo paisaje* [Seven Views of the Same Landscape]. In only one of the seven stories, "En la ciudad sin mar" [In the City without a Sea], do we find the common protagonist of the collection, Sara, living a passionate lesbian relationship. In contrast to Tusquets's first novel, the story ends with Sara's certainty that she has committed the greatest error of her life by abandoning Roxana, thus validating the lesbian relationship depicted.

Published almost simultaneously with Tusquets's collection of short stories, *12 relatos de mujeres* [12 Women's Short Stories] (1982), compiled by Ymelda Navajo, contains three stories that center on lesbian desire: Carme Riera's "El reportaje" [The Report], Ana María Moix's "Las virtudes peligrosas" [Dangerous Virtues], and Marta Pessarrodona's "La búsqueda de Elizabeth" [Searching for Elizabeth]. In all three the lesbian characters appear to be much more independent than in the first period described, but they still lack complete freedom to pursue their desires. Still, the lesbian relationships represented during this second period are no longer the result of an abnormal psychology that must be clinically justified or morally condemned but rather are presented as an integral part of female experience, and as such, as worthy of being recognized and validated. Along the same lines we can cite an additional short story from this period, Monserrat Roig's "Mar" [Sea], written in 1980 but published in the 1990 collection *El canto de la juventud* [Youth's Song], which describes the profound love and friendship between two young friends, who both recognize its lesbian nature. Marina Mayoral's 1982 novel, *Recóndita armonía* [Hidden Harmony], likewise recounts the friendship that unites two women, portraying their sexual encounters as a logical extension of the love they share.

The social and political changes of the 1980s and 90s in Spain were vertiginous and brought with them new attitudes toward equality for gays and lesbians in Spain. Our anthology addresses many of these achievements as we attempt to situate the diversity of Spanish lesbians in politics, society, the media, and literary works of the 1990s and the new millennium.

OVERVIEW OF THE CRITICAL ESSAYS IN THE ANTHOLOGY

Lesbian Realities/Lesbian Fictions in Contemporary Spain is dedicated solely to the emergence of lesbian identities and cultures in Spain since the late 1980s. Although this is not the first academic study to examine such issues, we believe that it is unique in its singular focus and range of topics. To demonstrate the originality of our collection, we should like to offer an overview of major earlier and contemporary texts that contain studies on Spanish lesbian identities and cultural production. One of the first academic publications in English (or Spanish) to focus explicitly on lesbian desire and the lesbian body in contemporary Spanish culture is Paul Julian Smith's *Laws of Desire: Questions of Homosexuality in Spanish Writing and Film 1960–1990*.[10] This pioneering study presented radically new readings of the lesbian subject in the works of the author Esther Tusquets and director Pedro Almodóvar. Subsequent to this, a number of multidisciplinary texts have been published in English and Spanish, addressing issues such as the Spanish gay and lesbian movement, Hispanic lesbian literature, Spanish lesbian identities, and sociological studies and self-help for gays and lesbians.

Two English-language volumes published by Duke University in the 1990s provide an extensive range of essays on Hispanic culture. The first, *¡Entiendes? Queer Readings, Hispanic Writings*, explores issues around gay and lesbian Spanish and Hispanic literature, with specific contributions on lesbian identity focusing on Cervantes' *Don Quijote,* Latina cultural production, and the works of Latin American writers Gabriela Mistral, Teresa de la Parra, Alexandra Pizarnik, and Carmen Lugo Filippi.[11] Only one study in the volume, an essay by Brad Epps, examines more recent Spanish lesbian literature—in this case a text published at the time of the Transition—the writer suggesting that Carme Riera's *Te deix, amor, la mar com a penyora* presents a lesbian subject and lesbian sexuality in a virtual state.[12] The essays that constitute the second anthology, *Hispanisms and Homosexualities,* embrace a remarkable geographical and historical scope in their examination of gay, lesbian, bisexual, transgender, and queer themes within the context of the Spanish-speaking world.[13] Lesbian identity and desire are analyzed in texts from Spain's Golden Age and from Puerto Rican narrative of the mid-twentieth century, as well as in the work of Argentinean film director María Luisa Bemberg. However, in this volume there is no specific focus on similar cultural manifestations from present day Spain. In *Reading and Writing the Ambiente: Queer Sexualities in Latino, Latin American and Spanish Culture,* published at the turn of the millennium, just over half the essays explore lesbian themes within the contexts of early modern Spanish literature, Spanish Golden Age texts, the work of Chilean poet Gabriela Mistral, Chicana lesbian literature, and Cuban performance art.[14] As with *¡Entiendes?,* only one contributor discusses lesbian desire within the context of Spanish texts produced in the late 1970s. Thus, in focusing exclusively on contemporary Spanish lesbian cultural production, *Lesbian Realities/Lesbian Fictions in Contemporary Spain* offers a significant body of research into the contemporary Spanish lesbian subject, as redress for an absence evident in previous volumes published in English.

Analyses of lesbian identities and cultures in Spanish society have also been included as part of other publications, yet almost all of these volumes have been published in Spanish, with little information available to the non-Spanish speaker. Of such works, Xosé M. Buxán's edited volume, *conCiencia de un singular deseo: estudios lesbianos y gays en el estado español* [Consciousness/With Science of a Singular Desire: Lesbian and Gay Studies in the Spanish State], often deemed one of the earliest significant academic texts on the subject, presents perhaps the first collection of scholarly essays published in Spain to examine male and female homosexuality, in literature, art, history, politics, and sociology.[15] A further pioneering text, *Identidad y diferencia: Sobre la cultura gay en España* [Identity and Difference: About Gay Culture in Spain], examines aspects of the gay and lesbian collective as a symptom of societal change that had occurred since the reestablishment of democracy in Spain in the late 1970s.[16] A more recent publication, Jordi Petit's *25 años más:Una perspectiva sobre el pasado, el presente y el futuro del movimiento de gays, lesbianas, bisexuales y transexuales* [25 More Years: A Perspective on the Past, Present and Future of the Gay, Lesbian, Bisexual and Transsexual Movement], provides an analysis of the main factors contributing to the emergence and development of Spain's gay, lesbian, transgender, and bisexual movement, from 1977 to the present, as well as the author's views about how the movement is still relevant and what it should do to bolster its campaign for equal rights.[17] Published first in 2004 and now in its second edition, *De Sodoma a Chueca: Una historia cultural de la homosexualidad en España en el siglo XX* [From Sodom to Chueca: A Cultural History of Homosexuality in Spain in the Twentieth Century] presents an in-depth study of the history of homosexuality in Spain. However, in this volume Alberto Mira presents little, if any, treatment of lesbianism, defending this approach as being due to the constraints of focusing specifically on male homosexuality, and subsequently calling for a dedicated study of "la historia del lesbianismo en nuestro país" [the history of lesbianism in our country].[18] Therefore, while the importance of these texts is not in question, the tokenism of any references to lesbians or lesbianism and the texts' evident gender/sexuality imbalance in favor of the male, points to the need for a text that directly addresses the lesbian subject.

Como se vive la homosexualidad y el lesbianismo [How Homosexuality and Lesbianism Are Lived] was published as one of a series of books on sexology, at a time when questions around homosexuality and same-sex relationships were beginning to attract more widespread public debate.[19] The author, Sonia Soriano Rubio, provided a sociological overview of what it meant to be living as a gay or lesbian in Spain at the end of the twentieth century. Another publication appearing in the same year, albeit with a more personalized tone, was Alfonso Llopart's *Salir del armario* [Coming Out of the Closet], containing first-hand accounts of experiences from gay and lesbian life, and focusing in particular on the concept and consequences of "coming out" in mainstream Spanish society.[20] Begoña Pérez Sancho's *Homosex-ualidad: Secreto de familia* [Homosexuality: The Family Secret] brought together the findings of an extensive period of sociological research focusing on how the issue of homosexuality is handled within the context of the family in Spain.[21] Thus, while mention is made of male and female experiences in all three of these publications, once again it is the gay male voice that considerably outweighs that of the lesbian.

Regarding publications whose core focus is on lesbians rather than gay men, there have been a number of key texts published during the current decade; however, these tend to focus either on one specific aspect of lesbian life or to include reference to lesbian cultures both within and outside Spain. Olga Viñuales's *Identidades lésbicas: Discursos y prácticas* [Lesbian Identities: Discourses and Practices], Jennifer Quiles's *Más que amigas* [More Than Just Friends], and more recently Inmaculada Mujika Flores's *Visibilidad y participación social de las mujeres lesbianas en Euskadi* [Visibility and Social Participation of Lesbian Women in the Basque Country] represent three groundbreaking Spanish-language texts.[22] The first publication offers a sociological analysis of lesbian identity and behavior in Barcelona, Spain, while the second provides a compendium of information regarding lesbianism and bisexuality, including references to lesbian cultural production from the Spanish-speaking world and beyond. This latter, easily accessible text, almost a lesbian handbook, addresses questions of sexuality, identity, lifestyles, and inequality. The third volume, the result of a fifteen-month sociological study carried out in the Basque Country, draws the somewhat perturbing conclusion that "la presencia de mujeres lesbianas con reconocimiento social, político, cultural o económico es casi nula" [the presence of lesbian women with social, political, cultural, or economic recognition is almost zero].[23]

With specific focus on the lesbian narrative, Inmaculada Pertusa's *La salida del armario: Lecturas desde la otra acera* [Coming Out of the Closet: Readings from the Other Sidewalk] contributes to the study of cultural manifestations of lesbian identities in Spain by presenting a close textual analysis of significant novels from three contemporary Spanish female writers and one Latin American novelist.[24] Also published in Spanish, *Un deseo propio: Antología de escritoras españolas contemporáneas* [A Desire of One's Own: Anthology of Contemporary Spanish Female Writers] addresses the theme of lesbian desire as manifested in the works of a range of Spanish female authors from the mid-1960s to the present day.[25]

To date, there have been perhaps only two important publications that engage with Spanish lesbian culture in the English language: *Tortilleras: Hispanic and U.S. Latina Lesbian Expression* and *Queer Transitions in Contemporary Spanish Culture: From Franco to la Movida*.[26] The former was the first anthology to focus exclusively on queer readings of the works of lesbian writers and performance artists throughout the Spanish-speaking world. *Queer Transitions*, on the other hand, studies the defining role that urban queer culture played in the cultural and political processes that helped move Spain from a premodern, fascist military dictatorship to a late-capitalist, parliamentary democracy in the late 1970s and early 1980s. This is one of the few texts which, while addressing GLTBQ culture overall, gives priority to the study of women authors and sequential artists dealing with lesbianism.

Finally, mention should be made of two anthologies in the Spanish language that focus on emerging lesbian identities and cultures. In 2007 the publishers Editorial Laertes brought out Angie Simonis's edited volume *Cultura, homosexualidad y homofobia, Vol. 2, Amazonia: Retos de la visibilidad lesbiana* [Culture, Homosexuality and Homophobia. Vol. 2. Amazonia: Challenges to Lesbian Visibility], perhaps the first work from Spain to focus exclusively on the question of lesbian visibility in Spanish society.[27] Even more recently *Lesbianas: Discursos y representaciones* [Lesbians: Discourses and Representations], edited by Raquel Platero, likewise focuses solely on lesbian cultures in Spain, offering a number of historical, literary, organizational, and theoretical perspectives on the subject.[28]

By presenting a volume in English, our collection, while covering similar aspects, parallels and complements the Simonis and Platero anthologies, bringing together a range of previously unpublished essays written specifically for this publication. *Lesbian Realities/Lesbian Fictions in Contemporary Spain* represents a valuable contribution to research in the field by bringing knowledge into the public domain that has hitherto lacked the same level of examination as gay male identities in Spain. Further, it provides access to this area of discourse to a readership that is interested in social and cultural change in Spain but is unable to access material in Spanish.

Those contributing to our project, some of whom are leading voices in the field, all have involvement in either researching or developing lesbian cultures in Spain. Throughout the anthology, the visibility of the lesbian subject in Spain, either within the media, literature, Parliament, or even within the gay-book-publishing industry, emerges as a key concept for analyzing the status of lesbians in Spanish society. Part I of *Lesbian Realities/ Lesbian Fictions in Contemporary Spain*, as the title suggests, focuses on the realities of lesbian lives at the turn of the millennium.

Our collection opens with essays from two of the most exciting voices emerging in the field from U.S. and Spanish academia. In the lead essay, "Representation and the Politics of Visibility," Margaret G. Frohlich presents a challenging analysis of the politics of lesbian representation in Spanish culture. Focusing predominantly on literature, she explores the problematic of lesbian narrative and representation. In addition, by examining instances of visually oriented culture, Frohlich provides a compelling study of the paradoxical combination of increasing lesbian visibility and persisting lesbophobia in postdictatorial Spain and the pervasive role of economics in this equation.

Similarly, with the second chapter, "Transitions and Representations of Lesbianism in the Spanish Media," Raquel Platero Méndez, one of the most interesting new queer-studies voices emerging from Spain, examines the way in which lesbians have been portrayed within the Spanish media, primarily in advertising, pornography, the news, and reality shows. Platero maintains that the media does not show reality but rather constructions of reality, in this case representations of an idea of what it is to be a lesbian. By examining such representations and how they become a part of the social imaginary, she demonstrates how lesbian identities in Spain are formed and reproduced.

With "Living Out/Off Chueca," Marta Sofía López Rodríguez andYolanda Sánchez Paz, a professor and a bar-owner respectively, combine social scientific methodology with the genre of interview and testimonial to provide an essay that challenges usual academic conventions. This inventive collaborative piece examines "lesbianism" as both a metaphorical sociosymbolic space from which heteropatriarchy can be contested and as a literal geographic reference to examine perceptions of lesbians and the construction of a lesbian community outside the Spanish capital with its highly visible gay neighborhood, Chueca. Offering a different perspective on lesbian lives and realities, situated at a distance from the more progressive major urban areas of

Spain, their conclusion echoes arguments presented by Frohlich, that achieving lesbian visibility perhaps comes at a price.

Sociolinguist Encarnación Hidalgo-Tenorio provides an essay from quite a different discipline from the others in the volume. "Politics and Language: The Representation of Some 'Others' in the Spanish Parliament" strives to document how homosexuals in general, and lesbians in particular, were represented in speeches delivered in sessions of the Spanish Parliament leading up to the 2005 legislation on same-sex marriage. Critical linguists and critical discourse analysts have proved how differently the same event or phenomenon can be represented by means of (linguistic) devices that suggest the ideology of the author as reflected in their discourse. Despite well-argued opposition by some scholars, Hidalgo-Tenorio maintains that it is the user's choice of vocabulary and syntactic structures (conscious or not) and the very way in which they arrange information (among other interesting features) that show how someone conceives of the world and other people and how they generally construct themselves and depict the Other. This essay also examines the visibility of lesbian subjects from a range of manifestations of Spanish popular culture.

Finally, in this section the essay "Lesbian Literary Identities in the Chueca Book Business" by the established critic and scholar Jill Robbins—which could be said to function as a transitional piece between Part I of the volume (lesbian realities) and Part II (lesbian fictions)—explores the role of a particular gay/lesbian bookstore, Berkana, in the construction of Madrid's "queer literary spaces," those areas of the city—the Chueca neighborhood, in particular—that have transformed and been transformed by queer social and cultural practices, including literary writing and reading. Drawing on the work of such theorists as Henri Lefebvre and Michel de Certeau, both of whom associate the social and symbolic construction of urban life with art, and specifically with literature, Robbins examines the image of lesbian Madrid that emerges where networks linking Spain's imperial past and neoliberal present intersect with gender, race, and sexuality in literary spaces. These cross-sections are implicit in the clash of economic, political, and aesthetic values in gay/lesbian bookstores, which manifest themselves in their layout, stock, location, and functions, as well as in their publishing policies, all of which have tended to maintain a homogeneous image of lesbianism, to eliminate bisexuality, and to marginalize women in relation to gay men.

Part II of *Lesbian Realities/Lesbian Fictions in Contemporary Spain* focuses on lesbian literature at the turn of the new century. The lead essay in this section, Jacky Collins's " 'Sisters are doing it for themselves': Lesbian Identities in Contemporary Spanish Literature," explores how, within the context of contemporary Spanish literature, the lesbian subject has begun to emerge from obscurity and is now challenging the system that for so long denied her existence. The significant increase in the number of lesbian texts that have emerged by Spanish lesbian authors in the last decade allows her to examine the textual configuration of a Spanish lesbian body. Collins maintains that these writings grant the lesbian body—or rather bodies—a corporeality or presence that works to resist the eradication always threatened by the dominant patriarchal order. She examines a variety of lesbian texts published in the last ten years to demonstrate how the once-marginalized lesbian body has moved to the center of the text, allowing for the construction of a lesbian subjectivity and the development of both social and sexual lesbian identities.[29]

The remaining essays focus on key individual lesbian authors. " 'All L Breaks Loose': Lola Van Guardia's Lesbian Trilogy," by Nancy Vosburg, provides an overview of this landmark trilogy from the perspective of its innovative approach in presenting and critiquing not only its target audience, the lesbian community in Spain, but the larger sociopolitical community that surrounds Van Guardia's humorous characters. The author demonstrates how these popular texts break with previous lesbian narratives, serving to "normalize" this previously demonized identity and to encourage real-life Spanish lesbians in prominent positions, who are still in the closet, to openly acknowledge their sexuality. Further, she suggests that through the use of parody and humor, this postmodern trilogy serves to offer an alternative reality that defies the constraints of the gender binary and heteronormativity.

Carme Riera has won critical acclaim as a provocative writer, one who began pushing the envelope around the consideration of feminine identity and cultural agency in Spain following Franco's dictatorship in 1975. Two of the writer's most examined tales, "Te dejo, amor, en prenda el mar" and "Y pongo por testigo a las gaviotas" dialogue with each other as each describes a lesbian love relationship between an adolescent girl and an older woman. Curiously, "Gloria," another tale of a lesbian relationship published around the same time as these, has received little critical consideration, this inattention perhaps due to the tale's emphasis on shifting erotic desire and gender identity. María DiFrancesco's "The Aesthetics of Murder in Carme Riera's 'Gloria': Writing Sexually Subversive Violence," casts a critical eye on what this story reveals about feminine identities and sexualities.

Flavia Company is another well-known Spanish writer and literary critic from Catalonia, whose novels affirm the possibility of sexual expressions that exceed the predominant heterosexual norms. In Company's creative universe it is less necessary to recognize the differences that make the works so original than to determine the similarities that connect them and, more concretely, to establish the subversive elements of each text that model the destabilization of the power strategies of the dominant heterosexual discourse in which they are inscribed. In the final essay in our volume, "Flavia Company: From Lesbian Passion to Gender Trouble," Inmaculada Pertusa-Seva draws on Judith Butler's theories of gender performance and gender trouble to skillfully examine three novels by this prolific author.

Finally, we would be negligent indeed if we failed to acknowledge in this volume two of the most influential Spanish texts to appear in recent years within the field of identity and sexuality, *Manifiesto contra-sexual* and *Testo yonqui*, written by the philosopher and queer activist Beatriz Preciado.[30] The first text is based on research undertaken by the author in France and the United States as part of her studies in the area of queer theory. With the later publication Preciado, focusing on constructs such as the body, sex, and sexuality, posits a new social and political order. Despite the undeniable importance of her writing and the relevance that it has for Spain's GLTB community and the wider population, its transnational scope does not allow for any detailed treatment of lesbian identities and cultural manifestations in contemporary Spanish society, the particular focus of this volume.

While queer theory undeniably removes the restrictions of fixed notions of identity, there is inevitably an inherent danger that such a powerful, all-embracing construct can overwhelm gay and lesbian identities along with their concomitant implications of self-identity and community. With that in mind, our intention in compiling this volume is not to deny, underestimate, or ignore the importance of 'queer' in the study of gender and identity in Hispanic studies; indeed many of the contributors here work with queer theory in their research and analysis.

However, as bell hooks cautions, 'It's easy to give up identity when you have one'; given that lesbian identities in present-day Spain are some way from being what could be considered established, we have chosen to privilege the term "lesbian" over "queer."[31] To apply the umbrella term "queer" to these fledgling identities could prove costly, for as María Castrejón remarks, "La teoría [queer] favorece a todos porque no habla de nadie en concreto, no excluye a nadie porque a nadie incluye" [queer theory privileges all because it talks of no one specifically, it excludes no one because it includes no one].[32] Consequently, whereas others rightly argue and employ the liberating properties of "queer," we wish to foreground a subject that we believe remains relatively silenced. Indeed as Simonis insists, when commenting on the lack of contributions in academic publications on the subject of lesbian identities and cultural manifestations in Spain, "un libro aparte merecíamos las lesbianas" [14; we lesbians needed a book just for ourselves].[33] To that end, with *Lesbian Realities/Lesbian Fictions in Contemporary Spain,* our aim has been to provide just such a volume.

NOTES

1. Annie Brooksbank Jones, *Women in Contemporary Spain* (Manchester: Manchester University Press, 1997), 118.
2. Chris Perriam, "Gay and Lesbian Culture," *Spanish Cultural Studies: An Introduction,* eds. Helen Graham and Jo Labanyi, 393–95 (Oxford: Oxford University Press, 1995).
3. Rosa Montero, "El misterio del deseo: Así son y así viven las lesbianas en España," *El País Semanal* (October 31, 1993):16–28. Further references to this publication will be documented parenthetically within text.
4. Carmen G. Hernández, "Al armario de nuevo: la invisibilidad de las activistas lesbianas en la construcción histórica del movimiento LGTB español," in *Cultura, homosexualidad y homofobia, vol. 2, Amazonia: Retos de la visibilidad lesbiana,* ed. Angie Simonis, 55–89 (Barcelona: Laertes, 2007).
5. Mili Hernández, "Voces y ecos de la comunidad gay en españa," in *Identidad y diferencia,* eds. Juan Vicente Aliaga and José Miguel G. Cortes, 201 (Barcelona: Egales, 1997).
6. Luz Sánchez Mellado, "Lesbiana sin complejos," *El País Semanal* (June 29, 2003). Further references to this publication will be documented parenthetically within text.
7. Diane Richardson, *Rethinking Sexuality* (London: Sage, 2000), 47.
8. Ricardo Llamas, *Teoría torcida: Prejuicios y discusiones en torno a la homosexualidad* (Madrid: Siglo XXI/De España Editores, 1998), 375.
9. Olga Viñuales, *Identidades lésbicas: Discursos y prácticas* (Barcelona: Edicions Bellaterra, 2000), 78. Further references to this publication will be documented parenthetically within text.

10. Paul Julian Smith, *Laws of Desire: Questions of Homosexuality in Spanish Writing and Film 1960–1990* (Oxford: Oxford University Press, 1992).

11. Emilie Bergman and Paul Julian Smith, eds., *¿Entiendes? Queer Readings, Hispanic Writings* (Durham, NC: Duke University Press, 1995).

12. Carme Riera's work was first published in Catalan under this title; subsequent publications in Castilian bore the title *Te dejo, amor, en prenda la mar*. Both titles appear in this introduction according to whether the Catalan or Castilian text is being cited.

13. Sylvia Molloy and Robert McKee Irwin, eds., *Hispanisms and Homosexualities* (Durham, NC: Duke University Press, 1998).

14. Susana Chávez-Silverman and Librada Hernández, eds., *Reading and Writing the Ambiente: Queer Sexualities in Latino, Latin American and Spanish Culture* (Madison: University of Wisconsin Press), 2000.

15. Xosé M. Buxán, ed., *conCiencia de un singular deseo: Estudios lesbianos y gays en el estado español* (Barcelona: Laertes, 1997).

16. Juan Vicente Aliaga and José Miguel G. Cortés, *Identidad y diferencia: Sobre la cultura gay en España* (Barcelona: Egales, 1997).

17. Jordi Petit, *25 años más: Una perspectiva sobre el pasado, el presente y el futuro del movimiento de gays, lesbianas, bisexuales y transexuales* (Barcelona: Icaria, 2003).

18. Alberto Mira, *De Sodoma a Chueca: Una historia cultural de la homosexualidad en España en el siglo XX*, 2nd ed. (Barcelona: Egales, 2007), 32.

19. Sonia Soriano Rubia, *Como se vive la homosexualidad y el lesbianismo* (Salamanca: Amarú Ediciones, 1999).

20. Alfonso Llopart, *Salir del armario* (Madrid: Temas de Hoy, 1999).

21. Begoña Pérez Sancho, *Homosexualidad: Secreto de familia* (Barcelona: Egales, 2005).

22. Jennifer Quiles, *Más que amigas* (Barcelona: Delbolsillo, 2002); Inmaculada Mujika Flores, *Visibilidad y participación social de las mujeres lesbianas en Euskadi* (Vitoria-Gasteiz, 2007).

23. Inmaculada Mujika Flores, "Las lesbianas deben darse a conocer para ofrecer referentes positivos," *http://www.diariovasco.com/20080115/al-día-sociedad/lesbianas-deben-darse-conocer-20080115.html*.

24. Inmaculada Pertusa, *La salida del armario: lecturas desde la otra acera* (Gijón: Llibros del Pexe, 2005).

25. Inmaculada Pertusa and Nancy Vosburg, *Un deseo propio: Antología de escritoras españolas contemporáneas* (Barcelona: Bruguera, 2009).

26. Lourdes Torres and Inmaculada Pertusa, *Tortilleras: Hispanic and U.S. Latina Lesbian Expression* (Philadelphia: Temple University Press, 2003); Gema Pérez Sánchez, *Queer Transitions in Contemporary Spanish Culture: From Franco to la Movida* (Albany: State University of New York Press, 2007).

27. Angie Simonis, *Cultura, homosexualidad y homofobia. Vol. 2, Amazonia: Retos de la visibilidad lesbiana* (Barcelona: Laertes, 2007).

28. Raquel Platero, ed., *Lesbianas: Discursos y representaciones* (Barcelona: Melusina, 2008).

29. Lola Van Guardia, *Plumas de doble filo* (Barcelona: Egales, 1999); Mabel Galán, *Desde la otra orilla* (Madrid: Odisea, 1999) and *Donde comienza tu nombre* (Madrid: Odisea, 2004); Lais Arcos, *72 horas* (Barcelona: La Tempestad, 2004); Illy Nes, *El lago rosa* (Barcelona: Edicions Bellaterra, 2004); Paz Quintero's *Destino programado* (Barcelona: La Tempestad, 2005).

30. Beatriz Preciado, *Manifiesto contra-sexual* (Madrid: Opera Prima, 2002); *Testo yonqui* (Madrid: Espasa, 2008).

31. bell hooks, *Yearning: Race, Gender and Cultural Politics* (Boston: South End Press, 1990), 28.
32. María Castrejón, *. . . que me estoy muriendo de agua: Guía de narrativa lésbica* (Barcelona: Egales, 2008), 17.
33. Simonis, *Cultura, homosexualidad y homofobia,* 14.

REFERENCES

Aliaga, Juan Vicente, and José Miguel G. Cortés. *Identidad y diferencia: Sobre la cultura gay en España.* Barcelona: Egales, 1997.

Arcos, Lais. *72 horas.* Barcelona: La Tempestad, 2004.

Bergman, Emilie, and Paul Julian Smith, eds. *¿Entiendes? Queer Readings, Hispanic Writings.* Durham, NC: Duke University Press, 1995.

Brooksbank Jones, Annie. *Women in Contemporary Spain.* Manchester: Manchester University Press, 1997.

Buxán, Xosé M., ed. *conCiencia de un singular deseo: Estudios lesbianos y gays en el estado español.* Barcelona: Laertes, 1997.

Castrejón, María. *. . . que me estoy muriendo de agua: Guía de narrativa lésbica.* Barcelona: Egales, 2008.

Chávez-Silverman, Susana, and Librada Hernández, eds. *Reading and Writing the Ambiente: Queer Sexualities in Latino, Latin American and Spanish Culture.* Madison: University of Wisconsin Press, 2000.

Galán, Mabel. *Desde la otra orilla.* Madrid: Odisea, 1999.

———. *Donde comienza tu nombre.* Madrid: Odisea, 2004.

Hernández, Carmen G. "Al armario de nuevo: La invisibilidad de las activistas lesbianas en la construcción histórica del movimiento LGTB español." In *Cultura, homosexualidad y homofobia. Vol. 2, Amazonia: Retos de la visibilidad lesbiana,* edited by Angie Simionis, 55–84. Barcelona: Laertes, 2007.

Hernández, Mili. "Voces y ecos de la comunidad gay en españa." In *Identidad y diferencia,* edited by Juan Vicente Aliaga and Jose Miguel G. Cortes, 201–37. Barcelona: Egales, 1997.

hooks, bell. *Yearning: Race, Gender and Cultural Politics.* Boston: South End Press, 1990.

Llamas, Ricardo. *Teoría torcida: Prejuicios y discusiones en torno a la homosexualidad.* Madrid: Siglo XXI/De España Editores, 1998.

Llopart, Alfonso. *Salir del armario.* Madrid: Temas de Hoy, 1999.

Mira, Alberto. *De Sodoma a Chueca: Una historia cultural de la homosexualidad en España en el siglo XX,* 2nd ed. Barcelona: Egales, 2007.

Molloy, Sylvia, and Robert McKee Irwin, eds. *Hispanisms and Homosexualities.* Durham, NC: Duke University Press, 1998.

Montero, Rosa. "El misterio del deseo: Así son y así viven las lesbianas en España." *El País Semanal* (October 31, 1993): 16–28.

Mujika Flores, Inmaculada. *Visibilidad y participación social de las mujeres lesbianas en Euskadi.* Vitoria-Gasteiz, 2007.

———. "Las lesbianas deben darse a conocer para ofrecer referentes positivos." *http://www.diariovasco.com/20080115/al-día-sociedad/lesbianas-deben-darse-conocer-20080115.html.*

Nes, Illy. *El lago rosa*. Barcelona: Edicions Bellaterra, 2004.

Pérez Sánchez, Gema. *Queer Transitions in Contemporary Spanish Culture: From Franco to la Movida*. Albany: State University of New York Press, 2007.

Pérez Sancho, Begoña. *Homosexualidad: secreto de familia*. Barcelona: Egales, 2005.

Perriam, Chris. "Gay and Lesbian Culture." In *Spanish Cultural Studies: An Introduction*, edited by Helen Graham and Jo Labanyi, 393–95. Oxford: Oxford University Press, 1995.

Pertusa, Inmaculada. *La salida del armario: Lecturas desde la otra acera*. Gijón: Llibros del Pexe, 2005.

Pertusa, Inmaculada, and Nancy Vosburg. *Un deseo propio: Antología de escritoras españolas contemporáneas*. Barcelona: Bruguera, 2009.

Petit, Jordi. *25 años más: Una perspectiva sobre el pasado, el presente y el futuro del movimiento de gays, lesbianas, bisexuales y transexuales*. Barcelona: Icaria, 2003.

Platero, Raquel, ed. *Lesbianas: Discursos y representaciones*. Barcelona: Melusina, 2008.

Preciado, Beatriz. *Manifiesto contra-sexual*. Madrid: Opera Prima, 2002.

———. *Testo yonqui*. Madrid: Espasa, 2008.

Quiles, Jennifer. *Más que amigas*. Barcelona: Delbolsillo, 2002.

Quintero, Paz. *Destino programado*. Barcelona: La Tempestad, 2005.

Richardson, Diane. *Rethinking Sexuality*. London: Sage, 2000.

Sánchez Mellado, Luz. "Lesbiana sin complejos." *El País Semanal* (June 29, 2003): 36–47.

Simonis, Angie, ed. *Cultura, homosexualidad y homofobia. Vol. 2, Amazonia: Retos de la visibilidad lesbiana*. Barcelona: Laertes, 2007.

Smith, Paul Julian. *Laws of Desire: Questions of Homosexuality in Spanish Writing and Film 1960–1990*. Oxford: Oxford University Press, 1992.

Soriano Rubia, Sonia. *Como se vive la homosexualidad y el lesbianismo*. Salamanca: Amarú Ediciones, 1999.

Torres, Lourdes, and Inmaculada Pertusa, eds. *Tortilleras: Hispanic and U.S. Latina Lesbian Expression*. Philadelphia: Temple University Press, 2003.

Van Guardia, Lola. *Plumas de doble filo*. Barcelona: Egales, 1999.

Viñuales, Olga. *Identidades lésbicas: Discursos y prácticas*. Barcelona: Edicions Bellaterra, 2000.

Part I

Representation and the Politics of Visibility
Margaret G. Frohlich

Many cultural productions clearly draw our attention to the marginal status of lesbians, the need for their heightened visibility in society, and the prejudices that facilitate economic, social, and political inequalities. Since the end of the Franco period, there have been textual and visual works that destabilize a tradition of silence and invisibility by depicting not only lesbians but also lesbians in the act of creating texts and images, shaping cultural imaginaries. But just what is the relation of visibility and speech to principles of equality? What is their relation to power? In saying what has been unspoken, uncovering what has been hidden, and critiquing the way that lesbians are spoken of and seen, lesbian representations address and deepen these questions.

Silence and invisibility can be linked to violence and oppression. Thus, a central aim of LGBT activist work is to increase visibility in society. In her critical essay on violence and mourning, *Precarious Life,* Judith Butler describes how speech and visibility are connected with political power: "The public sphere is constituted in part by what cannot be said and what cannot be shown. The limits of the sayable, the limits of what can appear, circumscribe the domain in which political speech operates and certain kinds of subjects appear as viable actors."[1] Visibility and speech within the context of identity politics, however, are not sufficient for breaking the dialectic of margin to center. That is to say, visibility and speech are linked to the system of relations that maintain marginalization. I am not arguing against the importance of speech and visibility but rather emphasizing that being seen and heard is a complex sociopolitical exchange that can both oppose and maintain exclusions. Understanding their effects requires a critical approach. Lesbian activist Beatriz Gimeno provides a case in point in her analysis of the continuance of lesbian invisibility within the increasingly visible "gay movement":

Es el momento de pararnos a reflexionar dónde han quedado las lesbianas en este asunto de la visibilidad y dónde están las lesbianas
cuando decimos población lgtb u homosexual o, simplemente, gay-
lesbiana. Miremos simplemente a nuestro alrededor: ¿dónde están
las lesbianas políticas? ¿Dónde las lesbianas famosas, presentadoras
de televisión, actrices? Si se habla constantemente del glamor gay
¿existe algo parecido asociado a las lesbianas?

[It is time to stop and reflect upon where lesbians have ended up in
this topic of visibility and where are lesbians when we say lgtb[2] population or homosexual or, simply, gay-lesbian. Simply looking
around us: Where are the lesbian politicians? Where are the famous
lesbians, television anchors, actresses? If they are always talking
about gay glamor, does something similar associated with lesbians
exist?][3]

Exclusions are part of identities, communities, language, and
naming, and traces of the center can be found in marginalized
groups. It appears then that difference will have to be had differently in order for what is spoken and seen to be able to change
the power relations that maintain marginalization. Part of what
is at stake in lesbian representations is the ability to speak lesbian specificity, to engage political power and viability, without
repeating harmful exclusions and entrenching a politics of absolute difference.

The desire to express oneself in one's own language, to express
the specificity of one's experience, is a topic of both lesbian and
feminist discourse that is evident in lesbian fiction. Both discourses present challenges to Freud's theory of sexual difference
and the female subject's alienation from the production of
meaning. Luce Irigaray underscores the impossibility of representing the feminine since it is trapped in a phallocentric signi-
fying system.[4] She argues for a "true" femininity outside the
limits of representation, an idealized feminine body outside this
constraining system. This feminine body, when united with another female in lesbianism, is introduced as a point at which
phallocentric language can be challenged. In her book *Lesbian
Utopics*, Annamarie Jagose addresses Irigaray's privileging of the
sameness of mothers and daughters and of lesbians in a shared
feminine body, noting that it is yet another utterance and rein-
forcement of the sameness that underpins phallocentrism (all
men are the same in their superiority to all women).[5] The struggle of women and lesbians to account for internal differences in
a way that does not reify the rhetoric of absolute difference at

the heart of the process that maintains their own marginalization haunts lesbian writing.

In Susana Guzner's *La insensata geometría del amor*,[6] for example, the characters Maria and Eva maintain a relationship
across their different sexual identities; Maria identifies as lesbian and Eva identifies as heterosexual. In spite of this difference, they are able to unite and search for a language that
describes their sexual experience. They find that words associated with sexual pleasure in a heterosexual encounter are unable
to describe their lesbian pleasure. As Maria notes, "En alguna
ocasión aislada yo había mostrado sutilmente mi desagrado por
determinadas palabras e iba desterrando expresiones como 'correrse,' 'polvo,' 'irse' u otras similares que entre mujeres carecen
de sentido" [In one isolated occasion I had subtly demonstrated
my dislike of certain words and I went about banishing expressions like 'correrse,' 'polvo,' 'irse'[7] or other similar ones that
lacked meaning between women].[8] Maria remarks on her lover
Eva's invention of new words to describe their encounter: "Con-
cibió una primorosa metáfora para expresar la proximidad de su
orgasmo: 'Estoy subiendo,' Me pareció muy elocuente y me
sumé a su hallazgo. 'Subir' connotaba con acierto la bella percepción de que el placer es alado y te transporta hacia arriba hasta
tocar el cielo con las manos" [She invented an exquisite metaphor for expressing the nearness of an orgasm: "I'm climbing."
It appeared very eloquent to me and I joined in her discovery.
"To go up" skillfully connoted the beautiful perception that
pleasure is winged and transports you upward until touching the
heavens with your hands].[9] Though this example of "subir" is
presented as a metaphor, it is a metaphor that attempts to refer
back to a feeling that reaches upward into a place without limits,
toward the heavens. This lesbian language represents an attempt
to escape patriarchal heteronormative discourse and its silenc-
ing of lesbian desire.

Though there is certainly no fully developed lesbian language,
there are a growing number of dictionaries of lesbian, gay, bisexual, transsexual culture and its "micro-languages," for example
*Para entendernos: Diccionario de cultura homosexual, gay y lés-
bica*[10] and *El cancaneo: Diccionario petardo de argot gay, lesbi
y trans*.[11] To surmise that "lesbian words" simply name what
has been unnamable would, however, fail to account for how the
binary suggested by separate heterosexual and homosexual languages maintains a dialectic of difference. The creation of new
words and modes of writing may not break the dialectic of gen-

der and sexual discourse, but it does make plain the close association between desire and language.

At times, what is desired of language is that it would express what others have misrepresented or ignored. Hence, taking up the pen is a prominent act in Hispanic lesbian fiction, and female protagonists are involved with language and writing in multiple ways.[12] They are novelists, writers of short stories or other genres, graduate students writing theses and literary criticism, poets, journalists, and/or translators. The novels *Julia*[13] and *Beatriz y los cuerpos celestes*,[14] for example, have female characters that are students or professors of language and literature. Oftentimes female protagonists fall in love with women via written communication, such as occurs in *Venus en Buenos Aires*[15] and *Desda la otra orilla*.[16] These novels share an explicit concern with language, representation, and identity.

Establishing some of the basic aspects of how writing functions in relation to power and identity will further aid our understanding of what is at stake in the portrayal of the act of writing in lesbian narrative. One function of literature in the modern nation-state is to reify the myth of relative homogeneity that comprises the apparent "natural" unity of the nation. Doris Sommer's *Foundational Fictions: The National Romances of Latin America*[17] attests that during the founding years of a nation literature consolidates and legitimates culture, depicting conflict and rupture only to build toward its resolution and the solidification of national identity. Nationality is a principal organizing theme of literary canons, and the close relationship between nation and writing echoes in the literature of emergent and contested identities of the twentieth and twenty-first centuries. Of such contested identities, marginal sexual identities are currently receiving much political attention, as are the growing number of narratives about them.

Literature is a representational space of nation, and as such writing is one way to participate in national projects and the social imaginary. Despite the existence of women writers both in Spain and Latin America over many centuries, women have not been granted the same access as their male counterparts to education and cultural production. In the postindustrial age of the women's movement, however, there has been an increase in the production of women's writing and critical attention to women-authored texts. The act of writing in the lesbian genre often functions to document, reify, and legitimate sexual identity in a nationalistic manner: lesbian writing solidifies "lesbianness" and Lesbian Nation[18] just as Spanish writing solidifies "Spanish-ness." The lesbian subject, excluded from national models of fe-male sexuality that stress biological reproduction within the heterosexual family, writes lesbian sexuality in mimetic na-tional terms. This process involves creative reworking of the system of codes and symbols traditionally bound to heterosex-ual desire and inventing specifically lesbian language. Secondly, this engagement of language and representation does not escape the difficulties of language as such, regardless of the sexuality of the subject that engages it.

Lesbian lore speaks of an origin that is indelibly marked by language and the act of writing, culminating in the poetess of Lesbos, Sappho. She is sometimes referenced explicitly in His-panic lesbian narrative and also indirectly when characters en-gage in the act of writing. Writing that relates Sappho directly to love between women is an act that counters what Marilyn R. Farwell describes as an intellectual effort to deny homosexual topics: "Sappho's lyrical poems and Shakespeare's sonnets are considered problematic homosexual texts. Vast intellectual ef-fort has been expended to prove that these two paradigmatic poets of Western love lyricism did not write on homosexual top-ics despite the seemingly obvious indications to the contrary."[19] Sappho appears as a clearly lesbian inspiration that helps to con-solidate relationships between women in the novel *Con pedi-gree,* written by Isabel Franc under the pseudonym Lola Van Guardia.[20] The character Adelaida, an author of lesbian novels, listens to three phone messages: the first from Tea, a journalist and literary critic interested in her work; the second from her editor; and the final message from Karina, a woman she is hop-ing to seduce. Writing and lesbian desire are clearly linked in this Sapphic scene: "Tea fue una de las voces que Adelaida oyó en su contestador aquella semana de alta intensidad telefónica. La otra era de su editora anunciándole que *Novias en la noche* sería traducida al griego (el sueño de Adelaida era ver sus textos impresos en la lengua de Safo). Y la tercera . . . la tercera era la voz de Karina" [Tea was one of the voices that Adelaida heard on her answering machine that week of high telephonic intensity. The other was her editor announcing that *Girlfriends in the Night* would be translated into Greek (Adelaida's dream was to see her texts printed in the language of Sappho). And the third was the voice of Karina].[21] Karina, aware of Adelaida's success as a novelist of lesbian fiction, invites her to the bar, Gay Night that she co-owns. Adelaida's talent with the pen is referenced in the scene in which she is finally able to comfort Karina, who is at odds with her mother, and eventually to seduce her: «No puedes seguir así—declaró con aquella rotundidad literaria que la caracterizaba—. Lo primero y más importante es que te reconcilies con tu madre.[. . .] Yo te ayudaré»—oyó que la escritora le susurraba al óido, acompañando la frase con una tanda de besos en el lóbulo" ["You cannot continue this way," she declared with that emphatic literary quality that characterized her. "The first and most important thing is that you reconcile with your mother. "I will help you," she heard the writer whisper in her ear, accompanying the phrase with a batch of kisses on her earlobe].[22] "La gran diva de las letras lésbicas," [The great diva of lesbian letters] as she is described on the back of the novel's dust jacket, is so talented in her seduction that Karina, who previously thought that she was heterosexual, declares that she is a lesbian.

Sappho also plays an important role in Maria-Mercè Marçal's first novel, *La passió segons Renée Vivien*.[23] The novel is a fictional account of the poet Pauline Tarn who was born in England and wrote in French under the pen name Renée Vivien. The novel combines multiple layers of fictionalization and narrative positions as it tells of a doctoral student, Sara T., and her investigation of the personal letters and works of Renée Vivien and her writing of a script about Renée's life. The unnamed author of the introduction refers to the narrator in the third person as "the narrator" and hence places the narrator in a fictional position along with Sara T. as a character in the narration: the unnamed author of the introduction is a narrator who narrates the also unnamed "narrator." This self-reflective writing explicitly manifests the process of representation and mediation within the text, aligning itself with feminist goals to raise awareness about representation. The novel's two parts are divided into oscillating narratives: the private papers of Sara T. in the 1980s, the notebooks of Salomon in the 1920s, sections that narrate particular people in Renée's life, and sections with titles that address the doings of the "narrator" in the first decades of the twentieth century. This narrative fragmentation facilitates an association between Sara T. and Pauline T. (or Tarn) as it cuts back and forth between the two.

Pauline does not identify with the English nationality, or assumed heterosexuality, assigned to her at birth. Renée (Pauline) expresses her lesbian identity and adopted national identity in the French language. Her friend Marie notes Renée's passionate

affiliation with France: "Ja li semblava bé aquell fervor cap a
França que ella mateixa compartia, i amb més causa. En darrer
terme, Pauline només era francesa d'adopció. Però amb quina in-
sistència reclamava que en els sobres de les cartes hi figurés *mademoiselle* i no *miss!* I l'anell que duia al dit petit, amb els tres
colors de la bandera . . .!" [By now it appealed to her, this fervor
toward France that she herself shared, and with more reason.
After all, Pauline was only French by adoption. But with what
insistence she demanded that *mademoiselle* and not *miss* appear on the envelopes of the letters! And the ring that she wore
on her pinky finger, with the three colors of the flag . . . !].[24]
Renée's act of writing symbolizes the freedom to identify, both
nationally and sexually, as one wishes to identify. *La passió segons Renée Vivien*'s contemporary character, Sara, finds that she
shares Renée's interest in creating links between women that
form a feminine genealogy beyond traditional national identification: "Cerca les baules d'una genealogia invisible que uneix
indestriablement feminitat, revolta i dolor" [She searches for the
links of an invisible genealogy that inextricably unites femininity, rebellion, and pain].[25] This genealogy of the feminine is ex-
emplified in the figure of Sappho, and both Sara and Renée make
pilgrimages to Lesbos.

La passió segons Renée Vivien incorporates multiple levels of
epistolary writing: letters written by Renée to various lovers as
well as Sara's letters to her lover Chantal. Sara continually references Renée's words and life experiences while she processes her
own emotions in relationship to the woman she loves. The act
of writing works to dissolve the boundaries and impositions
placed on lesbian desire, as one of Renée's lovers, Kerimée, says:

I la veritable connexió, la trobada, es produïa sens dubte en aquell
espai comú que generen dues quimeres trenades estretament a
través del mots. La irrealitat, en canvi, l'atmosfera de somni, va em-
bolcallar sempre la fugacitat intensa de les seves visites i el breu,
àvid, i lent incendi dels nostres cossos en l'amor. I de fet, des del cor
mateix del foc, el record de la paraula escrita n'atiava les flames, com
un vent poderós, i, després, la paraula escrita en perllongava encara
els dominis en el temps, fora del temps i, alhora, esdevenia llavor de
nous records incendiaris.

[And the true connection, the encounter, was produced without
doubt in that common space generated by two chimeras closely intertwined by words. Irreality, on the other hand, the atmosphere of
dreams, always enveloped the intense fleetingness of their visits and

the brief fire, avid and slow of our bodies in love: And in fact, from the very center of the fire, the memory of the written word fanned the flames like a powerful wind and, afterward, the written word prolonged still more its grasp on time, outside of time, and it became the seed of our incendiary memories.][26]

At the same time that *La passió segons Renée Vivien* affirms the lesbian identity of particular characters and their "lesbian nationality," i.e., Lesbos, it also complicates identity via the blurring of distinction between characters and time periods. Writing plays an integral part in both instances, and this dual act of affirming identity and rendering it ambiguous is a contradictory aspect of language that is part and parcel of understanding the problematic of lesbian narrative and representation.

Patrick Paul Garlinger relates a similarly powerful connection between women through writing in *Confessions of the Letter Closet: Epistolary Fiction and Queer Desire in Modern Spain.*[27] Garlinger describes how Carme Riera's "Jo pos per testimoni les gavine" opens with a letter written in 1977 to Riera's editor under Franco's dictatorship. The letter thanks Riera for her collection of stories *Te deix, amor, la mar com a penyora* (1975):[28] "The unnamed letter writer expresses her sense of indebtedness to Riera for the first story: seeing her life transposed into fiction has emboldened her to take an unprecedented step and voice her sexuality in the public sphere by publishing a letter of her own."[29] This ability of words to move past boundaries that the anonymous woman of the letter describes mirrors the importance of letter writing in *Te deix:* the text appears as a letter that the protagonist writes to her lover across the distance that her father, and society, have imposed between them. She recounts her father's words upon finding out about their relationship, "'Aquest és el camí de la depravació. T'enviaré a Barcelona, si això dura un dia més.'" [This is the way to depravity. I will send you to Barcelona, if this lasts one more day].[30] They write to each other when she goes to study in Barcelona: "Certament vaig passer tota la nit amb tu. A estones la ploma sobre el paper escrivia amb tanta morositat, tan delicadment que era com si t'acaronés en silenci" [I spent all night with you. At times the pen slid with such delay, so delicately over the paper, that it was as if I were caressing you in silence].[31] The text appears as a letter written to her lover later in life after she has married and is pregnant. This last letter ends with the wish that the baby be named after her lover, Maria, whose gender is only explicitly revealed at the end.

The representation of characters' creative use of writing in lesbian fiction, their attempts to speak what has been unspoken, echoes the common theme of the coming-out story, or making visible what was previously hidden. For sexual minorities that have been relegated out of sight, to the closet, the question of visibility is particularly cogent. Eve Kosofsky Sedgwick argues that the closet, in addition to being the "defining structure for gay oppression in this century," has marked many binary impasses (natural/unnatural; public/private; health/illness; same/different) that are central to epistemologies of twentieth-century Western culture and in which visibility plays an important role.[32] In its frequent representation of the act of "coming out of the closet," lesbian fiction hones in on the binaries equal/oppressed and visible/invisible, encouraging us to understand the role that visibility plays in sociopolitical constructions of the lesbian subject. For example, Carmen Nestares's *Venus en Buenos Aires* and Geovanna Galera's *El cielo en tus manos*[33] each depict the difficulties experienced by a young woman protagonist who comes out to her homophobic family during her first romantic relationship with another woman. Here visibility solidifies the formation of the characters' sexual identity. In the far more humorous *Diario de una aupair bollo en USA*[34] by Asia Lillo, a Spanish au pair confronts her Republican host family living in Washington, D.C. with her lesbianism. Mabel Galán's *Desde la otra orilla* puts a twist on the coming-out scenario through its depiction of the character Andrea's act of coming out to her own lover, Alicia. At first, Andrea cloaks herself in a textual interface on the Internet by using the alias Acuarela and seducing Alicia without having to reveal that she is a woman. These novels are compelled toward the culminating moment when the lesbian subject becomes intelligible as such to those around her. In these instances, the act of making oneself "visible" is an act that confronts social prejudices.

Novels such as these about individuals making their experience of lesbian desire visible in their personal and professional lives resonate with and are contemporary with the work of the Barcelona-based political activists that form *Grup de Lesbianes Feministes* (GLF) who aim to increase lesbian visibility within the larger context of society:

Since 1999, the GLF campaigned for "A street for lesbian women," denouncing that many streets in Barcelona are dedicated to famous writers, doctors, scientists, philosophers, mainly men; not a single one is dedicated to a lesbian and thus our contribution to history becomes invisible, and thereby our lives symbolically cease to exist in the public space. Lobby techniques ranged from actions in the street (sticking names of famous lesbians to the street signs) to exhibitions and publishing of materials, this continued every year until 2004, when Barcelona had finally named a street after Sappho, a major Greek poet.[35]

This publicly visible marker of the ancient Lesbian poet on state property functions as an historical documentation of lesbian existence and cultural contribution that extends visibility beyond the privately owned clothing shops, discotheques, cafes, and bookstores in gay neighborhoods throughout Spain, such as Chueca, in Madrid; *zona* Alameda, in Seville; and "Gaixample" (Eixample) in Barcelona, places that are commonly referred to as "gay ghettos."

In addition to lesbian novels, films, and activist work aimed at increasing the visibility of lesbian desire and contributions to history, there are a growing number of cultural productions that address the juridical, physical, and mental abuse of lesbians. We find this type of visibility represented in Susana Guzner's novel *La insensata geometría del amor* when the protagonist, Maria, and her friends risk the possible social repercussions of being identified as lesbians in order to protest the death of a friend. They are provoked to engage visual mass media in response to their friend's death from complications related to the electroshock therapy she received for being a lesbian: "Nos agrupamos frente a las cámaras. Amparo me dirigió una sonrisa que correspondí. Yo era consciente de que había tomado una decisión trascendente, el reportaje se haría público y corría el riesgo de ser etiquetada, pero lo asumí con decisión. Ya era hora de que mi elección amorosa dejara de ser un secretillo entre íntimos y sirviera para algo más que para engrosar mi propia biografía" [We gathered in front of the cameras. Amparo smiled at me and I reciprocated. I was aware that I was making a transcendental decision, the report would be made public and I was running the risk of being labeled, but I took it on with decision. It was time that my choice in lovers ceased to be a little secret between those close to me and served for something more than to enlarge my own biography].[36] This topic is also the central focus of Juan Carlos Claver's film *Electroshock*[37] based on the real-life events of a lesbian couple, Isabel M. and Carmen B., living in Spain during Franco's dictatorship.[38] Aired on Spanish television, this film depicts scenes of lesbian intimacy behind closed doors, positioning the viewers' gaze against the blinding effect of the proverbial closet. The spectator sees not only lesbian desire but also watches while parents and doctors see illness.

Visibility, then, is not simply related to equality, and not all aspects of lesbian visibility are focused on bringing what has been hidden into the light. Guillermo Olivera's analysis of discourses that make the homosexual subject possible in contemporary Argentina follows changes in critical discourse and gay activism from the '70s to the '90s. His analysis is also useful in distinguishing between practices of visibility in contemporary Spain. During the early years of the gay movement, gay politics were mostly concerned with transparency, "transparentar una identidad homosexual verdadera" [making a true homosexual identity transparent].[39] Later, the goal of gay politics began to expand to include an interest in the specific conditions of the homosexual subject's visibility and the limitations of terms used to socially identify oneself, "intervenir efectivamente sobre las condiciones que hacen posible tanto la transparencia como el exceso" [to really intervene in the conditions that make transparency as well as excess possible].[40] The work of feminist film scholars, such as Laura Mulvey and Judith Mayne, are more in line with this latter approach, and they explore the potential of film to question and disrupt the "transparency" of gender. Mayne extends her analyses to include cinematic representations of lesbianism, and she explains what is at stake in such visual representations,

> Lesbianism raises some crucial questions concerning identification and desire in the cinema, questions with particular relevance to female cinematic authorship. Cinema offers simultaneous affirmation and dissolution of the binary oppositions upon which our most fundamental notions of self and other are based. In feminist film theory, one of the most basic working assumptions has been that in the classical cinema, at least, there is an unproblematic fit between the hierarchies of masculinity and femininity on the one hand, and activity and passivity on the other. If disrupting and disturbing that fit is a major task for filmmakers and theorists, then lesbianism would seem to have a strategically important function. For one of the "problems" that lesbianism poses, insofar as representation is concerned, is precisely the fit between paradigms of sex and agency, the alignment of masculinity with activity and femininity with passivity.[41]

The film *Costa Brava: Family Album*[42] by director Marta Balletbò-Coll performs such a disruption. We watch as the protagonist of the film, Ana, performs a comedic monologue that she
wrote while another woman films her, actively controlling the
visual apparatus. Later, when Ana and her girlfriend Monserrat
are physically intimate inside their car, the camera angle takes
us around the edges of the car but does not let us see inside it,
making us explicitly aware of the frame that informs our view
of the lesbian subject. Mulvey explains the traditional framing
of the gaze that this scene disrupts: "The gaze of the spectator
and that of the male characters in the film are neatly combined
without breaking narrative verisimilitude."[43] In traditional
framing, the spectator can only see the woman through the gaze
of the man, who in a patriarchal system gives meaning to the
world and the woman. *Costa Brava* challenges this traditional
gaze by avoiding the traditional use of shot/countershot that su-
tures the spectator's gaze with that of the male onlooker. Instead, the two women appear in the center of the frame side by
side, reinforcing their similarity.[44] The film's constant reference
to the constructed nature of the visual image that in turn informs our knowledge of the characters belies the claim that invisible subjects can simply be made transparent; they are, rather,
inextricable from the frame.

Though rooted in an examination of male homosexuality, Michel Foucault's historical analysis of the relation of visibility to
the creation of the homosexual "species," versus sexual acts,
can also be related to the lesbian subject. Speaking of the nineteenth-century homosexual, Foucault notes that his sexuality
was "written immodestly on his face and body because it was a
secret that always gave itself away. . . . The machinery of power
that focused on this whole alien strain did not aim to suppress
it, but rather to give it an analytical, visible, and permanent reality," and this power "set about contacting bodies, caressing
them with its eyes."[45] Norman Bryson describes this shift that
Foucault mentions as "an epistemological turn or swerve into
the visual as the place where the signs of deviancy are now to
appear."[46] Attempts to make the lesbian subject visible do not
simply run counter to a history of invisibility but rather are part
of an historical "machinery of power" that constitutes the homosexual subject. In some cases, being invisible and even un-
imaginable has worked to lesbians' advantage: "Así las leyes
modernas contra la homosexualidad eran por lo general aplica-
bles, y aplicadas, únicamente contra la homosexualidad mascul-

ina" [In this way modern laws against homosexuality were generally applicable, and applied, only against masculine homosexuality].[47] Though references are frequently made to the role of invisibility in processes of social and political marginalization, there is a need for further analysis of visibility's role in the maintenance of the relation between margin and center.

In Geovanna's Galera's novel *El cielo en tus manos* the characters' experience of visibility highlights the complex and often negative aspects that it entails. The narrator, in a typically didactic passage of the novel, hones in on some of these complexities in the following description of the protagonist, Carlota, and her partner, Andrea, in Madrid's gay neighborhood, Chueca:

En aquella zona se sentían muy bien, aunque realmente no les gustaba tener que recluirse en un barrio para poder amarse. Si paseaban por el centro de Madrid, no se recataban en ningún momento, pero les incomodaban las miradas y más teniendo en cuenta que Andrea era famosa. Allí, al menos, todos eran de la misma condición, y los que no, lo suficientemente tolerantes como para no sorprenderse . . . o, bueno, en su mayoría. Era curioso que en determinados sitios también se sintieran observadas. Ellas eran distintas, demasiado femeninas como para ser lesbianas, y hasta que los demás no se aseguraban de que eran pareja no cesaban las miradas. Parecía que las lesbianas sólo podían tener aspecto masculino, o al menos una de la pareja; cada persona era de una forma distinta, no todas las mujeres de esa condición eran iguales, aunque en ocasiones pudiera parecerlo.

[In that area they felt comfortable, although they really didn't like to have to limit themselves to one neighborhood in order to be able to love each other. If they went through the center of Madrid, they never hid themselves, but gazes still made them uncomfortable and even more so taking into account that Andrea was famous. There, at least, everyone was of the same condition, and those that were not, sufficiently tolerant so as not to be surprised . . . or, well, most of them. It was strange that in certain places they also felt observed. They were distinct, too feminine to be lesbians, and until others were sure that they were a couple their stares didn't cease. It appeared that lesbians were only able to have a masculine aspect, or at least one of the partners; each person had a unique form, not all women of that condition were equal, although upon occasion they could appear to be.][48]

El cielo en tus manos underscores the comfort that privately owned social spaces in a gay neighborhood can provide. They are not, however, spaces where lesbianism is rendered invisible as the status quo but rather visibly marked, and variations in a woman's "markings" raise suspicions: coming out of the closet to step into a homogenized box. Visibility is also uncomfortable for the couple when they kiss in their car at a stop light and suddenly feel "miles de ojos que las incomodaban" [thousands of eyes that made them uncomfortable].[49] Carlota is equally disgusted by people's fear of the lesbian gaze, and ponders with sarcasm: "Cuando te encuentres en el vestuario a una lesbiana, para empezar, si eres capaz de encontrar la marca física que las diferencia, ¿acaso crees que se va a fijar en tu cuerpo? Seguramente tenga otras cosas mejores que hacer antes que intentar ligar contigo. No va a sorprenderse por ver un cuerpo femenino, ella también es una mujer, ¿lo recuerdas? Y está cansada de ver dos pechos y unas buenas curvas" [When you find yourself in a dressing room with a lesbian, to begin with, if you are able to find the physical mark that distinguishes them, do you really think that she is going to notice your body? Surely she has better things to do before trying to hook up with you. It is not going to surprise her to see another female body, she is also a woman, remember? And she is tired of seeing two breasts and good curves].[50] The novel closes with the success of the couple in creating a pleasing visual event with witnesses to their lesbianism; without the possibility of a legally sanctioned matrimony, they have their own wedding ceremony. Visibility is an undeniably important aspect of this ceremony's stated effect: "Se abrazaron llorando emocionadas, tanta alegría las superaba: había mucho tiempo que no se sentían tan arropadas por la gente, tan comprendidas. Se amaban hasta la muerte" [They embraced, crying emotionally, they were overcome by so much happiness: they hadn't felt so protected and understood by people in a long time. They loved each other to death].[51] Taking the previously mentioned scenes into account, however, *El cielo en tus manos* problematizes visibility and resists portraying it as a simple mechanism by which equality can be achieved.

In their film *A mi madre le gustan las mujeres*,[52] Daniela Fejerman and Inés París depict an example of when lesbian visibility does not favor lesbians. Sofia, a divorced mother played by Rosa Maria Sardà, makes the decision to come out to her daughters about her relationship with a Czechoslovakian woman named Eliska. Her daughters, Elvira, Jimena, and Sol, each react to the news in their own unique way. One night, Sofia and Eliska go to see one of Sol's vocal performances with a rock band. Sofia smiles at Eliska when Sol announces from the stage that her next song is dedicated to her family and especially her mother. Sol prances about the stage and sings, "Hoy les quiero presentar a la novia de mamá. Me quise suicidar cuando me dijo que tiene una mujer, tiene una mujer, lamiéndole el vientre" [Today I want to present Mama's girlfriend. I wanted to kill myself when she said that she has a woman, she has a woman, licking her belly].[53] Mortified by this publicly visible and explicitly sexual depiction of their relationship, Sofia and Eliska quickly leave the venue where the band is playing and hence disappear from sight. Though the film's overall treatment of lesbianism is favorable, it appears before the Spanish public as a subplot of the film's primary depiction of the heterosexual relationship that develops between Elvira and a male writer.

Also depicting some of the ways that visibility can be negative, Isabel Franc's novel *Con pedigree* uses humor to ridicule reductive positivism. One of the novel's characters, Amelia, is the leader of a political faction named GLUP (Group of United Lesbians and Pioneers) that decides in favor of creating a lesbian *carné*, or identification card. Concerned with the presence of heterosexuals and bisexuals in a popular nightclub, Amelia goes so far as to support the idea of bolstering the fidelity of the *carné* with a genetic test for the "gay gene" Xq28. An unnamed woman present during the discussion asks, «Y con el carné ¿nos harán descuentos?» [And with the identification card, will they give us discounts?].[54] *Con pedigree*'s critical treatment of lesbian visibility continues in its representation of the character Tea de Santos. As a reporter who has recently been given her own television show, Tea capitalizes on the intrigue of sexual identity by only conducting interviews of women who are clearly recognized in lesbian circles, "claramente reconocidas dentro del bollerío," without making direct reference to her own or her guests' sexual identity.[55] When questioned by her friend and author of lesbian novels, Adelaida Duarte, about how she will get the topic out in public, Tea responds, «Las telespectadoras lo advertirán en los entresijos de mis preguntas y de las potenciales respuestas de las entrevistadas que se precien. Tendrán que escuchar entre líneas, las 625 líneas de la pantalla» [The viewers will notice it in the details of my questions and the potential responses of the possible interviewees. They will have to listen between the lines, the 625 lines of the screen].[56] Functioning as a commercial gimmick for Tea's television program, the intrigue of lesbians who are visible but not "out" is emphasized above any concern for lesbian politics. The novel underscores that greater social visibility is not necessarily primarily motivated by an interest in addressing the social inequalities experienced by marginalized groups.

Indeed, not all visual images and markers of sexual identity that are recognized by members of the gay and lesbian community challenge the societal norms that maintain lesbian invisibility. Beatriz, the protagonist of Lucía Etxebarria's *Beatriz y los cuerpos celestes*, questions the benefits of the restrictive nature of communities and their visual markers:

> A veces tenía la impresión de que vivíamos automarginadas en nuestro propio gueto, que habíamos renunciado, sin conocerlo, a un intercambio que quizá nos hubiera enriquecido.
>
> Nuestros amigos y amigas hacían todo lo posible para hacerse fácilmente reconocibles: llevaban anillos en los pulgares, tatuajes en los antebrazos, pequeñas chapitas con triángulos rosas y collares con los colores del arco iris. La mayoría llevaba el pelo muy corto, sobre todo ellos, que además se lo teñían o lo remataban con un copete de Tintín. Todos los chicos tenían al menos un disco de Barbra Streisand; y las chicas, uno de K.D. Lang.

> [Sometimes I had the impression that we lived automarginalized in our own ghetto, that we had renounced, without knowing it, an exchange that perhaps would have enriched us.
>
> Our friends did everything possible to make themselves easily recognizable: they wore rings on their thumbs, tattoos on their forearms, pins with pink triangles and necklaces with the colors of the rainbow. The majority wore their hair short, especially the males, who also dyed it or finished it off with a Tintín crest. All the guys had at least one CD by Barbra Streisand; and the girls, one by k.d. lang].[57]

Beatriz questions the benefits of such visible markers and norms of social exclusivity, which solidify community boundaries. While they may make individuals that participate in the purchase of certain goods in certain venues more easily identifiable as gay or lesbian, they are also restrictive in their homogeneity and hence do not pose a challenge to the limits that maintain marginalization.

I agree with Alberto Mira when he insists in *De Sodoma a Chueca*[58] that the problems of consumerism are not specifically gay problems. They are, however, problems that gather particular meaning for a community that is superficially tolerated as long as it preoccupies itself more with spending money than with concerns for political equality and the eradication of homophobia. Directly addressing this problem, the work of the activists of *Grup de Lesbianes Feministes* of Barcelona provides us with an opportunity to consider the implications of wedding gay and lesbian politics with the market. While we have seen the group's concern for making lesbians more visible in society, they are also critical of extant images of the gay and lesbian community. In 2004, for example, they directed their work toward the visual display of the many retail shops and clubs that are scattered throughout Barcelona's neighborhood, Eixample, or "Gaixample" (gay-Eixample), as it is commonly called.[59] They plastered posters on almost every street corner of "Gaixample," an area that boasts a reduction in crime and augmented commerce since the '90s when the gay community started opening bars and shops there. The bright pink posters with radioactive symbols in the middle ironically congratulated the "normalized" gays and lesbians in the "controlled zone" of Gaixample for being glamorous, for going to the most "in" places, for having a Visa or MasterCard, and for being trendy. This criticism of fellow gays and lesbians occurs in a national context where it is not gays and lesbians that are being accepted so much as those individuals who best exemplify the values and consumer behavior of the middle class. As Alexandra Chasin says in *Selling Out:The Gay and Lesbian Movement Goes to Market*: "[T]he capitalist market makes possible, but also constrains, social movements whose central objective is the expansion of individual political rights."[60] Following the implications of commodifying gay and lesbian identity and increasing visibility in the market one step further, we can see that it amounts to commodity fetishism when the political aims of the gay and lesbian movement are obscured in the process of their commodification: "Visibility is still fetishized to the extent that it conceals the social relations new urban gay and queer identities depend on."[61]

In addition to GLF's pink posters, another example of the creative use of visual media to address the politics of sexual identity is the online game *A tortillazos con el mundo* [To tortilla strikes with the world].[62] On the game's webpage it is described as "el primer juego lesbi de la historia" [the first lesbian game in history], and players are encouraged to vent their frustrations by moving the graphic of a lesbian who holds a *tortilla* in her hands and hitting various targets over the head with it and making them disappear: "¡¡¡Desahógate a tortillazos!!!" [Vent your frustration with tortilla strikes]. Here "tortilla" references the slang term for lesbian, "tortillera." The "targets" vary, and in one

round the lesbian protagonist is confronted with a wave of "lesbis folklóricas." This sequence likely references highly visible
folkloric entertainers who are rumored to be lesbians but do not
openly declare a lesbian identity. Another round is titled, "La
doble vida de las yuppies lesbis" [The double life of yuppy lesbi-
ans]. This round refers perhaps to those lesbians who project an
image of themselves as interested in the lesbian community and
its politics in their private lives but whose more public life is
guided by materialism and superficiality and in which their lesbian identity is hidden.

There is a clear link between capitalism and visibility and representation in the market that does not always work to destabilize gay and lesbian stereotypes. During my field research in
Spain in 2004, I found that gay and lesbian literature is often understood to be erotica. Despite the presence in bookstores of gay
and lesbian novels of a nonerotic focus shelved by the last name
of the author, store clerks had difficulty indicating a single nonerotic lesbian novel. In a *Casa del Libro* in Barcelona, I was led
to a shelf containing two Spanish lesbian novels, one by Carmen
Nestares and one by Marta Fagés, as well as *Yestergay* by Miguel
Fernández. Nestares's novel, *Venus en Buenos Aires*, tells the
story of a young Spanish woman who falls in love with an Argentinean woman and focuses on the emotional difficulty she experiences as a lesbian in a homophobic family. *Venus in Buenos
Aires* had been shelved alongside the *Kama Sutra*. The majority
of the gay and lesbian novels shelved in the erotica sections of
bookstores were written by non-Spanish authors. The message
that such commercial practices send is that being lesbian is re-
ducible to erotic experience and that lesbian novels are almost
exclusively written by foreigners and rarely, if ever, in the Spanish language. During a return trip to Spain one year after the le-
galization of same-sex marriage, I noted that the retail store
FNAC in Madrid had installed a table for "famous gay writers,"
though the trend of displaying mostly male and mostly foreign
writers persisted. The works of Spanish lesbian authors were not
on the table, though Esther Tusquets would, for example, be a
clear candidate. The specific ways that lesbian literature has entered the marketplace makes plain that marketing practices are
culturally charged and politically motivated and not always to
the benefit of lesbians.

Marriage ceremonies are a lucrative market enterprise, and recently the topic of gay marriage has received an unprecedented
amount of publicity. Marriage ceremonies are marvelously pow-

erful visual events that represent a couple's legitimate emotional and sexual unity. The legitimacy afforded relationships under marriage is strongly reinforced by its visual components: wedding rings and a public ceremony. Spain's plans to legalize gay marriage, which were eventually passed in 2005, prompted many to celebrate what appeared to be a sure step forward for sexual rights. Though many gays and lesbians would agree that as long as marriage is the sole legitimating institution of intimate relationships that is recognized by the state, then gays and lesbians should be allowed to participate in it, not all agree that marriage furthers sexual equality, despite its visual cues that assure us that it does. Dominican-born activist Ochy Curiel questions the benefits of marriage and visibility:

La mayoría de las lesbianas feministas se inscribe en la política de la diferencia, del reconocimiento y del rescate de una identidad y ahí se queda. Si vemos las acciones políticas van en la línea de la visibilidad, de salir del closet, de sentir orgullo de ser lesbiana y muchas proponiendo el matrimonio o la unión civil. Esta parece ser la única política posible y no se entiende que estas políticas mantienen intactas las lógicas del sistema patriarcal. Es cierto que la visibilidad es importante, es fundamental para poder colocar nuestras posturas en el ámbito público; sin embargo, la visibilidad por la visibilidad no es suficiente si eso no contiene presupuestos políticos. Yo puedo ser visible como lesbiana, y sin embargo, la discriminación me puede seguir afectando, igual que la explotación económica, los estereotipos y prejuicios que se me imponen. El matrimonio, por ejemplo, es una de las instituciones en donde descansa el patriarcado, no entiendo cómo es posible que muchas aspiren a él. Creo que como la heterosexualidad es el referente válido muchas quieren gozar de sus privilegios sin cuestionar de fondo lo que significa para las mujeres y para las lesbianas.

[The majority of lesbian feminists subscribe to the politics of difference, of recognition and the recovery of an identity, and there they remain. If we look at political actions they go in line with visibility, with coming out of the closet, with feeling pride in being lesbian, and many propose matrimony and civil union. This appears to be the only politics that are possible, and they do not understand that these politics maintain intact the logics of the patriarchal system. It is true that visibility is important, it is fundamental in order to insert our posture in the political environment; however, visibility for visibility is not sufficient if it does not contain political motives. I can be visible as a lesbian, and even so, discrimination can continue to affect me, as well as the economic exploitation, the stereotypes, and the prejudices that are imposed upon me. Matrimony, for example, is one of the institutions in which patriarchy lies; I do not understand how it is possible that so many aspire to it. I think that as heterosexuality is the favorite referent, many want to enjoy its privileges without profoundly questioning what it means for women and for lesbians].[63]

In Barcelona, *Grup de Lesbianes Feministes* also questions the benefits of gay marriage and asserts that it would do little to address the socioeconomic inequalities of daily life or to guarantee sexual rights. They handed out a pamphlet at Barcelona's Gay Pride Parade in 2004 that called into question the benefits of marriage: "Rights must be based on persons, not on couples. The necessary measures should be adopted so that everyone's basic needs are provided for, regardless of whether they are in a couple or not."[64] As Curiel mentions, the close tie of political action to visibility often includes the occlusion of multiple layers of oppression. Beatriz Gimeno critically analyzes lesbian visibility, noting that lesbians are in many ways invisible in the "gay" (read male) movement and the women's movement, and not all lesbians have or want access to the visibility of same-sex marriage: "El matrimonio implica una salida del armario obligatoria que no todo el mundo querrá o podrá asumir, y no podrán especialmente las mujeres con una situación laboral, social o familiar inestable" [Matrimony implies an obligatory coming out of the closet that not everyone will want or be able to assume, and especially women in unstable working, social, or familiar situations will not be able to do so].[65] As certain kinds of visibility become possible, critical attention to the conditions of visibility is needed in order to understand what changes, if any, they imply.

Visual representations are often so powerful that we fail to address them critically. In *The Society of the Spectacle*, Guy Debord outlines the power of the spectacle in modern societies: "The spectacle presents itself as something enormously positive, indisputable and inaccessible. It says nothing more than 'that which appears is good, that which is good appears.'"[66] This moralizing logic of the spectacle implies that what is distasteful, inappropriate, or evil is invisible; it has not seen the light of reason and has been relegated to society's "closet." Debord asserts that in societies dominated by modern conditions of production, the spectacle is not only tied to the good but to the real and cannot be separated from objective reality. The spectacle collapses the distance between reality and representation: "The spectacle is not a collection of images, but a social relation among people, mediated by images."[67] So powerful is the spectacle, that fighting against inequality in democratic societies has become conflated with fighting for visibility.

Understanding how these inequalities are perpetuated within globalized economies requires that we understand how sexual discourses intersect both local and global frameworks. In her presentation given at the Center for Gay and Lesbian Studies at City University of New York, Kate Bedford argued that more critical attention needs to be given to the "norms, institutions, and structures that help to naturalize dominant forms of heterosexuality and make them hegemonic . . . make them appear universal and morally righteous."[68] One example of such an institution is Disney, a decidedly U.S. corporation with an unmistakable global scope that is evidenced in the reach of its theme parks, television and cable channels, films, stores, and in its incorporation of famous historical and mythical figures from nations around the world in its productions: Anastasia, Quasimodo, Aladdin, Pocahontas, and others. In their essay published in 1978, *Para leer al Pato Donald*,[69] Ariel Dorfman and Armand Mattelart perform an incisive critique of imperialist ideology in Disney's productions that can also be related to the sexual politics of the company's films. Clara Martin's short film made in Spain in 2004, *STUPENDA comerciaLes*, addresses this aspect of Disney, and it is described as "cine reciclado para entretenimiento y reflexión puramente comercial. Visión no-española del mundo lesbiano en los *spots*, en la que se evidencia la necesidad de convencer a un sector invisible social y comercialmente hasta ahora" [recycled cinema for purely commercial entertainment and reflection. A non-Spanish vision of the lesbian world in the spots in which there is an evident need to incite what has been, until now, a socially and commercially invisible sector].[70] One of the clips in the short film shows Disney's animated version of Cinderella kissing Snow White. Martin's film opposes lesbian invisibility and indicates the heteronormativity of Disney's "princess tales."

Contrasting with the humorous nature of Martin's short film, Amnesty International's advertisement campaign to stop violence against women also unites the topic of lesbianism with a global perspective. One advertisement of the campaign features a large photo of actress Patricia Vico who plays the lesbian doctor, Maca, on the prime time Spanish television show, *Hospital*

Central. Vico appears with ghastly bruises and lacerations all over her face along with a caption that reads, "Si Maca viviera en Colombia, podría acabar así. Salvajemente violada, torturada y tal vez asesinada por la guerrilla o los paramilitares, tan sólo por haber sido vista besando a otra mujer. En más de 70 países las lesbianas, gays, bisexuales y transgénero son víctimas de agresiones, asesinatos, persecución policial o incluso ejecuciones a causa de su orientación sexual, real o supuesta" [If Maca lived in Colombia, she could end up like this. Savagely raped, tortured and maybe even killed by guerrillas and paramilitaries, only for having been seen kissing another woman. In more than 70 countries lesbians, gays, bisexuals and transsexuals are victims of aggression, killing, political persecution, and even executions owing to their sexual orientation, real or imagined].[71] Despite its potent visual image, there is much left out of sight in the advertisement's wording, which all too easily suggests, given the broad scope of Amnesty International, that globally homophobia is everywhere but locally (in Spain) it is nowhere to be found. The advertisement also contains another level of invisibility:

> Los organizadores no hayan podido encontrar a ninguna actriz lesbiana española (que haberlas, *haylas* todas lo sabemos y tenemos una ligera idea de quiénes son). Y es curioso que haya tenido que dar la cara por todas nosotras una mujer que no lo es (Patricia Vico, con su personaje *Maca*). . . . A todas las actrices que se debaten entre el exterior o el interior de su solapado armario particular, sólo puedo aconsejarles una cosa: como dice siempre Shrek, *mejor fuera que dentro.*

> [The organizers have not been able to find any Spanish lesbian actress (they exist, there are . . . we all know it and we have a vague idea of who they are). And it is curious that a woman who isn't one has had to give face for all of us (Patricia Vico with her character *Maca*) . . . To all the actresses that debate between the interior and exterior of their particular whispered closet, I can only advise them one thing: as Shrek always says, *better out than in*].[72]

This observation, in addition to offering another queer ventriloquizing of an animation character, manifests a persistent longing for authenticity and identity, a haunting of nationalism in globalization that links to other more easily recognizable lesbian fictions and realities.

A spirit of optimism following Spain's approval of same-sex

marriage in 2005 could encourage a dubious reading of the uns-pecified "seventy" countries in Amnesty's ad, one that assumes that violence against lesbians occurs in many countries, espe-cially Colombia, but no longer in Spain. Leonardo Fernández, the head of Amnesty International's sexual minority division in Spain, said of the campaign, "Queríamos una campaña que no fuese dirigida exclusiamente a los homosexuales de Chueca—barrio gay de Madrid desde hace más de una década—sino diri-gido a la gente en general" [We wanted a campaign that was not directed exclusively toward the homosexuals of Chueca—a gay neighborhood in Madrid for more than a decade—but rather di-rected to people in general].[73] By stating that "Maca" could be hurt in Colombia, however, the ad not only directs our attention away from Chueca but also facilitates the false impression that homophobia is not a Spanish problem now that sexual discrimi-nation and related hate crimes can be legally prosecuted. Novels such as El cielo en tus manos by Geovanna Galera and Venus en Buenos Aires by Carmen Nestares, as well as continued reports of sexual discrimination, remind us that sexual minorities in Spain are susceptible to prejudice and violence. The president of the Association of Lesbians, Gays, Bisexuals and Transsexuals of Malaga (Colega-Málaga), David Cedeño, argues that greater so-cial liberty has not been associated with a drop in instances of intolerance but rather with more acts of violence on the part of intolerant people: "Antes, los gays, lesbianas y transexuales éra-mos más invisibles y no les molestábamos tanto" [Before, gays, lesbians and transsexuals were more invisible, and we didn't bother them as much].[74] While adopting a global perspective has long been a tradition of the gay movement, the adaptation of such a perspective is sometimes associated with a loss of per-spective "at home." This is not to imply that lesbian fiction, whether in a novel or an ad campaign, ought to depict local vio-lence done to sexual minorities—in fact many novels do not—but rather that insinuating its absence locally while pointing elsewhere (especially in the context of a European nation point-ing toward a former colony) is problematic. While many His-panic lesbian narratives critique utopian renderings of the United States and its cultural imperialism,[75] time will tell whether or not equally problematic utopias are erected as the visibility of lesbians increases.

Whether or not lesbian visibility is related to greater social equality depends upon the how, who, and where of lesbian im-ages, upon what kinds of exclusions and occlusions lesbian visuality[76] engages. Across a diverse array of lesbian texts and images we find the affirmation of marginalized identities, an affirmation that challenges the social inequalities that lesbians experience. It is in those works that extend this affirmation to a depiction and critique of the complex relation of margin to center, a critique of how mechanisms of exclusion are perpetuated and produced in both sites, that we find a hint toward the rupture of these power relations.

Notes

Portions of this essay appear in *Framing the Margin: Nationality and Sexuality across Borders* by Margaret G. Frohlich. Tempe, AZ: AILCFH, 2008.

1. Judith Butler, *Precarious Life: The Powers of Mourning and Violence* (London: Verso, 2004), xvii.
2. Here the author changes the order of the initialism GLBT in response to her observation that "gay" is prioritized above "lesbian."
3. Beatriz Gimeno, "La doble discriminación de las lesbianas," in *Cultura, homosexualidad y homofobia*, Vol. 2, *Amazonia: Retos de visibilidad lesbiana*, ed. Angie Simonis (Barcelona: Laertes, 2007), 20. Translations are mine unless otherwise noted.
4. Luce Irigaray, *This Sex Which is Not One*, trans. Catherine Porter and Carolyn Burke (New York: Cornell University Press, 1985), 69.
5. Annamarie Jagose, *Lesbian Utopics* (New York: Routledge, 1994), 29.
6. Susana Guzner, *La insensata geometría del amor* (Barcelona: Plaza y Janés Editores, 2002).
7. Both "correrse" and "irse" are used to refer to having an orgasm and "polvo" comes from the expression "echarse un buen polvo" or "to have a good screw."
8. Guzner, *La insensata geometría*, 222.
9. Ibid.
10. Alberto Mira Nouselles, *Para entendernos: diccionario de cultura homosexual, gay y lésbica* (Barcelona: Ediciones de la Tempestad, 1999).
11. Ferrán Pereda, *El cancaneo: Diccionario petardo de argot gay, lesbi y trans* (Barcelona: Laertes, 2004).
12. In addition to novels published in Spain, there are also many Latin American and Latina/Chicana novels that represent the act of writing: *En breve cárcel* by Sylvia Molloy, *Dos mujeres* by Sara Levi Calderón, *Margins* by Terri de la Peña, *Una mujer y otras cuatro* by Mireya Robles, and more. See Frohlich, *Framing the Margin*, for further analysis of how these novels represent the act of writing.
13. Ana María Moix, *Julia* (1970; repr., Barcelona: Muchnik Editores, 1999).
14. Lucía Etxebarria, *Beatriz y los cuerpos celestes* (1998; repr., Buenos Aires: Planeta Argentina, 2000).
15. Carmen Nestares, *Venus en Buenos Aires* (Madrid: Odisea, 2001).
16. Mabel Galán, *Desde la otra orilla* (Madrid: Odisea, 1999).
17. Doris Sommer, *Foundational Fictions: The National Romances of Latin America* (Berkeley: University of California Press, 1991).

18. "Lesbian Nation" is a term coined by Jill Johnston in her book by the same name: *Lesbian Nation* (New York: Simon and Schuster, 1973).

19. Marilyn R. Farwell, *Heterosexual Plots and Lesbian Narratives* (New York: New York University Press, 1996), 108.

20. Isabel Franc (Lola Van Guardia), *Con pedigree*, 3rd ed. (Barcelona: Egales, 2002).

21. Ibid., 23.

22. Ibid., 272.

23. Maria-Mercè Marçal, *La passió segons Renée Vivien* (Barcelona: Proa, 1994).

24. Ibid., 99.

25. Ibid., 92.

26. Ibid., 226.

27. Patrick Paul Garlinger, *Confessions of the Letter Closet: Epistolary Fiction and Queer Desire in Modern Spain* (Minneapolis: University of Minnesota Press, 2005).

28. Carme Riera, "Te deix, amor, la mar com a penyora," in *Te deix, amor, la mar com a penyora* (1975; Barcelona: Planeta, 1991).

29. Garlinger, *Confessions*, 88.

30. Riera, *Te deix*, 23.

31. Ibid., 32.

32. Eve Kosofsky Sedgwick, *Epistemology of the Closet* (Berkeley: University of California Press, 1990), 71.

33. Geovanna Galera, *El cielo en tus manos* (Madrid: Editores, 2003).

34. Asia Lillo, *Diario de una aupair bollo en USA* (Madrid: Egales, 2006).

35. Grup de Lesbianes Feministes, "Exploring new ways of insubmission in social representation," *Annual Review of Critical Psychology*, 4 (September 24, 2005), http: www.lesbifem.org/textos/ARCP05.pdf

36. Guzner, *La insensata geometría*, 348.

37. *Electroshock*, DVD directed by Juan Carlos Claver, Los Angeles: Picture This! Home Video, 2008.

38. The following report documents the real-life events: Lydia Garrido "Juntas hasta la muerte," *El País* (December 4, 2001), http://www.elpais.com/articulo/sociedad/Juntas/muerte/elpepisoc/20011204elpepisoc_4/Tes.

39. Guillermo Olivera, "Políticas de la representación homosexual en Argentina: de las utopías de la transparencia a las disputas por la visibilidad," in *Las marcas del género: configuraciones de la diferencia en la cultura*, eds. Fabricio Forastelli and Ximena Triquell (Córdoba, Ar: Universidad Nacional de Córdoba/University of Nottingham, 1999), 151.

40. Ibid., 152.

41. Judith Mayne, "Lesbian Looks: Dorothy Arzner and Female Authorship," in *Feminism and Film*, ed. E. Ann Kaplan (Oxford: Oxford University Press, 2000), 174.

42. *Costa Brava: Family Album*, VHS directed by Marta Balletbò-Coll and Ana Simón Cerezo (Tallahassee, FL: Naiad Press, 1995).

43. Laura Mulvey, "Visual Pleasure and Narrative Cinema," in *The Feminism and Visual Culture Reader*, ed. Amelia Jones (London: Routledge, 2003), 48.

44. María Dolores Herrero, "*Costa Brava:* Una comedia romántica lesbiana de los años noventa," *Antipodas: Journal of Hispanic and Galician Studies* 11–12, (1999–2000), 177.

45. Michel Foucault, *The History of Sexuality*, vol. 1, trans. Robert Hurley (New York: Random House Vintage Books Edition, 1980), 43–44.

46. Bryson, Norman, "Todd Haynes's *Poison* and Queer Cinema," *Invisible Culture* 1 (1999), http://www.rochester.edu/in_visible_culture/issue1/bryson/bryson.html.

47. Gimeno, "La doble discriminación," 20–21.

48. Galera, *El cielo*, 136.

49. Ibid., 126.

50. Ibid., 103.

51. Ibid., 200.

52. *A mi madre le gustan las mujeres*, DVD directed by Daniela Fejerman and Inés París (New Almaden, CA: Wolfe Video, 2005).

53. "A mi madre le gustan las mujeres" composed by Andy Chango.

54. Franc, *Con pedigree*, 194.

55. Ibid., 97.

56. Ibid., 80.

57. Etxebarria, *Beatriz*, 48.

58. Alberto Mira Nouselles, *De Sodoma a Chueca:Una historia cultural de la homosexualidad en España en el siglo XX* (Barcelona: Egales, 2004).

59. My field research was conducted in Spain during the summer of 2004 with the help of grants from the Tinker Foundation and the Program for Cultural Cooperation between Spain's Ministry of Culture and U.S. universities.

60. Alexandra Chasin, *Selling Out: The Gay and Lesbian Movement Goes to Market* (New York: Palgrave, 2000), xvii.

61. Rosemary Hennessy, *Profit and Pleasure: Sexual Identities in Late Capitalism* (New York: Routledge, 2000), 115.

62. Miren Itziar de Iñurria Garay, in collaboration with graphic designers Javier Royo and Patricia Izarra created *A tortillazos con el mundo: El primer juego lesbi de la historia* in July 2003. http://www.cebolla.net/juegolesbis/juegolesbi.html.

63. Ochy Curiel, interview by Erika Montecinos, "Ochy Curiel. Activista lésbica feminista y cantante: 'La visibilidad por la visibilidad no es suficiente,'" *Rompiendo el silencio: Revista virtual de culturas lesbianas* (September 2005), http://www.rompiendoelsilencio.cl/entrevistas/entrevistas_1sep05_1.htm.

64. Grup de Lesbianes Feministes, "Beyond Marriage" (2002): 2, http://www.lesbifem.org/textos/matrimoni/matrimoni_ENG.pdf.

65. Gimeno, "La doble discriminación," 25.

66. Guy Debord, *Society of the Spectacle* (1967; repr., Detroit: Black and Red, 1983), 12.

67. Ibid., 4.

68. Kate Bedford, audiotape of panel discussion presented at "Sex and the Global Economy Seminar," February 23, 2006 (New York: Center for Gay and Lesbian Studies at City University of New York).

69. Ariel Dorfman and Armand Mattelart, *Para leer el Pato Donald* (Valparaíso: Ediciones Universitarias de Valparaíso, 1971).

70. BarceDona: Programa Cine-Video-Forum de cortometrajes de temática lesbiana, (short film program, Barcelona, 2004).

71. "Nueva compaña de Amnistía Internacional, por los derechos LGBT," *Inforgay.com* (December 2005), http://www.inforgay.com/2005/12/nueva-campaa-de-amnistia-internacional.html.

72. Paz Quintero, "La caja tonta," *Stupenda: Revista mensual para entendidas (mujeres en general y lesbianas en particular)* 47 (2006), http://web.archive.org/web/20060715052349/http://www.barcedona.org/01-STUPENDA-REVISTA/01-TV-Paz_Quintero.htm.
73. Luis Repiso, "Famosos españoles, 'entre rejas' por ser gays," *20minutos.es* (February 21, 2006), http://www.20minutos.es/imprimir/noticia/92888/O/amnistia/internacional/homosexual.es/.
74. F. J. Pérez, "El casero incendia la vivienda de una transexual," *El País* (April 4, 2009), http://www.elpais.com/articulo/andalucia/casero/incendia/vivienda/transexual/elpepiespand/20090404elpand_1/Tes?print=1.
75. For further analysis of the topic of U.S. imperialism in lesbian narrative, see Frohlich, *Framing the Margin.*
76. Nicholas Mirzoeff's term that describes "the intersection of power with visual representation", "The Subject of Visual Culture," in *The Visual Culture Reader*, 2nd ed., ed. Nicholas Mirzoeff (London: Routledge, 1998), 4.

REFERENCES

A mi madre le gustan las mujeres. DVD directed by Daniela Fejerman and Inés París. New Almaden, CA: Wolfe Video, 2005.

BarceDona: Programa Cine-Video-Forum de cortometrajes de temática lesbiana. Short film program, Barcelona, 2004.

Bedford, Kate. Audiotape of panel discussion presented at "Sex and the Global Economy Seminar." February 23, 2006. New York: Center for Gay and Lesbian Studies at City University of New York).

Bryson, Norman. "Todd Haynes's *Poison* and Queer Cinema." *Invisible Culture* 1 (1999). http://www.rochester.edu/in_visible_culture/issue1/bryson/bryson.html.

Butler, Judith. *Precarious Life: The Powers of Mourning and Violence.* London: Verso, 2004.

Chasin, Alexandra. *Selling Out: The Gay and Lesbian Movement Goes to Market.* New York: Palgrave, 2000.

Costa Brava: Family Album. VHS directed by Marta Balletbò-Coll and Ana Simón Cerezo. Tallahassee, FL: Naiad Press, 1995.

Curiel, Ochy. Interview by Erika Montecinos. "Ochy Curiel. Activista lésbica feminista y cantante: 'La visibilidad por la visibilidad no es suficiente.'" *Rompiendo el silencio: Revista virtual de culturas lesbianas* (September 2005). http://www.rompiendoelsilencio.cl/entrevistas/entrevistas_1sep05_1.htm.

de Iñurria Garay, Miren Itziar, Javier Royo, and Patricia Izarra. *A tortillazos con el mundo: El primer juego lesbi de la historia* (July 2003). http://www.cebolla.net/juegolesbis/juegolesbi.html.

de la Peña, Terri. *Margins.* Seattle: Seal Press, 1992.

Debord, Guy. *Society of the Spectacle.* 1967. Reprint, Detroit: Black and Red, 1983.

Dorfman, Ariel, and Armand Mattelart. *Para leer el Pato Donald.* Valparaíso: Ediciones Universitarias de Valparaíso, 1971.

Electroshock. DVD directed by Juan Carlos Claver. Los Angeles: Picture This! Home Video, 2008.

Etxebarria, Lucía. *Beatriz y los cuerpos celestes*. 1998. Reprint, Buenos Aires: Planeta Argentina, 2000.

Farwell, Marilyn R. *Heterosexual Plots and Lesbian Narratives*. New York: New York University Press, 1996.

Foucault, Michel. *The History of Sexuality. Vol. 1, An Introduction*. Translated by Robert Hurley. New York: Random House Vintage Books Edition, 1980. First published as *La Volonté de Savoir*. Paris: Editions Gallimard, 1976.

Franc, Isabel (Lola Van Guardia). *Con pedigree*, 3rd ed. Barcelona: Egales, 2002.

Frohlich, Margaret G. *Framing the Margin: Nationality and Sexuality across Borders*. Tempe, AZ: AILCFH, 2008.

Galán, Mabel. *Desde la otra orilla*. Madrid: Odisea, 1999.

Galera, Geovanna. *El cielo en tus manos*. Madrid: Entrelíneas, 2003.

Garlinger, Patrick Paul. *Confessions of the Letter Closet: Epistolary Fiction and Queer Desire in Modern Spain*. Minneapolis: University of Minnesota Press, 2005.

Garrido, Lydia. "Juntas hasta la muerte." *El País* (December 4, 2001). http://www.elpais.com/articulo/sociedad/Juntas/muerte/elpepisoc/20011204elpepisoc_4/Tes.

Gimeno, Beatriz. "La doble discriminación de las lesbianas." In *Cultura, homosexualidad y homofobia. Vol. 2, Amazonia: Retos de visibilidad lesbian*, edited by Angie Simonis, 19–26. Barcelona: Laertes, 2007.

Grup de Lesbianes Feministes. "Exploring new ways of insubmission in social representation." *Annual Review of Critical Psychology* 4 (September 24, 2005): 107–14. http://www.lesbifem.org/textos/ARCP05.pdf.

———. "Beyond Marriage" (2002): 1–3. http://www.lesbifem.org/textos/matrimoni/matrimoni_ENG.pdf.

Guzner, Susana. *La insensata geometría del amor*. Barcelona: Plaza y Janés Editores, 2002.

Hennessy, Rosemary. *Profit and Pleasure: Sexual Identities in Late Capitalism*. New York: Routledge, 2000.

Herrero, María Dolores. "*Costa Brava:* una comedia romántica lesbiana de los años noventa." *Antipodas: Journal of Hispanic and Galician Studies* 11–12 (1999–2000): 171–86.

Irigaray, Luce. *This Sex Which Is Not One*. Translated by Catherine Porter and Carolyn Burke. Ithaca, NY: Cornell University Press, 1985. Originally published as *Ce Sexe qui n'en est pas un*. Editions de Minuit, 1977.

Jagose, Annamarie. *Lesbian Utopics*. New York: Routledge, 1994.

Johnston, Jill. *Lesbian Nation*. New York: Simon and Schuster, 1973.

Kosofsky Sedgwick, Eve. *Epistemology of the Closet*. Berkeley: University of California Press, 1990.

Levi Calderón, Sara. *Dos mujeres*. México: Diana, 1990.

Lillo, Asia. *Diario de una aupair bollo en USA*. Madrid: Egales, 2006.

Marçal, Maria-Mercè. *La passió segons Renée Vivien*. Barcelona: Proa, 1994.

Mayne, Judith. "Lesbian Looks: Dorothy Arzner and Female Authorship." In

Feminism and Film, edited by E. Ann Kaplan, 159–80. Oxford: Oxford University Press, 2000.

Mira Nouselles, Alberto. *De Sodoma a Chueca: Una historia cultural de la homosexualidad en España en el siglo XX.* Barcelona: Egales, 2004.

———. *Para entendernos: diccionario de cultura homosexual, gay y lésbica.* Barcelona: Ediciones de la Tempestad, 1999.

Mirzoeff, Nicholas. "The Subject of Visual Culture." In *The Visual Culture Reader,* 2nd ed., edited by Nicholas Mirzoeff, 3–23. London: Routledge, 1998.

Moix, Ana María. *Julia.* 1970: Reprint, Barcelona: Muchnik Editores, 1999.

Molloy, Sylvia. *En breve cárcel.* 1981. Reprint, Buenos Aires: Ediciones Simurg, 1998.

Mulvey, Laura. "Visual Pleasure and Narrative Cinema." In *The Feminism and Visual Culture Reader,* edited by Amelia Jones, 44–53. London: Routledge, 2003.

Nestares, Carmen. *Venus en Buenos Aires.* Madrid: Odisea, 2001.

"Nueva campaña de Amnistía Internacional, por los derechos LGBT." *Inforgay.com* (December 2005). http://www.inforgay.com/2005/12/nueva-camp aa-de-amnistia-internacional.html.

Olivera, Guillermo. "Políticas de la representación homosexual en Argentina: de las utopías de la transparencia a las disputas por la visibilidad." In *Las marcas del género: configuraciones de la diferencia en la cultura,* edited by Fabricio Forastelli and Ximena Triquell, 143–58. Córdoba, Ar: Universidad Nacional de Córdoba/University of Nottingham, 1999.

Pereda, Ferrán. *El Cancane: Diccionario petardo de argot guy, lesbi y trans.* Barcelona: Laertes, 2004.

Pérez, F. J. "El casero incendia la vivienda de una transexual." *El País* (April 4, 2009). http://www.elpais.com/articulo/andalucia/casero/incendia/vivienda/ transexual/elpepiespand/20090404elpand_1/Tes?print=1.

Quintero, Paz. "La caja tonta." *Stupenda: Revista mensual para entendidas (mujeres en general y lesbianas en particular)* 47 (2006). http://web.arc hive.org/web/20060715052349/http://www.barcedona.org/01-STUPENDA-REVISTA/01-TV-Paz_Quintero.htm.

Repiso, Luis. "Famosos españoles, 'entre rejas' por ser gays." *20minutos.es* (February 21, 2006). http://www.20minutos.es/imprimir/noticia/92888/O/ amnistia/internacional/homosexual.es/.

Riera, Carme. "Te deix, amor, la mar com a penyora." In *Te deix, amor, la mar com a penyora.* 1975; Barcelona: Planeta, 1991.

Robles, Mireya. *Una mujer y otras cuatro.* San Juan: Plaza Mayor, 2004.

Sommer, Doris. *Foundational Fictions.* Berkeley: The National Romances of Latin America. University of California Press, 1991.

Transitions and Representations of Lesbianism in the Spanish Media

Raquel Platero Méndez

INTRODUCTION

IN SPAIN, THE SOCIAL PERCEPTION AND UNDERSTANDING OF SEXUAL-
ity, in particular non-normative sexualities, has rapidly evolved,
resulting in fundamental changes in the last thirty years. Those
changes have had a trickle-down effect on legislation. The starting point for this process can be located in recent references to
the punishment and prohibition of homosexuality by means of
the 1954 Slackers and Delinquents law and the 16/1970 Dangers
to Society law—which were rarely applied to lesbians.[1] The second most important advances took place regarding the Penal
Code in 1995, which was modified to protect sexual orientation.[2] Nowadays Spain is one of only a very small number of
countries allowing same-sex marriage, with the introduction of
Law 13/2005 and the registration of gender reassignment with
the introduction of Law 3/2007.[3] These legislative amendments
reflect changes in the social construction of sexuality, not only
through the creation of legal resources, but also of a certain collective imaginary.

Often, when referring to Spanish mass media and the representation of lesbianism the expression "lesbian invisibility"
arises, referring to the lack or negligible number of female images compared to the abundance of male homoerotic images, an
"invisibility" that could easily lead to the conclusion that lesbians simply do not exist. If we take a more accurate look, we can
find references, even before Franco's dictatorship.[4] For instance,
mention is made of the first lesbian film, *Mädchen in Uniform*,
in the magazine *Blanco y Negro*.[5] In the same magazine, there
are remarks about the masculine appearance of women like
Marlene Dietrich, using moralist terms, or about the Countess
d'Armonville, showing the upcoming fashion tendencies includ-

ing comfortable clothing such as trousers, clothing that became known as "sportswear," e.g., the emergence of sweaters, new garments with pockets for women.[6] Other lesbian-related news items are linked to women practising sports and the fear of masculinization. It is important to bear in mind that during the dictatorship Pilar Primo de Rivera promoted the prohibition of women's athletics, a prohibition that did not end until the 1960s. In addition, as Tatiana Sentamans explains, there are references to this fear in the Catalonian press of the Second Repub-

—Guaita: la senyoreta diu que vol ensenyar-me de fer una truita.
—Tant bé que les sabem fer tu i jo!

Guaita: la señorita dice que me va a enseñar a hacer una tortilla. [Guaita: the mistress says she's going to show me how to make a tortilla.]
! Con lo bien que las hacemos tu y yo! [Knowing how well you and I do it!]

lic. It is also worth mentioning images shown in the *revistas psicalípticas* (erotic magazines), published from 1900 to the 1930s (e.g., *La Traca, Papitu, La Tuies o KDT*), full of frivolous images, such as the one on the previous page, with references to the "tortilla" as slang for lesbianism.[7]

Most authors refer to lesbian invisibility when discussing the Spanish media of the 1970s, an absence only altered by some U.S. TV shows screened at unsociable times, up to the present when most TV shows now include a lesbian and/or gay character.[8] The 70s were known as the *años del destape* [uncorked years], when for the first time, nude women and sexuality were portrayed openly in Spanish media. Sexuality and gender norms were extremely stereotypical, showing pitiful, longed-for images to repressed Spaniards. In 1977 we find what is thought to be the first Spanish lesbian film, which was quite successful in terms of audience figures—*Me siento extraña* [I Feel Odd], featuring a torrid romance between Rocío Durcal and Barbara Rey. Soon after, both actresses regretted their involvement in the movie.[9]

The 1980s brought the *'movida madrileña'* [Madrid scene], an intellectual and artistic movement, which Pedro Almodóvar has shown to the entire world through his films. Meanwhile, Spanish audiences had to read ambiguous or gay attitudes in the media, mostly in foreign films dubbed in Spanish.[10] In 1988, the famous band *Mecano* surprised everyone with a song titled "Mujer contra mujer" [Woman on Woman], telling the love story of two women.[11] However, there has not been a song about lesbians or lesbianism since this release.

One of the largest national newspapers, *El País*, published in its Sunday magazine (*El País Semanal*) two substantial articles on lesbianism over a period of ten years. The first article appeared in 1993, written by the popular journalist Rosa Montero.[12] It pointed out that lesbianism was not a unique experience but rather very diverse, and it commented on the impact of invisibility. Montero stated that lesbian couples were more unstable than gay and straight couples, since they were less interested in sex as a result of differential gender socialization. The edition was also controversial because of the editorial ban on the original cover, which showed a couple consisting of a black woman and a white woman. The newspaper claimed that "it risk[ed] diverting attention" away from the main issue, and it subsequently chose a more conventional and representative white couple.[13] The second article, written by Luz Sánchez Mellado and published in 2003, focused on lesbianism from a heterosexual perspective.[14] This journalist highlighted the principal *clichés* and presented the stereotypical questions concerning the subject matter. Again, the representation and images of lesbians were controversial. She asked interviewees to dress in warm colours, wear makeup and pose in a garden, presenting soft photographs against a green background. This article was particularly derogatory in its treatment of masculinity in lesbians, depicting it as something eccentric and peculiar. Regarding masculine traits, the journalist described these as: "Pelo rapado, cara lavada, gafitas deportivas, camiseta cuadrada, pantalones anchos, andares resueltos, aire masculino" [44; shaved head, no makeup, sporty glasses, check shirt, wide trousers, a gentle swagger, a masculine air].

From the 1990s onward, television started to screen foreign movies, mostly from the United States, with some LGBT characters who were then copied by Spanish shows, adapting sitcoms to the Spanish context. There have been Spanish shows that followed the North American pattern of incidentally including a lesbian and/or gay and/or transgender character, only to subsequently transform them into stable characters, mostly in our decade. Some of the Spanish shows and TV programs that included a lesbian or gay character have been: *Todos los hombres son iguales* (1994) [*All Men Are the Same*], *Al salir de clase* (1997) [*Class is Out*] and *Compañeros* (1998) [*Buddies*]; all of them sitcoms which showed funny situations about homosexuality, the protagonists of which later turned into stable characters. This was the case of the Basque situation comedy *Hasiberriak* (2001) [*Beginners*], in which a lesbian relationship was portrayed.[15] The first Spanish show that showed a lesbian character was *Más que amigos* (1997) [*More than Friends*], in which a lesbian secretary worked in a law firm.[16] In 2000, dealing with LGBT issues became frequent. For example, in the family-oriented show *Médico de familia* [*Family Doctor*], a female friend of the protagonist is in love with a woman; in *Periodistas* [*Journalists*] two women journalists pretend to be lesbians in a adoption process. In *El comisario* [*The Police Chief*] the typical situation appears in which someone is mistakenly believed to be gay. In 2001, the sitcom *Moncloa, ¿dígame?* [*Moncloa, How Can I Help You?*] included a lesbian character known as María Fernanda.[17] It is worth noting that all these shows were designed to be watched by families in prime time.

Three prime-time sitcoms presented lesbians in a positive way: *Siete vidas* [*Seven Lives*], *Hospital Central* [*Central Hospi-*

tal] and *Aquí no hay quien viva* [*It's Impossible to Live Here*]. *Siete vidas* had a long run (with two hundred programs, ending in 2006), that included a lesbian character in 2000: Diana discovered her lesbianism, came out of the closet, tried to get pregnant, got married, and developed a number of amusing relationships. The shows *Aquí no hay quien viva* (2003–04) and *Hospital Central* (2000–9) presented lesbians who get married and undergo artificial insemination to become mothers or give birth to a child with the gay character of the show.

There were also shows in which explicit rejection of homosexuality was shown: *Motivos personales* (2005) [*Personal Reasons*] presented a gay character named Jaime who confessed love for Nacho. He experienced rejection and tried to pass as heterosexual. *Obsesión* (2005) [*Obsession*] presented a male actor, Javier, being discriminated against by Fabi and his family. Other series are more explicit in their rejection of defective performances of masculinity, becoming a joke. The family shows *Los Serrano* (2003) [*The Serranos*] and *Aída* (2005) are relevant in this sense. The latter is a pioneer in that it showed for the first time a young adolescent man as gay, but the representation included an explicit criticism of incipient homosexuality, showing the dominant discourses of rejection of feminine masculinity.[18]

Another kind of TV program that has played a relevant role in both stereotyping and showing the progressive access of LGBT individuals to Spanish public society are talk shows. The popular *Cruzando el Mississippi* (1998) [*Crossing the Mississippi*] used ridiculous and infamous images of flamboyant gay characters (Pepelú and Crispin) to cause laughter. Also this show allowed Pepe Navarro to ask the typical and narrow-minded question of which member of the lesbian couple performs the woman's role and which one the man's.[19] The perennial talk show *Crónicas Marcianas* (1994–2005) [*Martian Chronicles*] presented flamboyant Boris Izaguirre "performing gayness" as a permanent guest. Meanwhile *Big Brother* reality show lesbians Raquel and Noemí recounted their first sexual experience, later becoming permanent guests on other talk shows and commenting in the tabloids (2002–06). Also *Crónicas Marcianas* brought on male transgender guests to debate *Big Brother*. The reality show *Big Brother* introduced the audience to the debate over lesbianism in 2002, and later male transgenderism in 2004, by including lesbian and transgender participants. Often we cannot tell the difference between talk shows and reality shows. Both have used sexuality and the experiences of *Big Brother*–show participants as a source of debate or as an excuse to debate changes in legislation.

Some shows that represented homosexuality in Spanish versions were a resounding failure. This was the case with *Tio Willy* (1998) [*Uncle Willy*] and *Equipo G* (2005) [*The G Team*]. The first show presented a Spanish gay man who returns from San Francisco to encounter a homophobic society. The show *Equipo G* was the Spanish equivalent of the popular makeover show *Queer Eye for the Straight Guy*. More serious and successful shows were relegated to impossible times and were located on less relevant channels, such as the shows *Uno más* (2003) [*One More*], and *La otra* [*The Other*] on Channel Telemadrid. That was also the case of the show *Hasta en las mejores familias* (1995–97) [*Even in the Best of Families*] shown on the Telemadroño channel and the show *Uaiemsiei* (2004)— referring to the pronunciation of the famous song by Village People, "YMCA"—on Flaix TV Channel in Catalonia. In Andalucia, the show *De Frente* [*Head On*] on Channel 2 only lasted a few shows (2003–4).

Currently most media include lesbian, gay, bisexual, or transgender characters, which reflects the extent of recent social changes. They are not only present in fiction TV shows but also in advertising (underwear, ice cream, and cars, for example), and lesbianism has been used as part of the entertainment machinery of programs such as reality shows like *Big Brother*, the tabloids, and publicity for TV shows. If we look more closely at the press and news broadcasts, real events appear less successful in representing lesbianism. The news has shown a small number of lesbian activists getting married; some leading lesbian speakers of the LGBT rights movement and some foreign news reports have also focused on lesbians. Quoting Fernando Bruquetas, the proliferation of real or fictional homosexual characters is combined with the lack of reflection and analysis of gay problems and culture.[20] Indeed the little analysis that does exist is limited to a variety of problems within the mainstream political agenda.[21]

The narrative concerning the transformation of lesbian invisibility into a series of stereotyped images and later to a diverse representation is as yet incomplete. It ignores the relationship between gay subcultures and the media as generating gay and lesbian identities.[22] The media constructs identities by selecting which images to show or which to hide; mainstream images shown are consistent with heterosexual imaginary. Naomi Klein stated in her book *No Logo* that the media identifies certain identity groups as potential new market targets, focusing on those "collectives" that were previously ignored (e.g., non-heterosexuals, non-western, non-Catholics).[23] Therefore, visibility does not imply recognition of citizenship status but rather of consumer potential (a new market), which reinforces the social and economic order (for example, the creation of a "Pink market").

By telling happy stories about lesbians whose main dilemma is how their friends and families deal with their sexuality, this issue becomes a matter personal to the individual. The issue of homophobia as a structural problem then disappears. Equality is presented as having been obtained, while ignoring the general impact of homophobia or the unresolved issue of specific discrimination in the labour market. There has been a gradual increase in lesbian visibility that does not imply a positive or realistic representation. Instead, it has become a source of assimilation, presenting positively heterosexual majorities as accepting and dealing with their resistance, as part of social change. However, it is not only a matter of naming and being visible in the media, but also of having a debate regarding the quality of representation, highlighting the construction of gender and sexuality that underpins these images.

The (hi)story of sexuality in the media is not only linked to absence and repression but also to normativity and social discourses; images of homosexuality have existed since the emergence of television. Traditionally these representations have been limited by and constructed to reflect the dominant values of each historical and social environment.

This article sets out to examine the discourses and representation of lesbians in the Spanish media, pointing out their normative and disruptive elements. The text aims to challenge the invisibility argument which is often used to abandon the study of lesbianism in the media; often the arguments are that lesbians are represented just like women or like male homosexuals, or that they do not exist at all. As I will show, there is considerable evidence of representations of lesbianism that demonstrate that lesbianism is both a taboo and also an appealing resource. In addition, lesbianism in the media is presented as a cliché, often bringing together the concepts of masculinity, crime, and pathology. TV shows prefer to represent lesbians as women with a heterosexual past who perform lesbianism, get married, and become mothers. Thus becoming lesbian does not imply breaking down gender norms. Nonetheless, as the article unfolds I bring a critical analysis to show how the span of possible images and representations of lesbian experience is limited. The article is divided into four sections: a discussion around the field of representation as a theoretical framework; a consideration of the limits of lesbian visibility; the presentation of some elements of the most frequent representations, and finally my conclusions.

REPRESENTATION AS FRAMEWORK

The media, especially television and cinema, grant us vicarious access to experiences, feelings, places, and actions, along with constructions of daily issues. The media has become the lens that filters our view and generates an imaginary that interprets the world through known experience. The meaning of an image or of a text depends on our conceptual mapping, on the symbolic system in which it is inscribed, and therefore it is central to ascertain who has the power to represent and what is represented.[24]

We use knowledge, feelings, and past experience when interpreting reality. Meanings are produced within a concrete field of representation, in which the will intervenes to give the ultimate meaning.[25] What goes unrepresented does not exist in public life and lacks the legitimacy necessary for existence (Llamas 34). Therefore, both those realities that are absent and those that are represented as accessible for the mainstream audience serve to inform what the relevant societal values are. Representations are not innocent—they reflect heteronormativity, showing dominant values. Representation and sexuality constitute each other, how every person understands what is normal, what beauty means in relation to our bodies, what it means to be female/male within the norms of gender and sexuality. Therefore, in order to observe sexuality we need to be aware that sexuality is mediated and constructed actively through representations; in Tessa Boffin and Jean Fraser's words: "our bodies, our fantasies, come to be sexually organized".[26] It is our task to analyze representations: the emergence of excluded groups and identities in the media is not a result of demands for social justice, but rather of the recognition of a potential market.

There are many disciplines that deal with the field of "representation," from sociology and political science to visual arts and film theory, with many studies interrogating the concept of

audience identification: which constructions are more successful and why; which archetypes tend to be repeated in a given culture. Some authors—Catherine Belsey, John Berger and Laura
Mulvey, among others—see representation as a space for struggle along with political and cultural debate.[27] While analysing
the objectification of women, these authors found that images
and representations are not neutral; instead they depict certain
ideologies or particular ways of framing the world. It is currently
believed that representations comprise normativity in terms of
sexuality, gender, ethnicity, religion, and class, which intersect,
resulting in multiple discriminations.

The observer or ideal audience is conceptualized as male and
heterosexual, and images of women are designed to please him
(Berger, 46). That position is built on unequal gender relationships and compulsory heterosexuality. Nonetheless, there is
now a discussion about whether the overrepresentation of
women as objects from a male perspective, mainly in advertisements, is only directed at men or at women as well.[28] Michel
Foucault pointed out the relationship between power and
knowledge that makes individuals adopt the viewer's perspective, the so-called "panopticon," with an appearance of neutral-
ity and normativity.[29] The individual tends to police him/herself
within the boundaries of normativity regarding, among other
things, gender and sexuality, aware of when s/he is breaking the
rules. Although commercial images are made in general for the
heterocentered masculine gaze, it does not imply that individuals outside those parameters cannot enjoy them. There is much
written about the need to re-read mainstream information from
a gay perspective, in order to find gestures or a certain character
that remind us of experiences lived by LGBT individuals. Therefore, the male gaze provides information and shapes our experiences, even LGBT experiences.

There is considerable debate over the situation of women as
audience and passive subjects: a binary description of women as
opposed to men hides and ignores the multiple identifications
and desires of women. Women are depicted as an underrepresented group—and at the same time overrepresented through
stereotyped images—along with other people considered minorities in relation to power; but women are also presented in terms
that are blind to their own perceptions and relevant events in
their lives.[30]

Pilar López Díez has studied the representation of women in

the Spanish media, analyzing the news in 2001 and 2005.[31] The results were rather sad: women only made up 15% of people mentioned as protagonists on the radio and 18% on television. None of the reports in which women were protagonists concerned sexual orientation. This data confirms our worst expectations: real news is the least fruitful space to observe the representation of lesbians.

When studying the male gaze, Caroline Evans and Lorraine Gamman remarked on its complexity: they criticized essentialist perspectives of social relationships and proposed a queer perspective, searching for the most perverse and pleasurable relationships embedded in the act of looking.[32] They also suggested that the masculine gaze implicit in heterosexist constructions cannot be countered by merely increasing the number of LGBT images in the media, through a strategy of inclusion. Instead, they propose an alteration of normativity by problematizing identity categories (14–15). Ricardo Llamas in his theory of collapse remarked that representations of homosexuality are determined by a strategy to collapse possible gay and lesbian subjectivities. If there is a possibility of representing difference, there is a risk of building diverse subjectivities—and this could be threatening (26).

Teresa de Lauretis brought to our attention the representation of the lesbian subject and her capacity for self-representation, while located in a multiple intersection of gender and sexuality, between discourses and bodies.[33] On the one hand, lesbians have been outside dominant discourses, with very few self-representations. On the other hand, most representations of lesbians are immersed in heterocentered perspectives. Lesbians are not represented nor understood as women or as homosexuals, which makes them a source of contradiction and rich analysis.

As mentioned earlier, the aim of this chapter is to observe the construction and representation of lesbian identities in the context of Spanish media. From the most absolute invisibility to the current visibility, my purpose is to highlight the absence, the most repetitive clichés and normative discourses. My interest will be to focus on media productions for the mainstream audience, rather than on specific images or texts for LGBT audiences. Images and people referred to in the text are presented to illustrate the discourses and constructions in the Spanish setting; their sexuality or behavior is not assumed to be gay or lesbian.

SIDE EFFECTS OF VISIBILITY:
FROM INSULTS TO POLITICAL CORRECTNESS

LGBT activists often discuss media representations of LGBT reality and demands.[34] These debates include tensions between the more acceptable and normalizing images and the need to portray ones that are as diverse as possible, including the most subversive ones. The political changes that have placed Spain at the centre of media attention present Spain as a social lab for sexual freedoms.[35] Nonetheless, gay marriage and the fight against homophobia are regarded as issues exclusively related to gay men. It is gay men who appear, talk and recount their stories. Lesbians are either portrayed as "gay" women or as feminine homosexuals, their role being that of the exception that reinforces the norm. Both the construction of "the problems of gays and lesbians" in the political agenda and the choice of the forms of representation more in line with the mainstream place men at their center.[36]

The media do not reflect the lived reality of lesbians, offering instead certain constructs of lesbianism that are filtered by mainstream heterosexist images. I will discuss the impact of these representations of lesbianism on the social acceptance of this sexuality and the quality and diversity of such representations.[37] A study of qualitative changes in representations of LGBT people for mainstream audiences can serve to question normative values and perceive how these challenge or collide with heterosexist structures.

It is commonly thought that greater media representation of lesbians will have the effect of breaking traditional assumptions around women's—and, more specifically, lesbians'—sexuality. However, this sort of increased visibility does not automatically result in decreasing lesbophobia, nor does it break the stereotypes that homogenize lesbians and women more generally. As we will see, representations of lesbians are built around archetypes and stereotypical images. They are made by and for a heterosexual audience and promote images reinforcing lesbians' femininity while conceptualizing them as an erotic icon for men. These representations also portray them in desirable roles for women: those of mother and wife.[38]

As Walters maintained, lesbian visibility is made for heterosexual commercial consumption, for the de-lesbianization of lesbianism (15). Lesbian visibility is both an opportunity and an obstacle. It is a way of showing and promoting social change, but it also helps the creation of stereotypes by placing limits on lesbian behavior. Walters also pointed out that such portrayals convince gays and lesbians that they are accepted despite what they might hear on the news (20). That advertisements for tobacco, alcohol, or clothes show attractive lesbian poses or that televisions series such as *Hospital Central* and *Aquí no hay quien viva* display lesbian characters getting married or having artificial insemination does not prevent lesbians from suffering lesbophobia in their everyday lives. Despite the visibility generated by same-sex marriage, the permissiveness towards the homophobic attitudes and the aggression of extreme groups persists; all sorts of homophobic attacks occur repeatedly nowadays.

TV series portray happy stories in which lesbianism and homosexuality are personal problems with which the milieu deals successfully. However, they are disconnected from everyday acts of exclusion and from being questioned about their noncompliance to strongly imposed gender norms. Therefore, we could say that reductionist and stereotypical representations are responsible for the cognitive dissonance that lesbians experience, as well as for the lack of understanding of lesbophobia as a structural problem. Everyday problems and exclusions are then seen as completely removed from any structural or gender explanations.

One of the queer critiques of heterosexual normativity defining gay-lesbian categories is linked to romantic narratives; the scripts present narratives of liberation of gays and lesbians producing complacency both in straight and gay audiences. The fiction of "gay or lesbian authenticity" is a source of comfort in a homophobic society. For heterosexuals who sympathize with the LGBT cause, it means they can feel good because they are adopting a tolerant stance by accepting homosexuality. LGBT people in turn feel a change in values and that they are accepted. The narrative seems to be that lesbians should be honest with their milieu and "come out of the closet" to carry out the new roles available to them as a way of thanking the progressive society for accepting them. Such a narrative facilitates a social blindness towards heterosexism and homophobia by portraying conflicts as personal or temporary.[39] My argument is that there is a social desire to present ourselves as a progressive society with a progressive state while not altering to any real extent the understanding of otherness nor the intersectional experiences of citizenship and ignoring the consequences and exclusions that occur on a structural and everyday basis.

Anglo-American literature seeks similarities between lesbian and gay visibility and the impact of African-American visibility in famous television series such as *The Cosby Show*.[40] The series showed a middle-class African-American family, which marked a great difference from previous representations of African-Americans as slaves, servants, thieves, and other secondary characters that were commonplace in U.S. television at the time. However, this new representation did not put an end to racism nor did it generate a deep social transformation despite its being a very popular series even in apartheid South Africa (Walters 12). The series has been compared with *Ellen*, in which the main character comes out of the closet, as does the actress.[41] These televisual instances both produced a moment of visibility as never before seen in U.S. television that did not, however, put an end to racism or homophobia.

The representations of gays and lesbians in mass media show tensions that exist between representations of "otherness" and "normality," equality and difference (Walters 18). They outline a continuum ranging from depictions of lesbians as asexual, de-politicized women to those that portray lesbians adhering to the prescribed gender roles, the message being "I am normal like you (straight)." On the one hand, the representations that construe lesbians as other make the heterosexual majority feel at ease, as they can clearly identify the limits of "sexual normality," placed at female masculinity. As we will see later, a typical representation is that of masculine women—whether lesbian or not—as bad women. It is as though homoerotism among women and lesbianism were easily identifiable and easily revealed.

In contrast, when lesbianism is presented as a personal issue that a certain character faces, it is removed from its social and cultural context, in which structural explanations such as homophobia and patriarchy can arise. The drama that is generated around the acceptance of someone's gay or lesbian sexuality by heterosexual characters thus becomes a happy story of acceptance and progressiveness, in tune with mainstream social desires. The message of the narrative seems to be "put a lesbian or gay in your life" without, nevertheless, questioning the dominant heterosexual order.

Some Notes on the Representation of Lesbians in the Media

In order to discuss some of the features of the images of lesbians in the media, I will make use of both real and fictional representations in the press, advertising, and other media. Representations are embedded in a sexual dichotomy, with lesbians either appearing as asexual beings, resembling the "nymphs of the forest," or by showing signs of affection between women, *or* they are pornographic icons for the masculine gaze, appealing to hypersexualized lesbianism. Here individuality is disappeared with such representations becoming impersonal images that appeal to the heterosexual male audience as consumers. This dichotomy is true for the representation of women in general and not just lesbians. There is a thin and blurred line between mothers and whores. The constructions of women as bad or respectable are indeed very finely separated.

Advertising provides a good source for the analysis of binary representation. These images range from the contested homo-erotic images of Paz Vega with herself (see next page)—very similar to the portrayal of Linda Evangelista in a butch/femme play of images published in 1997—to the asexual women who hold hands while walking through idyllic locations.[42] Further mass media produce representations of reality that help shape people's ways of thinking and generate models of identification. Such representations often ignore and marginalize women by producing images that victimize them and that, more generally, do not reflect the wide range of roles they carry out.[43] Lesbians are not estranged to these processes of invisibilization and labeling. Representations of lesbians cover a narrow range with tensions between the feminine and masculine poles. These are more closely related to the perception of reality and social desirability often relegated to a discussion about dress code rather than being related to identitary and post-identitary processes.

The "more acceptable" images present lesbians as feminine women whose lesbianism is but an exotic element which does not affect their "normality." Their everyday experiences and how they face homophobia are then consigned to the private or personal spheres. As Patricia Vico—the actress playing Maca in *Hospital Central*—claims:

> When I was offered [the role of] Maca I liked her a lot. She's a doctor, with a strong character, with her own life experiences. And apart from that, she's a lesbian. What I mostly liked about her was her personality. Her sexual orientation was important to me but not essential, and that's how I looked at it. She's a well-defined character. We both wanted to convey the same thing: a love story between two people, not between two women or two guys, or between a guy and a girl. And that's what we're doing.[44]

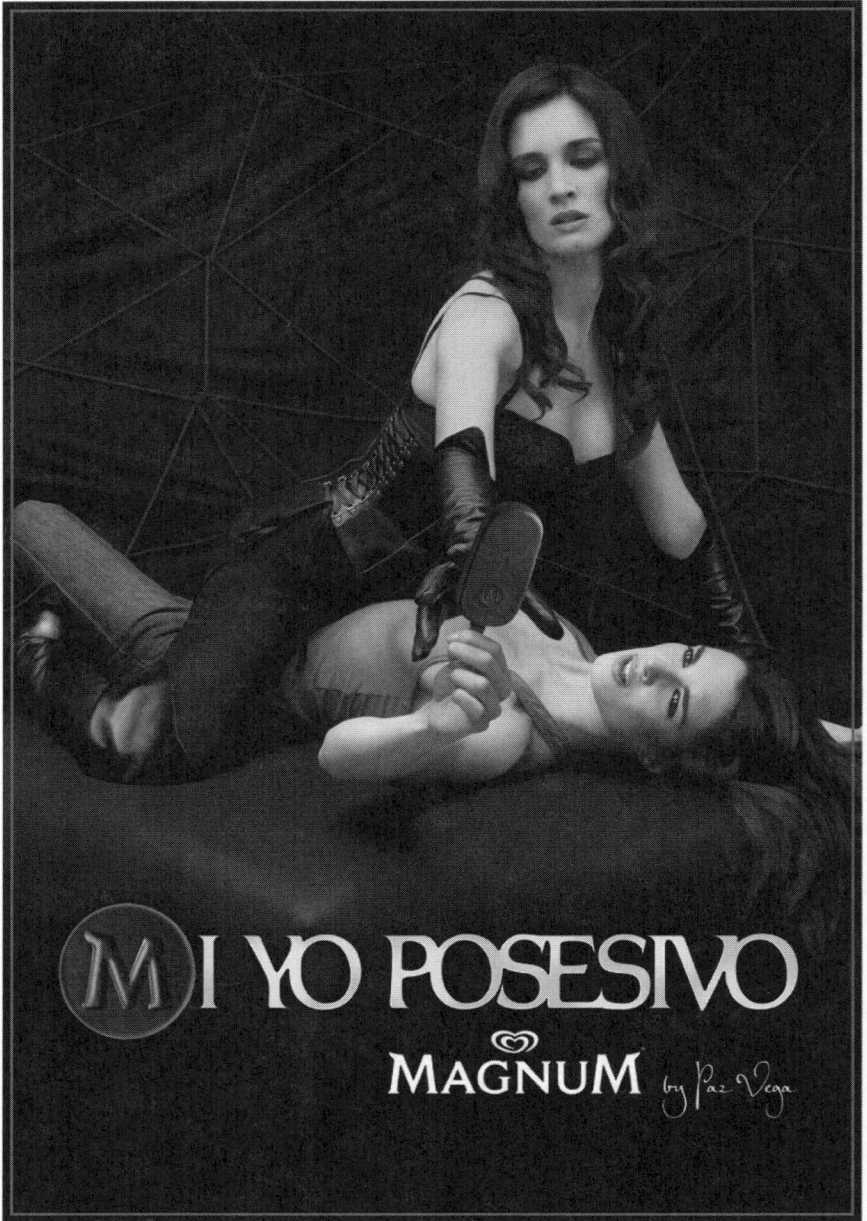

Brand: Magnum. Company: Frigo. Agency: McCann-Erickson. Year: 2006.

Photo by Gorka Postigo. B-Guided 23. Spring 2005. Patricia Vico as Maca

As the actress explains, lesbianism is but another element of the lesbian's fictional character. Lesbophobia then disappears from the dominant structure, as does the need for lesbian support networks or a social context showing LGBT cultural elements. The "power of love" is not seen as requiring either gender or sexuality distinctions or structural explanations.

While masculine representations are linked to increased credibility, they are also accompanied by rejection, conceptualizing them as maladjusted, bad, or just ugly (see an article extract by Salvador Sagaseta below). Representations and images of androgyny are more linked to commercial use. These are a resource and instrument for fashion and design (i.e., *CK One*, or *Benetton* with Jenny Shimizu).

Lesbian identity is constructed as a transhistorical, universal, and homogenous sexuality. It reinforces the idea that we can find it at different cultural spaces and historical moments. The social imaginary believes in a series of predetermined sexual options with a natural explanation. The identity processes thus reflected show a monosexual map, where the only plausible options are heterosexuality or lesbianism. Each is labeled and clearly situated. They exclude the possibility of bisexuality and other post-identitary processes. Lesbians symbolize the shattering of heterosexist norms, as a separate sexuality that generates a subjective threat and thus generates lesbophobic reactions. However, they also enter the realm of "normality" through the recreated rites of marriage and maternity. These representations are formed by Western, middle-class, white urban models. Hitherto the representations of the diversity of structural inequalities were monofocal. The lesbian cannot be represented as an immigrant, nor can the gypsy woman be disabled. Nevertheless, among all these forms of inequality, lesbianism, homosexuality, bisexuality, and transgenderism are more visible and more often represented than, for example, disability, ethnicity, and religion. It seems to be an aspect that can be changed more easily without altering the dominant sex and gender order.

The lack of real lesbian characters apart from a couple of famous women and a few known activists results in the overwhelming majority of lesbian representations in television, press and advertising being fictional and commercial characters. I will not analyze lesbian pornography, where we would find the majority of images or productions by lesbians since these merit specific research. Dichotomized representations are commonplace in advertisement. An example is the *Cutty Sark* advertisement in 2001 that asked, "Homosexuality or heterosexuality?" while showing a butch/femme couple. The more masculine, dark woman looks straight at us, in defiance, questioning us, while the blond femme has no face. She is only there in representation of the other pole and as a way of generating a homoerotic discourse. A Lucky Strike advertisement from the same period (2000) also shows a dark-haired, supposedly masculine lesbian looking at the audience while kissing a pretty blonde. Several interpretations might be offered here: these images could represent the assertive and defiant pose of lesbian masculinity, inviting us into the image, or the search for masculine validation through sexualizing her action. However, her gaze typically invites the male observer into the scene. In addition, the title "I choose" refers both to 'lesbian chic' as a fashion element and to the consumption of that particular brand of cigarettes.

Lesbian chic is the way in which lesbians have been inserted into gay glamor. They are then part of the trendsetting attributed to gay men, which differs greatly from the representations of lesbians as masculine, working-class women. This representation has allowed for the use of homoerotic images to sell objects which are considered glamorous, such as jewelry, certain brands of clothes, ice cream, and cars. Lesbian representations are often based on stereotypically feminized images. There is a clear absence of female masculinities when using lesbian chic. Series such as *The L Word* (first aired in Spain on January 12, 2006, with the title *L*) are consistent with that representation, as are Spanish TV series and advertising. Of the lesbian representations I mention here, only those that are shown to be punished

Brand: Cutty Sark. Company: Berry Brothers and Rudd. http://www.com mcercialcloset.org/cgi-bin/iowa/themes.html?agency = Year: 2001.

I CHOOSE
AN AMERICAN ORIGINAL

LUCKIES

LUCKY STRIKE

FILTERS

Las Autoridades Sanitarias advierten que el tabaco perjudica seriamente la salud.
Nic.: 0,9 mg. Alq.: 12 mg.

Brand: Lucky Strike. Company: British American Tobacco. Year: 2000.

as bad women or the few representations of real lesbians stray from the hyperfeminized lesbian model.

In TV series lesbians are never shown within a lesbian or gay social context. They are devoid of a lesbian social network or lesbian cultural references. As mentioned earlier, their lesbianism is seen as another aspect of their personality, free of consequences or reference points. Like Diana in *Siete vidas* or even *Ellen*, they are the "lesbian friend" in a heterosexual group, but interestingly, they never have any other LGBT friends. The function of lesbian characters is to show lesbian lifestyle. They go through the main points in the lesbian life narrative: coming out, getting a partner, motherhood, and so forth. However, gay men are treated differently. Their representation has somewhat matured, and they are therefore not so stereotypical. They do not need to continuously explain their homosexuality in the way lesbians do. Nevertheless, for both gay men and lesbians coming out *(salir del armario)* is a constant reference, being shown again and again, focusing on heterosexuals' reactions to the disclosure of the "secret." The heterosexual past of characters is shown as is the process of lesbian self-affirmation. Other common elements to these representations are the constant reference to gay pride marches, which are often presented as a humoristic resource and a universal gay point of identification. No real gay pride march is shown, but the idea of being part of it is a joke or proof of authentic gayness.

Homophobia is only shown in characters' attitudes. Homophobic characters show an exaggerated normativity, acting as the "baddies" (for example, the fruit monger in *Siete vidas* has strong sexist and lesbophobic attitudes). Problems are thus individual and generated by individuals, and the way to solve them is shown to be the lesbian's endurance and personal struggle to be accepted. Societal problems or solutions are thus avoided and excluded.

LESBIAN ARCHETYPES: THE MOTHER, THE BADDY, AND THE UGLY

When we look more closely at the representations of lesbians in the media, we see they are constructed from a limited number of archetypes. These stereotypical clichés reduce the diversity of social, cultural, sexual, and identitary experiences to a few examples that are repeated time and time again.

Lesbians as Mothers and Wives

> Esto supera la ficción;
> debe de ser la realidad
>
> *Ajo*, 2004[45]

When referring to the archetype of lesbian mothers and wives, fiction and reality become intertwined. They are present both in the lesbians in *Big Brother* (Mari, Nuri, Raquel, and Noemí) as well as in the characters of television drama (Diana in *Siete vidas*, Bea in *Aquí no hay quien viva*). In all, the ceremonies and stories showing the points of resistance and the key elements of debate around gay and lesbian rights are persistently repeated. This act of repetition creates a sense of reality and intelligibility, in which the viewer no longer has to go back to real life—a fact has been created. Reality imitated fiction when same-sex weddings were shown on screen before they were made possible by Law 13/2005. In *Siete vidas*, Diana marries a woman marine who has had a child from a previous relationship.

Reality also imitated fiction when Raquel Morillas and Noemí Ungría celebrated their engagement party (2003), followed by their wedding, divorce, and subsequent affairs. In TV series the representations of lesbians become more common after 2000. It is at the same time period that the LGBT movement and political parties were shifting their demands from civil partnerships (1993–2002) to same-sex marriage (2002–2005) and transgender rights (2005 onwards).[46]

The narrative of motherhood through artificial insemination follows the same path in reality and fiction. In *Aquí no hay quien viva* Bea plans her motherhood with Mauri. A typical dyad is formed between her and the camp gay of the show: he originally was not going to exercise his paternity but ends up having a leading role and displacing several potential couples—a pattern that repeated when *Queer as Folk* was aired in the summer of 2006. Reality then goes to show what we have already witnessed in fiction as Mari and Nuri announce they are going to have a child through artificial insemination following their marriage. Despite the novelty of such images, motherhood and lesbian weddings appear as climax points in the fiction series, a climax among an abundance of crazy comic situations. They show lesbians as being mostly asexual, so as not to question the heteronormativity of mainstream society.[47] It is straight characters who have to face the problem of acceptance, homophobia being a personal problem for them. In *Siete vidas* one of the representations of homophobia is through a character who stands in for traditional values—the military father of one of Diana's girlfriends. Once he has overcome his personal resistance, which is merely relational, homophobia disappears. Back in real life, weddings and maternity are also very present in the tabloids and talk shows. They imitate fiction, focusing on them as climax points that need to be examined and commented upon. Therefore, a point of closure is achieved when repeating the known rites of passage and all is reduced to the realm of personal experience.

Diana in *Siete vidas* is somewhat different from other representations of mothers and wives, because throughout the five years of the series, her sexuality has been more explicit, as she has had different partners, picks up women, and openly talks about sex and desire. She has had several very comical flings: a lesbian neighbor with whom she comes out, a famous actress, an exhibitionist with Opus Dei parents, a marine with a child. She flirts with straight women in the series, and her excitement is made explicit by having the character say, "I'm going to the bathroom. Back in a minute!" Despite the apparent liberal nature of the series, when explicit conversations about lesbian desire take place, they reproduce the debates taking place at the time: a lesbian is not a good influence for children, the acceptance of gay marriage, and so forth. They also reproduce the rites of passage: sleeping with a man to be sure one is a lesbian, being honest and coming out to one's parents, trying to be a lesbian mother, getting married. In contrast, the way lesbian sexuality is represented resembles more that of straight and gay men, as behaviors and conversations are created around the irrepressible nature of desire and a "predatory sexuality," treating all attractive women as a target or not recognizing the lack of reciprocity of the women targeted, for example. The lesbian is constructed as a masculine form or as a version of the representation of gay (masculine) sexuality.

If we look at lesbian characters as a whole, both in fiction and in reality, we can see they are remarkably feminine. Except for the women represented as masculine and therefore as bad women as we will see later on, most lesbian representations show aspects, forms, and manners understood to be feminine. Good examples of this are the characters Maca and Esther in *Hospital Central*, where a higher-class lesbian doctor seduces a hesitant nurse. They face their families' homophobia and that of some of their colleagues only to overcome this and achieve a happy marriage and insemination. Both characters are extremely feminine. We know both have a straight past, and we witness their process of coming out and of forming a lesbian home. This representation is very different from that of male gay characters. They are seen as more mature, as their representation is of already being gay at the start of the series, ignoring the complex personal identity processes that they had to go through.

This fictional representation of gay characters has been so accepted by LGBT organizations that it has received prizes for lesbian visibility and has been used as the main face for an Amnesty International publicity campaign.[48] In the absence of real famous lesbians who are open about their sexuality, Maca's fictional character representing all lesbians appears together with the famous gay man Jesús Vázquez in posters for human rights in Latin America. This situation calls our attention to two facts: the lack of known lesbians who are willing to be out to the public and how ideal fictional feminine characters are an acceptable representation of lesbianism.

"Si Maca viviera en Colombia, podría acabar así. Salvajemente violada, torturada y tal vez asesinada por la guerrilla o los paramilitares, sólo por haber sido vista besando a otra mujer. En más de 70 países las lesbianas, gays, bisexuales y transgénero son víctimas de agresiones, asesinatos, persecución policial o incluso ejecuciones a causa de su orientación sexual, real o supuesta. Haz algo.

La homofobia arruina vidas. No lo permitas. Amnistía Internacional."

[If Maca lived in Colombia, she could end up like this. Savagely raped, tortured and perhaps killed by the guerilla forces or the paramilitaries, only for having been seen kissing another woman. In more than 70 countries lesbians, gays, bisexuals and transgender and victims of aggression, murder, political persecution or even execution because of their sexual orientation, real or suspected. Do something.

Homophobia ruins lives. Don't let this happen. Amnesty International]

This archetype challenges normativity by representing an already existing, albeit unknown, reality, which is shown as new in an old role for women—that of wife and mother. Lesbianism has been one of the most transgressive experiences—a sexuality at the margins—that is, nevertheless, now part of one of the most conservative institutions. However, such a representation

"Si Maca viviera en Colombia, podría acabar así. Salvajemente violada, torturada y tal vez asesinada por la guerrilla o los paramilitares, sólo por haber sido visa besando a otra mujer. En más de 70 países las lesbianas, gays, bisexuals y transgénero son víctimas de agresiones, asesinatos, persecución policial o incluso ejecuciones a causa de su orientación sexual, real o supueesta. Haz algo. La homofobia arruina vidas. No lo permitas. Amnistía Internacional." [If Maca lived in Colomia, she could end up like this. Savagely raped, tortured, and perhaps killed by the guerrilla forces or the paramilitaries, only for having been seen kissing a woman. In more than 70 countries lesbians, gays, bisexuals and transgender are victims of aggression, murder, political persecution, or even execution because of their sexual orientation, real or suspected. Do something. Homophobia ruins lives. Don't let this happen. Amnesty International.]

has a limited capacity to generate new transgressions of sexual and gender norms. As occurs with women more generally, a dichotomy between good and bad lesbians is produced. The former are respectable and part of the social order—marked by monogamy, state regulation, and desire for children. The latter are second-class lesbians—non-monogamous, with no wish for state regulation of relationships, migrant workers, sleeping with men.

The Bad and Masculine

Unfortunately, this archetype is built out of many real events, in which the representation is of bad women who are identified as deserving punishment because of their masculinity. The association is not always clear, but it is the pattern that has appeared repeatedly in the lives of both Dolores Vázquez and Encarna Sánchez. Another case we will analyze is that of Raquel Morillas, from *Big Brother*, who was central in the first large-scale public discussion on lesbianism in Spain. If we examine how Dolores Vázquez and Encarna Sánchez have been discussed, we see that they have both been identified as masculine and as adopting roles of leadership and access to power. They both have jobs that imply a certain degree of power. They were both pointed out as visible, seductive, active, and recognized. And both received vociferous social condemnation for their sexuality. The press went into long discussions, descriptions, and judgments of them that were justified on the basis of their masculinity and their more or less explicit lesbianism.

More than ten years have passed since Encarna Sánchez's death (1996). The tabloids produced hundred of articles going into her partners and the presents she gave them, her lost fortune and the power she held. She was well known for her job as a radio journalist, her friends and contacts with famous women, and she was apparently feared by many. But what is of special interest to us is how she was found to be having intimate relationships or flings with famous flamenco singers and other well-known women who were presumably heterosexual. She was seen as using her powers of seduction, which journalists thought to be closely linked to money and gifts. The media did not believe it possible for her to have seduced her many (straight) lovers by any other means. In some popular talk shows it was said about her that "Encarna was a witch and treated everyone like shit," "she's Mafia (or uses Mafiosi techniques)," "a seductress," "milked money from everyone around her." She was connected to famous women like Massiel, Rocío Jurado, Isabel Pantoja, and Nuria Abad and is part of the debate around "lesbian folklore singers."

It is very relevant that she was represented as someone twisted, with her lesbianism forming part of her evil. At the present time she has been judged for her difficulty in accepting her lesbianism and not publicly declaring herself as such—as though it would have been possible to do so ten or twenty years ago without suffering serious personal and professional consequences. The media attention was even more present throughout 2007 when two controversial and frivolous TV shows (*Aquí hay tomate* [*Here's Trouble*]) and *Hormigas Blancas* [*White Ants*]) aired long documentaries based on Encarna Sanchez's relationship with Isabel Pantoja, as well as with other famous women.

Dolores Vázquez has similarly been portrayed as a bad woman.[49] She was arrested on October 7, 2000, and remained in prison for seventeen months. She was accused of the murder of her partner's daughter, which became known as the "Wanninkhoff Case." It is remarkable how the treatment given by the press included a subtext about her lesbianism, although the term or any explicit reference to lesbianism appeared much later.[50] For those following the news it was necessary to read between the lines when she was condemned to fifteen years in prison without any incriminating evidence. The decision was made by a jury in September 2001 based on thirty pieces of circumstantial evidence that included testimony from her employees saying she had torn up a picture of the victim, that she was a cold woman with a strong character, and that she did not have a single nervous breakdown during the trial. Ángel Acebes, the then Secretary of the Interior—of the Conservative Party (*Partido Popular*)—, stated in 2003 that "Dolores Vázquez had the most likely criminal profile."[51]

Her ex-partner told everyone willing to hear that Dolores was guilty and that she herself had been seduced.[52] After the charges were dropped in February 2005, Dolores claimed the right to four million Euros compensation for moral damage by the state.[53] On January 26, 2008, the Minister of Justice offered 120,000 Euros as compensation, although he admitted that what had happened was "especially distressing" (*especial penosidad*).[54]

Lesbophobia was personified in the mourning mother's public statements. Even after Tony King was accused of the murder and other deaths, she continued to insist that Dolores was guilty. We again find the archetype of a bad woman who seduces a poor woman—a straight mother—who welcomes the punishment the former receives for her actions. A good example of this is Salvador Sagaseta's statement for *La Provincia* on September 24, 2003:

> If I had been a juror, I would have probably condemned Dolores Vázquez. Death to the ugly! And even if it is now proven she was innocent she still seems such a repugnant character (short, with a big bum, a lesbian, always with a long face and looking like she did not like to shower), that I would have sent her to the lions without batting an eyelid. The saddest part of the whole thing seems to me that such a dirty woman was not the author of such a crime. . . . I still consider the lesbo in question so suspicious that I see her capable of another crime if not this one. Dolores Vázquez looks so bad that—if I wanted to say something nasty, which is what I would most like to do—I would even leave her in prison because I believe her capable of any obscenity in the near future. But it's also inconceivable to send someone to prison for their ugly face (my own translation).

We find here the typical association between lesbianism and lack of femininity that implies that such badness warrants punishment—with or without proof of a crime. Such a construction is based on the existence of an opposite pole upon which it is based: femininity as the true way of being a woman and straight, or at least a not-so-bad though less credible lesbian, who is seduced against her will by a perverse lesbian who deceives her with money and jewelry. Both representations are extremely harmful to women as they create a strong dichotomy between good and bad, feminine and masculine. They generate an impersonalizing dynamic that makes it impossible to show real women beyond the symbolic script. They maintain and reinforce the claim of men to the monopoly of masculinity. Accordingly, women's transgressive appropriation of masculinity is identified as pathological and is seen as an ever-greater social threat if accompanied by lesbian desire.[55] Statements like Salvador Sagaseta's are suspiciously close to what Albert Ellis said in 1928 about the "true lesbian invert": "Sudden and energetic movements, the posture of the arms, direct speech . . . there is also unfriendliness and an inability for sewing and other domestic endeavours and, often, certain athletic capacity."[58] Both Havelock Ellis and Radclyffe Hall, in the classic *Well of Loneliness* (1928) conceptualized lesbianism in a way that would persist until the 1970s.[57]

A further instance that offered the representation of lesbians as bad and masculine was that of the popular TV program *Big Brother*. Spain is the country where this show has aired the longest and where sexuality has been a key issue. Several winners have been bisexual, gay or transsexual (the Netherlands in 2000; the UK in 2001 and 2004). In 2002 Raquel Morillas was one of the contestants. She was a masculine woman with a strong character that soon polarized the debates. Once the show was over we saw her fall in love with another of the contestants, Noemí Ungría and admit to their relationship on the talk show *Crónicas Marcianas*. Before long there were those stating that Noemí was not a credible lesbian because of her heterosexual past and feminine appearance. The two women used their popularity to become the image of lesbian clubs in Barcelona. They had a car accident, as a result of which Raquel's face was severely disfigured while Noemí was intact. In the meantime, the rumours grew about Noemí having the relationship out of convenience. However, Raquel and Noemí celebrated a commitment party, as an imitation of a wedding, since same-sex marriage was still not legal in 2003. Suddenly, there was an unexpected turn of events when the couple split up, and the unconvincing lesbian entered into a relationship with an even more masculine woman—Judd. Everyone, including Raquel, spitefully said she was "a guy." The story goes on, with more break-ups and affairs, and in 2006 Judd came out as a transsexual man. What is most interesting about this story is that in the whole debate about masculinity it is presented as something negative that must be corrected by the same sort of glamor that gay men have, even by those defined as masculine.

For the first time ever, we witnessed how the tabloids treated and were capable of processing such a story. An array of friends, ex-lovers, and colleagues filed on screen and talked about the love triangle. Barcelona's nightlife was discussed, different lesbians took sides, even their parents were interviewed. The public had access through the press and television to a story as horrible as any other, but it had at its center something never before witnessed. The women were devoid of political discourse, and their experiences were treated as personal questions. It was the first time that lesbianism was lived and represented on TV as live-TV, their lives and experiences were broadcast as a daily soap. All involved were aware of the media impact of their sexuality and have exploited it in a number of ways: by lending their

Promotional flyer for a new lesbian bar depicting Noemí and Judd. Year: 2004.

LAS DOS JÓVENES SELLAN SU AMOR EN UNA ÍNTIMA Y EMOTIVA CEREMONIA, RODEADAS POR SU FAMILIA Y AMIGOS MÁS QUERIDOS

cturas

26 de Diciembre de 2003

ncipe y doña
a, íntimo fin de
na en Londres

ista
ermo
, papá
50 años

rma y Miriam
í viven las Fiestas

Canarias: 1,90 € (Only Spain)

02700

428019 000019

Raquel
y Noemí

Su día más feliz

Ferran Adrià, Juan Mari Arzak, Ramón Roteta, Benjamín Urdiain...

8 FICHAS CON LAS RECETAS DE ARGUIÑANO Y SUS AMIGOS

Front cover of the gossip magazine *Lecturas*. Year: December 2003. With permission of the magazine.

image to web pages and bars in Barcelona and by taking part in television programs.

We learned through this story that masculine lesbians such as Raquel have relationships with women who are perceived as more feminine and less credible as lesbians. The former "have always been that way"; their lesbianism has not been chosen and is therefore more genuine. We also learn that such masculinity and such relationships have negative consequences, such as a car accident. As Raquel appeared more and more on television, her image became less masculine, and when she suffered the car accident, she became secondary. Her popularity decreased with the accident: once Raquel lost her space on the largest evening talk show, she moved to afternoon talk shows with a lower profile. These shows included both ex-lovers: Raquel and Noemí, being asked to talk about each other, but also commenting on events in *Big Brother*.

These representations of bad women who deserve suicide or jail are similar to the way that many contemporary lesbian films end, in which the lesbian protagonists are portrayed as tormented, mad, and sad, and where they suffer and die. These portrayals contribute to the construction of masculinity as pernicious to women and lesbianism as tragic, becoming mechanisms that justify lesbophobia as a form of social control.

LESBIAN FOLKLORE SINGERS: AUDIENCE AND GOSSIP

At the end of 2005, we witnessed the creation of a new term: *lesbianas folclóricas* [lesbian folklore singers]. It was produced by the tabloids in programs such as *Aquí hay tomate.* According to the station, it had a 28.5% increase in audience as a consequence of the story on lesbian folklore singers. Some have branded this phenomenon as "outing for profit" in clear reference to its commercial use.[58] This is a new version of the old idea of lesbian folklore singers linked to the traditional world of music and folklore, and of their being not very credible as lesbians but generating a lot of "twisted curiosity." Not only *Aqui hay tomate* but other TV shows and tabloids reproduced and promoted the debates that were presenting them as lesbians.[59] The comments about Encarna Sánchez, mentioned previously, were quite simply based on rumor. We could say then that folklore singer lesbians are "fictional characters," a TV product that makes profit out of the stigma attached to lesbianism, as we know of their lesbianism only through third parties, none of them having openly declared their sexuality as lesbian. The suspected lesbian folk singers are among the circle of Encarna Sánchez's supposed lovers. These include singers about whom there have been previous rumors, such as Isabel Pantoja and María del Monte.[60] One such rumor used images related to Encarna Sánchez and the fact that Isabel had adopted a child whose godmother is María. Other names mentioned have included La polaca, Imperio Argentina, Gracia Montes.

This journalistic treatment is based on the overrepresentation of folklore singers as a feminine archetype, as one that is diametrically opposed to the masculine lesbian. Both representations of folk singers and masculine women as lesbians created a lot of unhealthy curiosity because of the popularity of these women. It is perhaps most interesting that in the representation "lesbian" has been used as an insult. It is a negative term which is used to denigrate famous women, who then defend themselves by showing their "normality." They show that they have not been seduced by bad women such as Encarna Sánchez or that they resisted it. Any expression other than heterosexuality seems unconvincing or even incomprehensible, a source of twisted curiosity and material for countless newspaper articles. The same negative treatment of lesbianism has been seen in other not-so-lucky *Big Brother* contestants, like Elba or even Mila Ximenez, Encarna Sánchez's ex-lover. Here we come up against a lesbian visibility that is meant to be insulting. Tabloids and television are interested in this topic only because of the destructive interest it generates among the heterosexual audience, which understands the accusation of lesbianism as an insult. Consequently the media use this issue exclusively to get a better position on primetime television.

Lesbians for Him

This notion is far from a new archetype. It has been used in all sorts of media to sell a wide range of articles. It is based on the idea that women's sexuality is passive and receptive, constructed in opposition to men's active and assertive sexuality, and with no autonomy from men. Homoerotic images are thus created that invite or show a third person: the heterosexual, white, Western, able-bodied, urban male gaze. This conceptualization is not far removed from the one prevalent in Francoist times, which stated that a woman should be at her husband's or father's service. During the time of the dictatorship, women were conceptualized as a source of male satisfaction, at the same time as naturalizing this order and refusing women's desire to be independent or to acknowledge its very possibility.[61] Therefore, such representations show extremely feminine women posing as in ecstasy while showing their availability. Their mouths are half open, their pupils dilated, inviting the male gaze. The images are accompanied by slogans such as "¿Quién dijo que es sólo para hombres?" [Who said it was just for men?], "Los amigos no son nunca casuales" [Friends are never by chance]. In the latter we can see a third person—the man who watches and controls the scene. Such scenes invite us into moments of presumed intimacy, where we practice an intrusive voyeurism that imitates pornography. It is the context of a sexual moment that appeals directly to men (and some women!) who feel that the subtext speaks to them.

Conclusion

Mass media shows the main socioeconomic changes of Spain's recent history. These range from the new social roles available to women to changes in the construction of sexuality. We can also see the transformations in the way that lesbians are represented. They have gone from being invisible and completely taboo to a gradual inclusion that can be found mainly in lesboerotic fiction. Advertising and television series reproduce novel images that, like representations of women as a whole, are subject to an andro- and heterocentric perspective.

Representations of lesbians attract the audience's attention. Media use their novelty and ability to invoke a desire constructed as masculine in order to sell numerous products, and they generate a self-righteous debate about society's acceptance of non-normative sexualities. The use of such images generates a fiction of acceptance and openness that fits well with the desire to belong to a modern and liberal state. Lesbian visibility thus appears as a qualitative change. However, the images shown are reduced to a specific repertoire linked to a very precise set of meanings.

Lesbians and society as a whole learn from representations in the media what lesbian identity and lesboeroticism are about, and these become the main models of (self)reference.[62] The collective imaginary is built on lesbian (in)visibility. Women's roles are limited to being bad mothers or wives—and there are also lesbian images used as a source of pleasure for the masculine gaze. Such stereotypical images delegitimize lesbian sexuality as pleasurable or even possible, allowing it but a few representations. The stereotyping and homogenization of lesbian representations reduce the possibilities of the imaginary of these diverse and fluid realities, which become restricted to images generated for men or which are presented as a problem for the individual, or just as something that is no longer a problem. They give a certain sense of comfort both for LGBT people and for society as a whole, through a discourse of tolerance and acceptance, albeit with limits. In television series homophobia and patriarchy disappear when discrimination is represented. It then becomes a personal and temporary issue demanding personal and temporary solutions. Another set of attributes comes into play: that of rendering the lesbian herself responsible for the effects of her own discrimination by being depicted as a bad or a defective woman.

In order to show the process of reduction of lesbians' and women's erotic experience, this chapter has sought to present archetypical representations, showing how these are constructed on a *monosexual* type of sexuality. This means that the only possibilities given are identity processes within heterosexuality or a conservative or illegitimate lesbianism. The former is conservative because of the restrictions imposed on the roles available, while the latter is rendered illegitimate by being presented as "sex for him." The images show a tension between the construction of lesbian otherness and the representation of utter normality. Both maintain the sexual order, since they do not question the values inherent to compulsory heterosexuality.

Most archetypes analyzed in this essay present lesbians in the roles of mothers and wives, rehearsing the new social roles that current Spanish legislation allows. These images create a certain degree of self-satisfaction by discussing our resistance to regarding lesbians as mothers and wives, which coincides with the desire to mainstream culture as tolerant and inclusive. It also assigns lesbians within a normativity marked by monogamy, state regulation of relationships, and the gender order (i.e., by showing all women as potential mothers).

Another archetype we often find is that of lesbians as bad women, their masculinity proving they deserve punishment. Dolores Vázquez is one such unfortunate case, her murder accu-

sation having been based upon the prejudices of society as a
whole, which saw her as straying from the conventions of normative heterosexuality and therefore warranting punishment.
The lesbian triangle formed by Raquel, Noemí, and Judd in *Big
Brother* introduced the audience to lesbian nightlife, masculinity as a negative attribute, and to the barrier between lesbianism
and transgenderism. The representations of Encarna Sánchez are
also an example of the construction of the "bad woman." She
was at the center of the media creation of the "lesbian folk singers," which has produced considerable profit shares for television channels. The use of the term "lesbian" as an insult is the
central point of the debate around lesbian folk singers. Therefore, this representation is far from breaking stereotypes; rather
it is used as a means to attract the audience to the tabloids and
to reality talk shows.

The third most common archetype is that of lesbians as a
product for heterosexual male consumption. This archetype
conceptualizes sexuality as making an instrumental use of
women. It is a very common representation in advertising,
which uses sexualized and hyperfeminine images that invite us
as men to engage in a voyeuristic act, a presumed intimate moment between two women. Moreover, none of the archetypical
constructions show lesbians or women in relationships with
women as citizens with certain experiences and an alternative
sexuality. We are rather trained to accept the gaze of those producing the constructions. They show a social desire for lesbian
women to be feminine and available, within a certain range of
liberal roles as women and mothers that we can now play, and
from which not even folk singers are free. Masculine women are
represented as bad, or simply nonexistent, as they are not desirable and lack gay glamor.

Television shows lesbians as women with a heterosexual past
who must come out of the closet in order to be honest to people
around them, who, after all, deserve this. We must also strive to
be sure that we are lesbians, maybe by trying to be with men.
Then, after being sure, we must take up roles which are coherent
with society's demands. Lesbian characters become treatises on
lesbianism. They become examples of all that is possible within
our cultural imaginary, including which roles are available to us.

As we have seen, lesbian representations share with those of
women in general the effects of stereotyping, which confine us
to very limited behavioral patterns and identity processes. These
are not solved by increased lesbian visibility but through the

transformation of such representations. Lesbian lives and the homoerotic relationships between women are fortunately more complex, messy, and fluid than the behaviors prescribed. I am not suggesting that one set of representations be replaced by another, but I would seek to problematize such representations and identities. Organizations, leaders, and lesbian women have the power to generate new images, transform stereotypes, and decide in which spheres they want to be signified and in what way. Some good practices to be suggested to the media would be questioning standard identitary processes, enabling the representation of more fluid and less homogenizing sexual representations, and presenting real people. We also need to be braver when it comes to showing homophobia in diverse situations. Homophobia is real, it is news, and discussing it is of public interest. Lastly, it is vital to diversify the images of women's homoeroticism. For example, we might include images of female masculinity without linking masculinity to the notion of being a bad woman. Or we might represent motherhood and other feminine roles within a much wider spectrum of possible roles. In the near future it remains to be seen what the new legislation, the changes in the conceptualization of sexuality, the impact of queer studies, and the proliferation of images and discourses generated by LGBT people, can produce—not only in terms of new lesbian representations, but also in terms of new ways of understanding non-normative sexuality.

NOTES

This article is a result of my long-standing interest which started with my presentation of the paper "Lesbophobias" at the First Conference on Lesbianism of 2003 (organized by National Federation of LGBT organizations, FELGT in Madrid). As time has gone by I have had the chance to contact different authors and learn. I am especially grateful for the support I have received from Didi Herman and Davina Cooper at the Research Centre for Law, Gender and Sexuality (University of Kent) under the grant given under the "Associate Fellow Scheme" in October 2005, which resulted in the present article. A previous version of this chapter has been published in: Raquel Platero, "Las lesbianas en los medios de comunicación: madres, folclóricas y masculinas," in *Lesbianas: Discursos y representaciones,* ed. Raquel Platero, 307–38 (Barcelona: Melusina, 2008).
    1. In 1954 the original 1933 Vagrants and Delinquents law was reformed to include and punish homosexuality. With regard to the 16/1970 Dangers to Society law, according to Jordi Petit, between 1974 and 1975 the law was applied to approximately one hundred fifty-two gay men and two lesbians, reflecting the conceptualization of sexuality regarding women (*25 años más: Una pers-*

pectiva sobre el pasado, el presente y el futuro del movimiento de gays, lesbianas, bisexuales y transexuales (Barcelona: Icaria, 2003), 27–28). To date only one police record from the Franco regime (1968)—showing the state repression of a female-bodied person dressed as a man—in which lesbianism and crime are associated and judged as delinquent has been exposed (Raquel Platero, "Opuntes sobre la represión organizada del lesboerotismo y masculinidad de las mujeres en el período franquista," in *Homosexuals i transsexuals: Els altres represaliats i discriminats del frauquismo, des de la memòria històrica,* ed. José Benito Eres Rigueira and Carlos Villagrasa Alcaide, 85–114 (Barcelona: Bellaterra, 2008). Nonetheless, legislation and its application impacts on self-perception, the symbolic representation and self-censorship of women and sexuality, interpreted within the limits of marriage and maternity. During the dictatorship, imprisonment was the punishment for wives in cases of infidelity—but not for husbands—, along with soft legal measures against honour crimes committed by those husbands in case of infidelity (known as 'Uxoricidio') (Amparo Rubiales Torrejón, *La evolución de la situación jurídica de la mujer en España,* Club Antares de Sevilla, Instituto Andaluz de la Mujer 2003)).

2. The "Democracy Code" is a progressive text introducing advanced and democratic penal legislation that respects and protects a citizen's sexual orientation.

3. These two groundbreaking legal amendments are expressed thus in Spanish: Ley 13/2005, de 1 de julio, por la que se modifica el Código Civil en materia de derecho a contraer matrimonio, BOE de 2 de julio de 2005, nº 157; Ley 3/2007, de 15 de marzo, reguladora de la rectificación registral de la mención relativa al sexo de las personas, BOE 65 de 16 de marzo de 2007 nº 11251.

4. I would like to thank Tatiana Sentamans from Miguel Hernández University for her guidance and her research contribution on the representation of lesbian images in the early twentieth century, which she has generously shared with me for this article.

5. *Mädchen in Uniform* (1931) is the first film in the history of cinema that explicitly shows lesbianism. This German film, directed by Leontine Sagan and Carl Froelich, depicts the love story between a young woman and a teacher at a girls' boarding school. The Spanish magazine *Blanco y Negro* reported on the film (Marquina, 1933: 99–104), as well as its relevance for the career of Dorothea Wieck (Marshal, 1934: 97–99).

6. *BN,* año 45, nº 2.273, d-10-II-1935.

7. Tatiana Sentamans, *Viragos en acción, señoritas ante el obturador: La imagen de la mujer deportista en la fotografía documental de la España prebélica (1923–1936)* (Diploma de Estudios Avanzados, Universidad Politécnica de Valencia, 2007).

8. I still remember the summer evening in the late 90s when *Ellen* came out of the closet. The program was shown as part of the evening schedule, when children's programs are also shown (between 5 and 8 p.m.). My family was watching the show while having a snack. My grandmother was becoming visibly uncomfortable, while my brother and I were pleasantly surprised. *Ellen* was coming out of the closet during a time slot in which we all expected to see youth sitcoms. That was also the case with *Roseanne,* which caught us off guard. Both shows produced a great impact in North America, but they were shown here with little comment or prior warning, to an audience craving gay and lesbian stories.

9. *Me siento extraña*, dir. Enrique Martí Maqueda, with Rocío Durcal and Barbara Rey (Suevia, 1977).

10. Some of the foreign shows with lesbian and gay characters that were shown on Spanish TV used a translated (or creative) title, whereas other kept their original names: *Dinastía* [*Dynasty*], *Enredo* [*Soap*], *Cheers*, *Las chicas de oro* [*Golden Girls*], *Roseanne*, *Treinta y tantos* [*Thirty something*], *Sensación de vivir* [*Beverly Hills 90210*], *Melrose Place*, *Ellen*, *La ley de los Ángeles* [*L.A. Law*], *Doctor en Alaska* [*Northern Exposure*], *Seinfield*, *Frasier*, *Los Simpson*, *Friends*, *Urgencias* [*E.R.*], *Xena*, *Buffy la Cazavampiros* [*Buffy the Vampire Slayer*], *Felicity*, *Dawson Crece* [*Dawson Creek*], *Allie McBeal*, *Nikita*, *A dos metros bajo tierra* [*Six Feet Under*], *House*, *Mujeres desesperadas* [*Desperate Housewives*], for example.. Recently, we have had access to shows that are promoted as "gay" or "lesbian," such as: *Will and Grace*, *"L" (The "L" Word)*, and *Queer as Folk* (2005–6).

11. The album, "Descanso Dominical," was recorded in 1988.

12. Rosa Montero, "El misterio del deseo: Así son y así viven las lesbianas en España," *El País Semanal* (October 31, 1993): 16–28.

13. Colectivo de Feministas Lesbianas de Madrid, "¿Quién te ha visto y quién te ve? Como nos presentamos las lesbianas en los medios de comunicación," in *Juntas y a por todas*, 207–8 (Madrid: Federación de Organizaciones Feministas del Estado Español, 1993).

14. Luz Sánchez Mellado, "Lesbiana sin complejos," *El País Semanal*. (June 29, 2003): 36–47. Further references to this article will be documented parenthetically within the text.

15. Paloma Fernández-Rasines, "Lesbianas en el mercado: Homoerotismo y mujeres en las pequeñas pantallas," *Cultura y Política*. *Actas IX Congreso de la Federación de Asociaciones de Antropología del Estado Español FAAEE* (Barcelona, 2002).

16. Illy Nes, *Hijas de Adán: Las mujeres también salen del armario* (Madrid: Hijos de Muley-Rubio, 2002), 141.

17. Ibid.

18. Carlos Arnanz et al., "¿Series o Telenovelas?" *Revista del Guión: Guionactualidad* (Barcelona: Universidad Autónoma Barcelona, 2006), *http://antalya.uab.es/guionactualidad/article.php3?id_arti cle = 1243*.

19. Ricardo Llamas, *Miss Media: Una lectura perversa de la comunicación de masas* (Barcelona: La Tempestad, 1997).

20. Fernando Bruquetas, *Outing en España: Los españoles salen del armario* (Majadahonda: Hijos e Muley-Rubio D.L., 2000), 108.

21. Raquel Platero, "¿Invisibiliza el matrimonio homosexual a las lesbianas?," *Orientaciones* 10 (2006): 103–20.

22. Suzanna Danuta Walters, *All the Rage: The Story of Gay Visibility in America* (Chicago: University of Chicago Press, 2001). Further references to this publication will be documented parenthetically within the text.

23. Naomi Klein, *No Logo* (Barcelona: Paidós, 2001).

24. Sentamans, *Viragos en acción*.

25. Victoria Seldón de León, "Y el verbo se hizo imagen," in *Publicidad: La imagen de la mujer en la publicidad y su influencia en los medios de comunicación* (Madrid: AMECO, 2001), 11.

26. Tessa Boffin & Jean Fraser. *Stolen Glances: Lesbians Take Photographs* (London: Pandora, 1991), 10.

27. Catherine Belsey, *Critical Practice* (London: Methuen, 1980); John Be-

rger, *Ways of Seeing* (Harmondsworth: Penguin Books, 1972); Laura Mulvey, "Visual Pleasure and Narrative Cinema," *Screen* 16.3 (1975): 6–18. Further references to these publications will be documented parenthetically within the text.

28. Isabel M. Menéndez Menéndez, "Bellas y radiantes: Aproximación al mensaje publicitario dirigido a las adolescentes," in *Publicidad: La imagen de la mujer en la publicidad y su influencia en los medios de comunicación* (Madrid: AMECO, 2001), 105; María García, "Investigación para el cambio de la imagen de la mujer en la publicidad," in *Mujeres y hombres y medios de comunicación*, Vol. 1 (Valladolid: Junta de Castilla y León, 2002), 57–58. There is a paradoxical simultaneous relationship of overrepresentation and underrepresentation of women. On the one hand, there is a generous presentation of women in all media, as objects of the male gaze used to sell a huge range of products. In contrast, women are simultaneously underrepresented in their access to power. Therefore, they are not part of the content of the news or the main spheres of social participation.

29. Michel Foucault, *Discipline and Punish: The Birth of the Prison* (Harmondsworth: Peregrine Books, 1979). Caroline Evans and Lorraine Gamman ("The Gaze Revisited, or Reviewing Queer Viewing," in *A Queer Romance: Lesbians and Gay Men in Popular Culture*, ed. Paul Burston and Colin Richardson (London: Routledge, 1995), 49) pointed to the contribution of Foucault's "panopticon" in his text published in Colin Gordon, ed., *Power/Knowledge: Selected Interviews and Other Writings 1972–77* (Brighton: Harvester, 1980).

30. Sentamans, *Viragos en acción*; Rebecca Johnson, *Taxing Choices: The Intersection of Class, Gender, Parenthood, and the Law (Law and Society).* (Vancouver: British Columbia University Press, 2002), 4.

31. The research conducted by Pilar López Díez analyzed the TV and radio news over a period of two weeks chosen randomly out of six weeks. She focused on two midday news broadcasts during weekdays (forty radio programs and thirty-five news programs between June 11 and June 29, 2001. The channels studied were *TVE1, La2, Tele5, Antena3*; the radio stations were *RNE, SER, ONDA CERO* and *COPE*. Pilar López Díez, *Representación de género en los informativos de radio y televisión* (Madrid: Instituto de la Mujer: 2001); Pilar López Díaz, *Segundo informe representación de género en los informativos de radio y television* (Madrid: Instituto de la Mujer, 2005).

32. Evans and Gamman, "The Gaze Revisited." Further references to this article will be documented parenthetically within the text.

33. Teresa de Lauretis, ed., *Diferencias* (Madrid: Horas y horas, 2000).

34. Raquel Osborne, *Entre la rosa y el violeta: Lesbianismo, feminismo y movimiento gay: Relato de amores difíciles* Labrys, 2006. http://www.unb.br/ih/his/gefem/labrys10/espanha/raquel.htm.

35. Raquel Platero, "¿Invisibiliza el matrimonio?"

36. Kathleen Battles and Wendy Hilton-Morrow, "Gay Characters in Conventional Spaces: *Will and Grace* and the Situation Comedy Genre," *Critical Studies in Media Communication* 19.1 (2002), 102; Walters, *All the Rage.*

37. My work is preceded by other authors such as Kathleen Battles and Wendy Hilton-Morrow and Suzanne Danuta Walters.

38. I am not saying that lesbian mothers or lesbian marriages are not transformative. I wish rather to highlight the impact of limiting lesbian representation to these roles.

39. Bonnie J. Dow, "Ellen, Television and the Politics of Gay and Lesbian

Visibility," *Critical Studies in Media Communication* 18.2 (2001): 123–40;
Battles and Hilton-Morrow, "Gay Characters."
	40. Among others, see articles by Battle and Hilton-Morrow, "Gay Charac-
ters,"; Dow, "Ellen, Television," 128; and Herman Gray, "Television, Black
Americans, and the American Dream," in *Television: The Critical View*, ed.
Horace Newcomb, 176–87 (New York: Oxford University Press, 1994).
	41. The impact of this show was present in the Spanish press. See for exam-
ple: R. Rivas, "La 2 emite *Ellen*, la primera telecomedia de EE UU con protagonista homosexual," *EL PAÍS* (July 2, 1997) and J. Cavestany, "Primera serie en
EE UU con protagonista homosexual," *EL PAÍS* (October 2, 1996).
	42. The most conservative sectors of society started a boycott against the
advertising campaign 'Descubre tu propio Yo' because it presents two women
in homosexual poses. The boycott was launched through the website *Hazte
Oir*, the same that was involved in the demonstration against same-sex marriage on June 18, 2005. See http://hazteoir.org/modules.php?name = Noticia-
sandfile = articlea ndsid = 2706.
	43. Pilar López Díez, *Representación de género*, 9.
	44. Patricia Vico and Fátima Baeza. *Mundo Joven LGTB* (Madrid: Fundación
Triángulo, October–November, 2005), 11.
	45. *Ajo*, "Micropoemas" (Madrid: La luz roja, 2004).
	46. Raquel Platero, "Overcoming Brides and Grooms: The Representation
of Lesbian and Gay Rights in Spain," in *Multiple Meanings of Gender Equality: A Critical Frame Analysis of Gender Policies in Europe*, ed. Mieke Verloo,
207–32 (Budapest: Central European University Press, 2007).
	47. Fred Fejes, "Making a Gay Masculinity," *Critical Studies in Media
Communication* 17.1 (2000): 116.
	48. The Gay and Lesbian Visibility prize was granted by Fundación Trián-
gulo in the context of the 2005 Gay and Lesbian Film Festival (Lesgaicinemad).
	49. There is one interesting article that compares the process experienced
by Dolores Vázquez with the "Arny Case," highlighting the use of sexuality as
a reason for punishment: Vicente Molina Foix, "El 'caso Wanninkhof': lo
oculto," *EL PAÍS Opinión* (October 10, 2003).
	50. Beatriz Gimeno, *Historia y análisis político del lesbianismo: La libera-
ción de una generación* (Madrid: Gedisa, 2006).
	51. "Dolores Vázquez tenía el perfil delincuencial más verosímil," *EL PAÍS*
(October 2, 2003).
	52. Dolores remained silent for most of the trial; in one of the few state-
ments to the press she alluded to homophobia without naming it. Because it
shows a lack of maturity, the propensity of Spanish society to conduct witch
hunts and to lynch more times than not, lacking any kind of evidence, without
information or any sense of caution, is worrying. We would have to dive into a
collective pathology created during centuries of inquisition to be able to understand these shallow judgments and this cruelty that enables individuals to ban
a movie without having seen it and at the same time point at someone as
guilty. ["Es preocupante, por lo que supone de falta de madurez, la propensión
de la sociedad española a la caza de brujas y al linchamiento las más de las
veces sin tener pruebas, ni información, ni el más mínimo sentido de la prude-
ncia. Habría que bucear en una patología colectiva creada por siglos de Inquisi-
ción, para entender esa ligereza en los juicios y esa crueldad en la condena que
lo mismo exige la retirada de una película sin haberla visto que señala a ojo y
con el dedo a los culpables de cualquier crimen"], *Noticias de Navarra* (September 20, 2003).

53. F.J. Pérez, "Dolores Vázquez exige cuatro millones por daños morales. Pide una indemnización al Estado por sus 17 meses en prisión por el 'caso Wanninkhof,'" *EL PAÍS* (January 25, 2006).

54. F.J. Pérez, "Justicia ofrece 120.000 euros a Dolores Vázquez por su calvario. Pasó 17 meses en prisión por error en el "caso Wanninkhof,'" *EL PAÍS* (January 26, 2008).

55. Judith Halberstam, *Female Masculinity* (London: Duke University Press, 1998).

56. Havelock Ellis, *Studies in the Psychology of Sex, Vol. 1, Sexual Inversion* (Philadelphia: PA: Davis, 1928), 250.

57. Anne Fausto Sterling, *Cuerpos sexuados* (Barcelona: Melusina, 2006), 316.

58. Alba Colomer, Susana Font, and Marta Taurina, "Outing: El largo viaje de la homofobia al orgullo," *Sales* 3 (2006): 16.

59. José Manuel Martín de la Plaza stated that "half of the Spanish folklore singers are lesbians." *EUROPA PRESS*, Madrid (November 14, 2005).

60. The talk show *Aquí hay tomate* took a further step by setting a date in which the relationship started, along with generating a discussion about their relationship, stating that folklore singers Isabel Pantoja and María del Monte lived together from 1995 until their break-up in 1999.

61. Gema Pérez Sánchez, *Queer Transitions in Contemporary Spanish Culture: From Franco to La Movida* (Albany: State University of New York Press, 2007).

62. Llamas, *Miss Media.*

REFERENCES

Ajo. "Micropoemas." Madrid: La luz roja, 2004.

Arnanz, Carlos, et al. "¿Series o Telenovelas?" *Revista del Guión: Guionactualidad.* Barcelona: Universidad Autónoma Barcelona, 2006. http://antalya.u-ab.es/guionactualidad/article.php3?id_article = 1243.

Battles, Kathleen, and Wendy Hilton-Morrow. "Gay Characters in Conventional Spaces: *Will and Grace* and the Situation Comedy Genre." *Critical Studies in Media Communication* 19.1 (2002): 87–105.

Belsey, Catherine. *Critical Practice.* London: Methuen, 1980.

Berger, John. *Ways of Seeing.* Harmondsworth: Penguin Books, 1972.

Boffin, Tessa, and Jean Fraser. *Stolen Glances: Lesbians Take Photographs.* London: Pandora, 1991.

Bruquetas, Fernando. *Outing en España: Los españoles salen del armario.* Majadahonda: Hijos de Muley-Rubio D.L., 2000.

Colectivo de Feministas Lesbianas de Madrid. "¿Quién te ha visto y quién te ve? Como nos presentamos las lesbianas en los medios de comunicación." In *Juntas y a por todas*, 207–8. Madrid: Federación de Organizaciones Feministas del Estado Español, 1993.

Colomer, Alba, Susana Font, and Marta Taurina. "Outing: El largo viaje de la homofobia al orgullo." *Sales* 3 (2006): 11–17.

de Lauretis, Teresa, ed. *Diferencias.* Madrid: Horas y horas, 2000.

Dow, Bonnie J. "Ellen, Television and the Politics of Gay and Lesbian Visibility." *Critical Studies in Media Communication* 18.2 (2001): 123–40.

Ellis, Havelock. *Studies in the Psychology of Sex. Vol 1, Sexual Inversion.* Philadelphia, PA: Davis, 1928.

Evans, Caroline, and Lorraine Gamman. "The Gaze Revisited, or Reviewing Queer Viewing." In *A Queer Romance: Lesbians and Gay Men in Popular Culture*, edited by Paul Burston and Colin Richardson, 12–61. London: Routledge, 1995.

Fausto Sterling, Anne. *Cuerpos sexuados.* Barcelona: Melusina, 2006.

Fejes, Fred. "Making a Gay Masculinity." *Critical Studies in Media Communication.* 17.1 (2000): 113–16.

Fernández-Rasines, Paloma. "Lesbianas en el mercado: homoerotismo y mujeres en las pequeñas pantallas." *Cultura y Política. Actas IX Congreso de la Federación de Asociaciones de Antropología del Estado Español FAAEE.* Barcelona, 2002: 1–16.

Foucault, Michel. *Discipline and Punish: The Birth of the Prison.* Harmondsworth: Peregrine Books, 1979.

García, María. "Investigación para el cambio de la imagen de la mujer en la publicidad." In *Mujeres y hombres y medios de comunicación*, Vol. 1, 55–68. Valladolid: Junta de Castilla y León, 2002.

Gimeno, Beatriz. *Historia y análisis político del lesbianismo: La liberación de unageneración.* Madrid: Gedisa, 2006.

Gordon, Colin, ed. *Power/Knowledge: Selected Interviews and Other Writings 1972–77.* Brighton: Harvester, 1980.

Gray, Herman. "Television, Black Americans, and the American Dream." In *Television: The Critical View*, edited by Horace Newcomb, 176–87. New York: Oxford University Press, 1994.

Halberstam, Judith. *Female Masculinity.* London: Duke University Press, 1998.

Hernández, Carmen. "De la hoguera a la cárcel: culpable por ser lesbiana e independiente. El caso de Dolores Vázquez." *I Congreso Internacional sobre Mujeres Malas. Percepción y representación de la mujer transgresora en el mundo luso-hispánico.* Universidade Fernando Pessoa. Oporto, June 26–28, 2003.

Johnson, Rebecca. *Taxing Choices: The Intersection of Class, Gender, Parenthood, and the Law (Law and Society).* Vancouver: British Columbia University Press, 2002. h Colombia.

Klein, Naomi. *No Logo.* Barcelona: Paidós, 2001.

Llamas, Ricardo. *Miss Media: Una lectura perversa de la comunicación de masas.* Barcelona: La Tempestad, 1997.

López Díez, Pilar. *Representación de género en los informativos de radio y televisión.* Madrid: Instituto de la Mujer, 2001.

———. *Segundo informe representación de género en los informativos de radio y televisión.* Madrid: Instituto de la Mujer, 2005.

Menéndez Menéndez, Isabel M. "Bellas y radiantes: Aproximación al mensaje publicitario dirigido a las adolescentes." In *Publicidad: La imagen de la mujer en la publicidad y su influencia en los medios de comunicación*, 93–116. Madrid: AMECO, 2001.

Mädchen in Uniform. Directed by Leontine Sagan and Carl Froelich, with Hertha Thiele, Dorothea Wieck. Filmchoice, 1931.

Marquina, Rafael. "Señoritas de uniforme." *Blanco y negro,* (August 7, 1932): 99–104.

Marshall, Eddie. "Figuras de pantalla Dorotsa Wieck." *Blanco y negro* (January 21, 1934): 97–99.

Me siento extraña. Directed by Enrique Martí Maqueda, with Rocío Durcal, Barbara Rey Suevia, 1977.

Montero, Rosa. "El misterio del deseo: Así son y así viven las lesbianas en España." *El País Semanal* (October 31, 1993): 16–28.

Mulvey, Laura. "Visual Pleasure and Narrative Cinema." *Screen* 16.3 (1975): 6–18.

Nes, Illy. *Hijas de Adán: Las mujeres también salen del armario.* Madrid: Hijos de Muley-Rubio, 2002.

Osborne, Raquel. *Entre la rosa y el violeta: Lesbianismo, feminismo y movimiento gay: Relato de unos amores difíciles.* Labrys, http://www.unb.br/ih/his/gefem/labrys10/espanha/raquel.htm.

Pérez Sánchez, Gema. *Queer Transitions in Contemporary Spanish Culture: From Franco to La Movida.* Albany: State University of New York Press, 2007.

Petit, Jordi. *25 años más: Una perspectiva sobre el pasado, el presente y el futuro del movimiento de gays, lesbianas, bisexuales y transexuales.* Barcelona: Icaria, 2003.

Platero, Raquel. "Apuntes sobre la represión organizada del lesboerotismo y masculinidad de las mujeres en el período franquista." In *Homosexuals i transsexuals: Els altres represaliats i discriminats del franquisme, des de la memòria històrica,* edited by José Benito Eres Rigueira and Carlos Villagrasa Alcaide, 85–114. Barcelona: Bellaterra, 2008.

———. "Intersecting gender and sexual orientation. An analysis of sexuality and citizenship in gender equality policies in Spain. 'Contesting Citizenship: Comparative Analyses.'" *Critical Review of International Social and Political Philosophy,* 10.4 (2007): 575–97.

———. "¿Invisibiliza el matrimonio homosexual a las lesbianas?" *Orientaciones* 10 (2006): 103–20.

———. "Las lesbianas en los medios de comunicación: madres, folclóricas y masculinas." In *Lesbianas: Discursos y representaciones,* edited by Raquel Platero, 307–38. Barcelona: Melusina, 2008.

———. "Lesbofobias." *I Jornadas de Lesbianas de la FELGT.* Madrid (November 29–December 1, 2003).

———. "Overcoming Brides and Grooms. The Representation of Lesbian and Gay Rights in Spain." In *Multiple Meanings of Gender Equality: A Critical Frame Analysis of Gender Policies in Europe,* edited by Mieke Verloo, 207–32. Budapest: Central European University Press, 2007).

Rubiales Torrejón, Amparo. *La evolución de la situación jurídica de la mujer en España.* Club Antares de Sevilla, Instituto Andaluz de la Mujer (October 31, 2003).

Sáez, Javier. *Los gays y las lesbianas en los medios de comunicación.* Vitoria, 2000. http://www.hartza.com/vitoria.htm.

Sánchez Mellado, Luz. "Lesbiana sin complejos." *El País Semanal* (June 29, 2003): 36–47.

Sentamans, Tatiana. *Viragos en acción, señoritas ante el obturador: La imagen de la mujer deportista en la fotografía documental de la España prebélica (1923–1936).* Diploma de Estudios Avanzados. Universidad Politécnica de Valencia, 2007.

Seldón de León, Victoria. "Y el verbo se hizo imagen." In *Publicidad: La imagen de la mujer en la publicidad y su influencia en los medios de comunicación,* 9–26.Madrid: AMECO, 2001.

Spender, Dale. *Man Made Language.* London: Routledge and Kegan Paul, 1985.

Toledano, Hilda de. "Marlene Dietrich." *Blanco y Negro* (September 5, 1933).

Vico, Patricia, and Fátima Baeza. *Mundo Joven LGTB.* Madrid: Fundación Triángulo (October–November, 2005): 11–12.

Walters, Suzanna Danuta. *All the Rage: The Story of Gay Visibility in America.* Chicago: University of Chicago Press, 2001.

Living Out/Off Chueca

Marta Sofía López Rodríguez and
Yolanda Sánchez Paz

THE TWO OF US: IN HER BOOK *HISTORIA Y ANÁLISIS POLÍTICO DEL LES-bianismo* [*History and Political Analysis of Lesbianism*], 2005, Beatriz Gimeno, former president for the FELGTB (Federación Estatal de Lesbianas, Gays, Transexuales y Bisexuales) asserts: "Lesbianism is not an essence, it is a place."[1] She is obviously using the word "place" in a metaphorical sense; to her "lesbian-ism" is a sociosymbolic space from which heteropatriarchy can be contested and where a fight against oppression can be grounded. But what if we were to take the word "place" in a more literal sense, as a locale, a specific geographical reference? How does "place" affect your perception of yourself as a lesbian, how does it interact with the construction of community; how does it constrict or expand your mental and social universe? It is our intention in this paper to reflect on these and other issues from the complementary perspectives of a bartender and an aca-demic, who happen to be a couple.

Yolanda owns the first and longest-lasting lesbian and gay bar in León, a small conservative town in northern Spain, with a population of 150,000 people. When she opened it ten years ago, she did not intend to create a specifically queer[2] bar, but a place of peaceful coexistence for all sorts of people; however, since most of her friends were gays and lesbians, they soon became her most faithful patrons. La Barraca has been and still is a crucial spot for many queer people in León.[3] For about four years, it was the only lesbian and gay bar in town. Although gay men have always had their own meeting places (the park, the bus station . . .), lesbian women did not have many options for so-cializing and meeting each other. Thus, the bar has been for many people, but particularly for the women, a haven in a rather hostile environment. La Barraca was also the place where the local community of activists, COGALE, was founded and developed, and one of the crucial axes in the formation of a group identity for the queer family in León.

Marta is the academic (suspect her!). For more than fifteen years, she has been studying and teaching, among other subjects, lesbian literature and criticism. She has written on authors like Djuna Barnes, Radcliffe Hall, and Jeanette Winterson, among others, and is currently working on a book-length study on the Sapphic tradition in English. As an activist she has been collaborating for some years now with a feminist association close to the local branch of the Socialist Party, mainly assisting in the organization of literary and other cultural events.

Both of us have tried to contribute to creating, in our different ways, spaces of lesbian (and gay) visibility in this city, whose former Popular Party mayor was one of those who, after the passing of the gay marriage law, refused to marry non-heterosexual couples—even though this is the hometown of President José Luis Rodríguez Zapatero, whose government has granted lesbian and gay couples and families a status of legal equality with heterosexual ones for the first time in the history of this country. We have been partners for almost four years now. For us the occasion to get to know each other better was a course on various queer topics (theory, literature, cinema, civil rights, transsexuality), which Marta had co-organized, together with the then-socialist municipality and the local community of activists, COGALE, for which Yolanda was the treasurer at the moment.

MARTA: For me, it was the first contact with the local group of queer activists; I had never felt the need for an immediate, actual community. I had my books, my conferences, my friends all over the world . . . But my relationship with Yolanda has changed everything; I have found myself in the midst of a relatively small but multifarious group of lesbians, gays, bisexuals, and transsexuals. I have had to negotiate the gap between high theory and daily existence and in the process have (un)learned many things. Yolanda has been a most reliable guide throughout this (ongoing) trip: her experience is first-hand, down-to-earth, practical.

YOLANDA: It is important to underline that the association represents only a very small part of the LGTB collective in León; at the moment, it has about thirty associates.[4] At the beginning, it was very difficult to get people to participate in it: they felt it was a kind of stigma, and they didn't believe in associations: what for? In big cities, these groups offer freedom and support to their members; in a place like León, belonging to an LGTB association implies proclaiming aloud your sexual preference, and many people are not ready to do that, although in the last two years the gay pride demonstration has attracted many more people than it used to, for example. This reflects, I think, the increasing social acceptability of "sexual dissidence." Being Marta's partner has given me a new perspective on all these matters and has made me even more visible as a lesbian.

THE TWO OF US: There will also be other voices in this essay: those of Spanish theorists and researchers, Beatriz Gimeno and Olga Viñuales, and those of local activists, with whom Yolanda has always been in close contact: as we mentioned above, COGALE was formed in the bar, and before they had a proper meeting place the premises were both their legal and practical headquarters. But above all, we want the voices of our friends and patrons to be heard. When this paper was accepted for its eventual publication (2006), we elaborated a questionnaire which was completed by women who have been regulars at the bar for some time. The first questions deal with sociobiographical information: age, occupation, studies . . . Then, there are questions about sexual identity, coming out, level of visibility, and community. We also ask about the possibility of marrying their partner, if they have one. Finally, we ask about party politics and feminist consciousness. But before going on, and in order to try to clarify where each of us locates herself vitally and politically, we will start by going through the questionnaire ourselves.

YOLANDA: I am thirty-seven, I studied bookkeeping at a polytechnic, and have mainly worked as a bartender for many years and in different places all over Spain. I have no hesitation in defining myself as a lesbian. To me, the word basically means "a woman who (sexually) loves other women." Except for a teenage relationship with a man, all my relationships have been with women. I came out in my late teens, when I fell in love with my best friend. As a lesbian, I am mostly visible in my workplace; my seven siblings know that I am a lesbian, but my mother doesn't (or pretends not to, more probably). My community is formed by the people who surround me in my daily life: my family, my friends, the regulars at the bar, my neighbors. I want to marry Marta because she is the person who has given me stability and because I want my family to understand that she is the woman I want to grow old with. I am a left voter. I agree with most of the tenets of feminism, but I don't like to define myself as a feminist, because I am aware that to most people "femi-

nism" suggests above all conflict, being hostile to men just because they are men. To me, there is not an obvious connection
between being a lesbian and being a feminist: most of the lesbians I know do not see themselves as feminists.

MARTA: I am forty, hold a doctoral degree in English language
and literature and teach at the university. Until quite recently, I
have had problems with defining myself as a lesbian; on the one
hand, I had in the past long and reasonably satisfactory relationships with men, although I feel much more comfortable with
myself since I gave them up as potential sexual or emotional
partners; on the other hand, the word is so politically charged for
me that I have always felt I must handle it with care; maybe I
am too self-conscious in this respect. I was nine when I first fell
in love with a schoolmate, and in my almost exclusively homo-
social context girls were the only available love objects almost
until I went to university. I was then married to a man for five
years and afterwards had both male and female lovers. My parents refuse to name my current lifestyle as lesbian, but I guess
they are actually as aware of it as anybody else in my family or
in my wider social and professional environment. I feel I am part
of many overlapping communities, from my family and close
friends to the women's associations I'm involved with, to the
transhistorical, transnational community of women writers and
thinkers whose work has nurtured me. I want to marry Yolanda
because it seems a good way of sharing our mutual commitment
with our friends and (at least part of) our family. I am a socialist
voter and an unrepentant feminist. I have been involved with
feminist theory and activism for a long time, and probably "a
feminist" would be my most motivated answer to the question
"Who are you?" In this sense "becoming-lesbian" seems the
most coherent choice for me: my feelings, my thoughts, and my
way of living are at last one.

THE TWO OF US: Our debates about the meaning of both
"feminism" and "lesbianism" have been intense since we
started from almost opposite stands. At this stage, we could
probably say that Yolanda is a lesbian-becoming-feminist,
whereas Marta is a feminist-becoming-lesbian; two years ago,
Yolanda would have said, "I defend women's rights, but I am not
a feminist," and Marta would have said, "I love women, but I am
not a lesbian, I am bisexual." Yolanda's un-self-conscious way of
naming herself "lesbian" has taught Marta that things might be
easier than they seem. Yolanda has learned in turn that femi-

nism is important and that she is more of a feminist than she would have thought.

THE WOMEN WHO ANSWERED THE QUESTIONNAIRE: In a period of about two months, between January and March 2006, twenty women completed our questionnaire. Although it is a reduced group, it is quite representative of our local reality in its internal diversity. These women belong to various age groups, ranging from eighteen to forty, with most of them being between twenty-five and thirty-five. As we said above, they are regulars at La Barraca, and all of them either currently have or definitely prefer women partners. Other than this, their profiles are rather diverse: two of them have primary studies; ten have obtained professional diplomas in different areas: hair-dressing, computing-science, social work, nursing; eight of them hold or are studying for a higher degree. They work in all sorts of places, from the university or high schools to bakeries, travel agencies, call-centers or hospitals. About half of them could be defined as working class or lower middle class, whereas the other half can be considered middle class. Thirteen defined themselves as left voters, six as uninterested in politics, and one as a right voter. Some of them (three, to be precise) are involved in public LGTB activism; the other seventeen are not.

Compared to the universe of study of Olga Viñuales, whose *Identidades lésbicas* [*Lesbian Identities*], 2000, is one of the very few research works to have this far been undertaken on Spanish lesbians in Spain, our group seems to be almost incongruously heterogeneous. Viñuales, a social anthropologist, worked in close contact with members of the Coordinadora Gai-Lesbiana in Barcelona for a period of about five years. Her findings, which are extremely valuable, are also very difficult to export to our context, at least in some respects: whereas the very notion of "Coordinadora" presupposes a multiplicity of groups, there is only one association in León, with a women-only branch founded about one year ago. Viñuales also explicitly mentions the existence of "a wide network of bars and meeting places for lesbian women," as well as the anonymity provided by the big city as preconditions for her study:[5] none of this can be found in León. Furthermore, her informants (or, as she would rather call them, participants) are highly articulated and politicized lesbians, who have been involved in the life of associations and collectives for a long time, and as she hypothesizes, "women collectives play a crucial role as generators of identity and are essential for the consolidation of a feeling of group belonging"

(22).[6] For these women, their lesbian identity, and with it the feeling of belonging to a particular group built around sexual preference, would seem to have been "already there," waiting for the anthropologist to explore and analyze, even if that identity proved in the end to be less homogeneous than she would have expected.

It is not so in this case. As a matter of fact, the answers to our questionnaire revealed a rather diffuse sense of either individual or collective lesbian identity. To the question, "How would you define your sexual orientation?" only six women answered, "Lesbian." Five of them defined themselves as "bisexual" and one as "homosexual." To our amused puzzlement, three people replied, "normal," one, "very normal," and another one "person." These last answers reveal two things simultaneously: first, a certain lack of familiarity with the expression "sexual orientation" but, secondly, a self-defensive attitude which speaks volumes about the moral censorship and medicalization to which lesbian women have been traditionally subjected. The rest of the group defined their orientation as "attraction for women," "rejection towards men," "love for one particular person, independently of his or her sex," and finally "not missing any train."

To the question about the implications of the word "lesbian" to them, whether they defined themselves as lesbians or not, the answers were remarkably varied, and we would like to quote them in full in order to offer an idea of this diversity of responses; to us, this was one of the most crucial questions, and the answers reveal a mixture of self-definitions, perceptions of oneself from the outside, received ideas about lesbianism, and political attitudes:

1. "The woman who in a natural way wants to share her daily life with another woman."
2. "The woman who likes other women."
3. "The only implication that the word 'lesbian' has for me is that of a woman who likes other women, it doesn't have any further transcendence, and it shouldn't, because, after all, this is the only thing that makes us different (or should make us different) from heterosexual women."
4. "Sexually I feel attracted to women, while I feel rejection towards men."
5. "At the moment I define myself as lesbian because my partner is a woman."
6. "She is the person (obviously a woman) who likes women, and she is still a lesbian even if she also likes men."

7. "Sometimes, not being understood by people who do not accept these relationships."
8. "Not being able to enjoy openly the same rights as heterosexuals."
9. "I am a lesbian, but I deeply dislike the word itself, it has been used in a wrong way and this is why I dislike it."
10. "'Lesbian' is a closed word, it implies going always to gay and lesbian bars, being always surrounded by homosexuals; it is very reductive. I do not consider myself a lesbian."
11. "It is a way of feeling and being. It is a word that, once you say it aloud, means that you are being cured from your own internal homophobia."
12. "It is, besides a sexual orientation, an attitude to life, it is a vindication."
13. "I define myself as a lesbian; to me, it doesn't have any other implication apart from a personal choice."
14. "None."
15. "I don't like labels. I feel comfortable with everybody and with myself. I think that the best way to fight is to respect other people and to be respected yourself, however you are."
16. "I define myself more as a bisexual, because I still like men, even if only a little . . ."
17. "The same as if I were heterosexual, but with a woman."
18. "Simply, I feel attracted to women, I don't go any further."
19. "None at a personal level; at a social level, I'm not interested."
20. Blank.

Expressive as they are in themselves, we think these answers deserve some comment; they are a criss-cross of different discourses about lesbianism, some rather unsophisticated, but all very suggestive, particularly if slightly contextualized. The most obviously political answers are numbers 11 and 12, and they correspond to a recently married couple with a historical connection to activism, at both local and national levels. One of them defines herself as lesbian, the other as bisexual. To both of them lesbianism is perceived as an integral part of their subjective and political being, a distinctive way of being in the world: in other words, an identity.

Then, there are some (let's say) "neutral definitions": those that could be summarized by the idea of "women loving other women," although the nuances are also suggestive: it is really remarkable that the word "sexually" appears only once attached to the idea of loving women. This seems to confirm what most studies suggest, namely that as opposed to gay men, lesbian women tend to characterize their commitment to women in emotional or political terms rather than sexual ones (Gimeno 227). Obviously, sexual attraction is suggested or implied in many answers, but not openly mentioned. As a matter of fact, a majority of the group discovered that they liked women when they fell in love with a woman in particular. This seems to reinforce the thesis maintained by Beatriz Gimeno: "All the studies indicate that while gay men generally know themselves to be gay before having any homosexual relationship, many women discover themselves feeling homosexual desire in the framework of a relationship with another woman, or with other women, relationships not necessarily, or not exclusively, or not primarily sexual, although no doubt sexual" (227).[7]

It is also interesting to note that some of these women want above all to normalize their sexual orientation, which is not only revealed by their answers to the previous question, but also by their emphasizing that lesbianism is the same as heterosexuality, "but with a woman." For three of the respondents, lesbianism does not exclude having sexual relations with men; apparently they perceive themselves as "contingent" lesbians, a definition determined by the sex of their current partner. However, the idea of lesbianism as a choice, a personal option rather than a fixed and immutable identity, is only explicitly mentioned once. On the other hand, the idea of lesbianism as something "genetic" is also mentioned only once, by one of the respondents who asserts in her answer to the question about her sexual orientation: "[Being a lesbian] is not a question of choice, it is something genetic."

In any case, what is really worth noticing is the number of answers that reveal internalized lesbophobia in various guises: to some, the social stigma of lesbianism is still painfully present, implying rejection from society at large and material exclusion from rights that heterosexuals enjoy. The dismissal of the word "lesbian" by some of these women involves both suspicion about the persistent depreciative connotations of the term and a willingness to dis/identify oneself as a member of a closed group. In this respect, it is also interesting to remark that for most of these women lesbianism is a purely individual issue.

This conclusion makes itself evident in the answers to the questions: "To what extent do you feel part of a community? Who belongs to your community?" Only two persons, the current and the former presidents of COGALE, offered a response which was couched in political terms: PILAR feels part of a community "insofar as there are people fighting together and joining efforts to work for a better society." ISABEL feels that community is organized around segregation, and it is about "sharing a stigma of exclusion and rejection that all lesbians suffer." Eleven women answered that their community was their family and friends, a reply probably to be expected in a context where, as opposed to the Anglo-Saxon world, family ties are still very strong and people tend to maintain connections based on a shared life history rather than any "civil" commonality of interests. Six women felt that their community was society at large, or could be as soon as certain rights are acknowledged: they just felt like citizens of the world. Only in one case was a negative answer to the idea of community expressed as a "dislike for ghettos."

Therefore, we must conclude that the very notion of "community" in the Anglo-American sense of a "politically motivated group" doesn't seem to be even meaningful for many in this particular group of women. Since for most of them "lesbianism" is basically a question of sexual orientation or choice of (sexual) partner, and not a political issue, a community structured around activism is almost automatically ruled out. However, eighteen of these women answered positively to the question of whether they socialized with other lesbians and gays; as to where, most mentioned bars and pubs. Of course, all of them feel that they are part of "el ambiente," a word that Viñuales describes with great precision: "['Ambiente'] designates the meeting places (bars and discos) frequented by lesbians. However, . . . this term comprises something that goes beyond the physical space. It is a social space where gossip is implacable, which serves as a mechanism of social control and which offers, to those who participate in it, a sense of group belonging. The term 'ambiente' makes reference to an idea of community: a community organized in terms of a social network" (Viñuales 25).[8] The idea of an informal social network, articulated around the three lesbian and gay bars in town, is probably the closest we could get to a feeling of community in our particular context. In "el ambiente" everybody knows who "understands" and who doesn't.[9] Everybody knows who's been involved with whom, who is looking for a partner and who has a long-lasting relationship, who is available for sex and who isn't. In such a small place as this, all the information about the life and "herstory" of any given woman can be quite easily gathered.

"El ambiente" is almost the only sphere of visibility for most of the women who answered our questionnaire. "Friends," and in some cases "workmates," are for all but six of them the only people who are aware of their sexual preferences. Only three women said that they were totally visible as lesbians in all the aspects of their lives; the three of them are activists, and they celebrated a double lesbian wedding which appeared in all the local media as prime-time news. Many people stressed, on the other hand, the fact that their families didn't know about their lesbianism. Olga Viñuales asserts that for many gays and lesbians a public acknowledgment of their identity starts with the family.[10] Rejection or the fear of rejection by the family is one of the most paralyzing feelings for the women who answered our questionnaire. From hours of conversations held with them and with many others, we know that the family is the greatest obstacle for many people at the time of making public their sexual preferences.

However, for those who are more visible, coming out has meant above all a profound liberation. These are some answers to the question "What have been for you the consequences of coming (or not) out of the closet?": "At the beginning, problems with my friends and family; in the long run, a liberation." "To the moment, all positive. More closeness with everybody around me, a wider and better relationship with them all." "I have felt much freer and confident with myself." "All positive. The first and most important one, I live at peace with myself." On the other hand, there were also three answers emphasizing rejection and family conflicts. To the rest of the people, nothing had changed, they could not perceive any consequences or hadn't actually come out of the closet.

On the question of marriage, three women asserted conclusively that they didn't want to marry, as a question of personal choice. Most of them considered marriage a feasible option in the future or near future, but only three of the women who answered the questionnaire have actually married, two of them between themselves. These are their answers to the question, "Are you married or do you intend to marry soon?": "I am married. First of all, for love, but also as an act of vindication and visibility. Besides, I have acquired the legal support I deserve." "Yes, we have married because we love each other and out of militancy." "We have married because of love and also because we were thrilled with the idea of joining our lives to all effects. In order to have security and the acknowledgement of our couple in delicate situations, in which not being married would mean not having legal support. And also to give some strength to this very young law which grants us legal equality." Obviously, for the three of them there was, besides the personal commitment to each other, a very strong political motivation.

THE TWO OF US: We were at the wedding, and apart from being a double lesbian wedding it was a most proper one. The brides wore clearly recognizable wedding gowns, there was an ample presence of members of the Socialist Party, and the banquet was held at the most luxurious hotel in town. The press and the local media took great interest in the event, which appeared in all newspapers and on radio and television. At the reception, we were dancing a *pasodoble* (namely, "La española cuando besa" [When a Spanish woman kisses]) under the attentive look of one of the brides' grandmothers: at that precise moment, we both understood at once the meaning of the word "normalization" and deeply celebrated it, even when our personal option at the time of getting married will go exactly in the opposite direction.

The fact that nonheterosexual marriage has become a parliamentary and political issue in the last two years has contributed to the mainstreaming of the discussion about the rights of queer people and with it of gay, lesbian, bisexual, and transsexual reality in this country. The debate, from the ranks of the Socialist Party, has been of course posed in terms of civil liberties and privileges; if lesbian and gay couples do exist, and they pay their taxes like their best neighbor, they should not be deprived of the legal right to kinship, inheritance, social security benefits, and so on. This could not seem more reasonable to a wide majority of Spaniards, actually about seventy percent, who are much less obedient to religious authority than they were in the past. However, since the Popular Party and the Catholic church have so actively campaigned against the lesbian and gay marriage and adoption law, organizing demonstrations to defend "the family," and grandiosely receiving the Pope for the "World Encounter of the Family" in Valencia in July 2006, it has become politically incorrect from the left to criticize or even question the very idea of lesbian and gay marriage. This has had a salutary effect on many people who, being convinced leftists, were also deeply homophobic. After Zapatero, you cannot be a left voter and homophobic.

But, on the other hand, one of the quickest actors to co-opt this movement towards visibility and legal equality was El Corte Inglés, the biggest chain of department stores in Spain; well before the law was passed, they had already designed all sorts of products and services for queer couples (wedding lists, honeymoons, and so on). Normalization and mainstreaming thus pose a double bind for us, lesbian feminists. Do we really want to be exactly like the rest? Do we want to spend our Saturdays at the mall or the shopping center? Do we want to be part of the establishment to all effects? We know that we are simplifying the terms of a much more complex debate, but these are some of the questions which many queer people are posing to themselves and/or their partners at this point.

MARTA: I concur with Beatriz Gimeno in considering that we are going through a dangerous political moment. She asserts: "The revolutionary and transformative potential that lesbianism might have had, as a menace to patriarchal ideology and the institution of heterosexuality, disappeared when liberalism managed to impose its thesis in which the political has disappeared from the sphere of the personal" (263).[11] For her, sexuality is no longer discussed and analyzed in terms of power, or to be precise, in terms of the unequal distribution of power between men and women, heterosexuals and nonheterosexuals, but in terms of individual practices; a queer[12] "poetics" has done away with the political content of radical identity politics. And this is so even in this country where, as we have just said, the issue of civil rights has been and still is being publicly debated. The younger generation in particular seems to ignore that behind any historical achievement there are years of hard strife. And sometimes it is also forgotten that there are many countries in the world where you can be convicted and even killed for being homosexual, lesbian, or transsexual.

Indeed, I still feel that there are many fights ahead that cannot be fought in the absence of a collective sense of identity *qua* members of an historically oppressed and discriminated group. But this sense of collective identity, as Gimeno remarks, is disappearing, and a new model of lesbian is emerging; that of, in her words again, "twenty-first-century lesbians who embody the depolitized model that refuses to acknowledge any problem with gender, willful and individualistic women, postcapitalists, who ran away from any ideological or vindictive position, who do not see any difference between being gay and lesbian (both things are cool); they feel accepted, capable of succeeding in any thing they want to achieve and do not see what relationship can possibly exist between sexuality and politics; indeed, they believe they know there isn't any. They are not either interested in the LGTB cause, because there is no cause, and the vindications of this movement seem old-fashioned to them; they maintain that they never had any problem because of being lesbians, much less for being women" (292).[13]

Historically, both in the Western world in general and in Spain in particular, the emergence of lesbian political movements is almost coterminous with the emergence of the wider women's liberation movement, and even when lesbian women suffered the subtle or outright rejection of heterosexual feminists, they did not renounce the ideological and political tools of feminism. But to my immense surprise, the answers offered by our group to the questions, "Are you a feminist" and "Do you see any connection between being a lesbian and being a feminist?" were mostly negative. Only four women defined themselves as feminists, five were indifferent, and eleven clearly emphasized that they were not feminist. Twelve stated that they couldn't see any connection between both terms, and these included some of those women who did define themselves as feminists. Two remarked that they were feminists as women, not because they were lesbians. These results clearly reveal that lesbianism has indeed lost its revolutionary edge as an ideological and political stance against heteropatriarchy.

Like the "daughters of educated men" in the thirties, when they started to gain access to the professions, lesbian feminists are now "between the devil and the deep sea."[14] We have to celebrate mainstreaming and normalization, political achievements like the lesbian and gay marriage and adoption law, and our augmented visibility in the media. At the same time, we are aware that the price we are paying is an increased depolitization of lesbianism. In small places like León, where circumstances have prevented the formation and consolidation of strong political and social networks, this situation is even more evident and to me quite worrying. But this is just a personal appreciation, made from the standpoint of a (privileged) academic, which might not be shared by most members of the lesbian community in this town.

YOLANDA: I think that Marta's diagnosis of the situation is quite accurate, but I have to insist on the context. In such a small city as this, being lesbian or gay can still mean having serious problems in your daily life; coming out of the closet is still not for free. It is true that people have become much more open and liberated throughout these ten years that I have had the bar, and the youngsters in particular behave in a freer and less prejudiced way. But those people in their thirties who haven't come out of the closet are even more closeted now, because although apparently society at large is more tolerant with gays and lesbians, we have to face a very old-fashioned mentality here. The possibility of living comfortably out of the closet is related to your social and economic status, and there are many people who cannot really afford it: they risk losing their jobs, being rejected by their families, being mocked and made fun of at their workplace or their neighborhood. . . . I can only hope that things become easier for the younger generation, and that society keeps on changing for the better in this country, and in this town.

$\backsim$

P.S.: On December 15, 2006, we got married in a discreet ceremony attended by our siblings and a small number of very close friends. It was really like a dream to us, being able to celebrate the occasion surrounded by the people we love best, although our parents were not there (supposedly, even today they do not know that we are married, although they clearly accept our lifestyle, and we are perfectly integrated into each other's families).

NOTES

1. "El lesbianismo no es una esencia, es un lugar." Beatriz Gimeno, *Historia y análisis político del lesbianismo: La liberación de una generación*, (Barcelona: Gedisa, 2005), 33.

2. Throughout this essay, "queer" is just meant as short-hand for lesbians, gays, bisexuals, and transsexuals.

3. Since the time of this writing, Yolanda closed La Barraca to open a new, larger bar, Spectrum, in the heart of Leon. The opening was celebrated in 2008.

4. Unfortunately, the association has disappeared since the time of this writing.

5. "La ciudad proporciona un anonimato que favorece la existencia de redes sociales lesbianas y también ayuda a la construcción de diversos colectivos públicos de carácter homosexual. En Barcelona, a principios de los noventa, coexistían tres grandes organizaciones: el grupo de Lesbianes Feministes de Ca la Dona, el grupo de lesbianas del Casal Lambda y el Grup Lésbia, posteriormente Grup Lesbos, de la coordinadora Gai-Lesbiana. Y también existe una amplia red de bares y locales de encuentro para mujeres lesbianas."

6. "[L]os colectivos femeninos juegan un gran papel como generadores de identidad y son decisivos en la consolidación del sentimiento de pertenencia grupal."

7. "Todos los estudios indican que, mientras que los gays generalmente se saben gays antes de tener ningún tipo de relación homosexual, muchas mujeres se descubren sintiendo deseo homosexual en el marco de relaciones con una mujer, o con otras mujeres, relaciones no necesariamente, o no exclusivamente, o no primariamente sexuales, pero sin duda sexuales."

8. "Ellas utilizan el término 'ambiente' para designar los espacios de encuentro (bares y discotecas) frecuentados por lesbianas. Sin embargo, [. . .] este término comprende algo que va más allá del espacio físico. Se trata de un espacio social en el que el cotilleo es implacable, que sirve como mecanismo de control social y que proporciona, a quienes participan en él, sentido de pertenencia grupal. El término 'ambiente' hace referencia a la idea de comunidad: una comunidad organizada en términos de red social." Olga Viñuales, *Identidudes lísbicas: Discursos y practicas* (Barcelona: Bellaterra, 2000),   .

9. "To understand," *entender*, is the slang word for being lesbian or gay.

10. "Para muchos gays y lesbianas el reconocimiento público de la identidad empieza por la familia."

11. "El potencial revolucionario y transformador amenazante para la ideología patriarcal y para la institución de la heterosexualidad que pudiera tener el lesbianismo desapareció al conseguir el liberalismo imponer sus tesis en las cuales la política ha desaparecido del ámbito de lo personal."

12. On this occasion, I use the term "queer" in its more theoretical/academic sense.

13. "Lesbianas del siglo XXI que encarnan el modelo despolitizado que niega que exista ningún problema con el género, mujeres voluntaristas e individualistas, postcapitalistas, que huyen de cualquier posicionamiento ideológico o reivindicativo, que no ven ninguna diferencia entre ser gay y ser lesbiana (ambas cosas son *cool*), se sienten aceptadas, capaces de triunfar en lo que se propongan y no ven qué relación puede tener la política con la sexualidad; de hecho, ellas creen saber que no tiene ninguna. Tampoco les interesa la causa LGTB porque no hay causa, y las reivindicaciones de este movimiento les parecen antiguas; aseguran no haber tenido nunca ningún problema por ser lesbianas y mucho menos por ser mujeres."

14. Virginia Woolf, *Three Guineas* (New York: Oxford World's Classics, 1998).

REFERENCES

Gimeno, Beatriz. *Historia y análisis político del lesbianismo. La liberación de una generación.* Barcelona: Gedisa, 2005.

Viñuales, Olga. *Identidades lésbicas: Discursos y prácticas.* Barcelona: Bellaterra, 2000.

Woolf, Virginia. *A Room of One's Own* and *Three Guineas.* 1929; 1939. New York: Oxford World's Classics, 1998.

Politics and Language:
The Representation of Some "Others"
in the Spanish Parliament
Encarnación Hidalgo Tenorio

BACKGROUND

AFTER THE SPANISH PARLIAMENT INTRODUCED LEGISLATION PERMIT-
ting same-sex marriage in 2005, given my interest in the linguistic representation of the so-called "other," I felt it would be op-
portune to study the textual construction of those whom the
new regulation was expected to benefit, being same-sex couples
who were afforded similar rights to those that straight couples
enjoy.

Language, a miraculous (although imperfect) means of communication, is a powerful instrument that influences people's
attitudes and views. It is used to comprehend and structure the
world into manageable sets of entities. Thanks to language, we
can classify objects and subjects for the purposes of inclusion
and exclusion; thus, as Norman Fairclough argues, each person
becomes a recognizable member of a particular group, a collective that can be under- or overrepresented, silenced, or given
voice to.[1]

When depicting the world around us, our perceptions turn
into (partial) truths that reveal our ideology. Our identity is con-
cealed behind our language usage; or, conversely, observing people's linguistic behavior must necessarily help to uncover who
they are, their prejudices and presumptions. In the analysis of
discourse practice, notions such as power and manipulation appear unavoidable and are particularly prevalent in contexts such
as the one in which I have developed my research: the political
arena.[2] If in general terms representation is power, within the
public sphere there is a manifest correlation between these two
factors. Those who hold a position of power can determine the

119

extent and nature (whether positive or negative) of such representation—of others, as well as of themselves. By obscuring or
giving more prominence to the role of certain participants, those
in power build scenarios that may privilege only the few. No
doubt, all speakers behave in this way, but the effect of such positioning is all the more significant when it occurs within socially influential domains such as the one under discussion.

AIMS AND METHODOLOGY

In the eyes of the addressee, individuals exist in terms of their
verbal performance. It is through what they say and the way in
which they express it that they become subjects. Critical linguists and critical discourse analysts, as well as other linguists
who do not define themselves by either label, have proved how
differently the same event or phenomenon can be represented by
means of (linguistic) devices that suggest the ideology of the author of a text.[3] Despite very well-argued opposition by some
scholars, I consider that each linguistic choice individuals make
explicitly (and, what is more interesting, unconsciously) is instrumental in identifying the way in which those individuals
wish to be perceived.[4] At the same time, it is evident that each
linguistic option embodies how speakers view other members
of society and the role ascribed to those others in their verbal
configuration of reality. In this particular approach to appreciating self and other individuals, certain images will be perpetuated
and others discarded, so that a social character involved in this
discourse practice may become either an agentive force or simply stand in the background as passive objects or mere circumstance. It is this sociolinguistic phenomenon that will be
explored in this chapter.

In the last five years important changes have been taking place
in Spain. Following the end of the Conservatives' (*Partido Popular*) second term of office and the advent of the new Socialist
(*PSOE*) administration, key issues such as immigration, domestic violence, and same-sex marriage have begun to be (re)consid-
ered. Here, I present data taken from a study on how the Spanish
parliamentarians have been dealing with the "minority" mainly
affected by one of these issues—that is, gays and lesbians. By analyzing the minutes of parliamentary sessions in which homosexuality is discussed or homosexuals mentioned, I examine
how these subjects are represented (if indeed they are at all)

through the speeches delivered by Spanish political representatives. I will also take into account other corpora of Spanish that will augment the final result.

The research context is the Spanish senate and parliament; the speaking individuals include mainly members of the respective houses, as well as others invited to participate in the proceedings of various committees; the materials, a 5,471,408-token non-lemmatized corpus that collects all the official documents containing the lemmas "gay," "lesbian," "homosexual," and derivatives. The search engine of the Spanish parliament allows the user to look for all types of texts produced there from 1977.[5] The time span of my investigation is only eight years, from February 2, 1997 to June 30, 2005; that is, from the first moment that reference to any of these terms can be demonstrated to the day when same-sex marriage was legally sanctioned by a vote of 187 in favor, with 137 against and 4 abstentions.

In order to be able to cope with this large amount of data, it was necessary to resort to corpus linguistics and one of the tools devised within this framework, the concordancer *WordSmith*, which is extremely useful for studying key words in context, collocational patterns, and lexical sets.[6] I focused my attention mainly on the latter elements. Once I had selected all the texts relevant for the purpose of this analysis, they then had to be made computer-readable. It was necessary to convert the PDFs to text files, so that any incompatible formatting features could be removed. The materials, once computerized, could be analyzed.

The philosophy behind corpus linguistics makes the contribution of this new methodology relevant not only to the field of syntax or morphology, but also to lexicography, language variation, language acquisition and teaching, contrastive analysis and pragmatics. The key is that it is essential to study and have access to real data, rather than fabricated examples or intuition.[7] With all the statistical information provided by software programs, frequency of usage becomes one of the principles endorsed by corpus linguists in language description. This does not mean, however, that these perform quantitative analysis alone. Figures need to be interpreted, and constructions must be assigned to the linguistic values under scrutiny.

Here I should like to add an observation that is essential to this research project. I believe that someone's identity is built verbally. Individuals define their social persona through several means, especially language; and, as maintained earlier, the traces of their ideology are identified by detecting verbal preferences.[8] Nonetheless, in making these options, other alternatives are disregarded; thus, absence also becomes essential.[9] Political correctness has taught us to examine and interpret choices as well as dispreferred expressions or terms.[10] Corpus linguistics can also prove most useful in this respect, owing to the word lists that software programs can generate.[11] A presupposition from which research starts can be validated this way, and further findings can encourage us to modify and reformulate our initial hypothesis.

ANALYSIS OF THE DATA

Introduction

The table below displays the data concerning how often the lemmas "lesbian," "gay," and "homosexual" have been used in the Spanish parliament over a period of eight years. The most frequently mentioned is "homosexual," a word that in this language tends to be a hypernym of both "gay" and "lesbian." Meanwhile, the 462 occurrences of "heterosexual" make up 0.008% of the total.

Considering that, in the minutes of the sessions collected, speakers discussed matters other than homosexuality (e.g. adoption by same-sex couples), the lower frequency of appearance of these four lemmas was not surprising. In the first one thousand words some of the main focal points of the speakers can be detected, which ultimately happen to be closely connected with the main concern under discussion. The most frequently used lemmas are "persons," "rights," "security," "women," "society," "protection," "development," "citizens," "the Constitution," "marriage," "education," "reforms," "problems," "freedom," "couples," "young people," "families," "children," "pensions," "truth," "men," "adoption," "cohabitation," "dis-

Table 1. Statistics of usage of sexual orientation-related terms in the Spanish Parliament, 1997–2005.

Gay/s		Lesbian/s		Heterosexual/s		Homosexual/s	
%	Occurrences	%	Occurrences	%	Occurrences	%	Occurrences
0.0068	361	0.007	370	0.008	462	0.026	1,366

crimination," "orientation," "health policy," "criminality," "terrorism," "sex," "prostitution," "accommodation," "students," "immigrants," "the elderly," and "AIDS." The word "homosexuals" was one of these (ranked at 612). As for "lesbians," "heterosexuals," and "gays," although numerically less frequent (their rank number of frequency was 1,563, 1,725, and 1,743, respectively), they were still important in a corpus of this size.

The collocations of some of these words are very telling. We find repetitive patterns such as the following: "persons of the same sex," "marriage of persons," "the rights of persons," "couples of persons," "persons of homosexual orientation," "homosexual persons," "handicapped persons," "old persons," "heterosexual persons," "persons of homosexual conduct," "deaf persons," "persons with dependency problems," "persons of Spanish nationality," "free and equal persons," "young persons," "single persons," "immigrant persons," and "foreign persons." It cannot escape our notice that many of these phrases are redundant expressions, since we all assume that the lexical decomposition of "the deaf," "the elderly," "the handicapped," "immigrants," "foreigners," or "homosexuals" and "heterosexuals" implies semantic components such as (+ANIMATE) (+HUMAN); that is, they are already persons. This initially unnecessary repetition cannot be a mere mistake due to haste or lack of preparation. It is possible to explain this trend in at least two ways. On the one hand, by adding the noun "persons" to these phrases, the speaker makes it explicit that they want to emphasize that they are speaking about a group of human beings with all the attributes typical of rational creatures (including obligations and especially rights). As a result, on the other hand, this generalization may hinder the mental construction of these groups as characterized by some (possibly negative) features associated with the stereotypes in terms of which they may be often described. What they all share in common is the fact that they are members of the human race. Their subsequent subcategorization indicating the collective they belong to, within the main category "human being," does not seem to convey (at least directly) any pejorative values. To test this assumption and what it may imply, I will pick up two apparently similar examples: "las personas extranjeras" [foreign persons] and "las personas de nacionalidad española" [persons of Spanish nationality].

In order to prove my point, I will use the 150,778,934-token synchronic corpus of Spanish (CREA, or *Corpus de Referencia del Español Actual*), sponsored by the Royal Academy of Spanish Languages.[12] The CREA consists of oral and written texts from 1975 onwards (books, newspapers, emails, advertisements, blogs, TV and radio recordings). The main areas covered are science, politics, economy, arts, health, and fiction. In this corpus I retrieved five cases of the phrase "foreign persons" and 762 of the phrase "foreigners." Clearly, the first is very infrequent in Spanish. Its contexts of usage are neutral; no controversial evaluative connotations are implied. That is why speakers in my corpus appear to show a preference for using such terminology. The term "foreigners," on the other hand, is linked in these examples to having vices, committing crimes, and being the victims of violence.

In the Parliament corpus, speakers prefer referring to their fellow countrymen and -women as "Spaniards" or "the Spanish," when these are supposed to be engaged in quite positive activities, for the same reasons mentioned above. Bearing in mind the role of most of the speakers as political representatives and their own nationality, the generic term here essentially conveys a compilation of all the virtues the people born in this country are traditionally known for. However "persons of Spanish nationality" is a phrase mainly used to refer to those whose involvement in illegal actions is prosecuted. The focus of the addressee's attention shifts and seems to be on the fact that these are first of all people. The information concerning their citizenship, which in a way the speakers are trying to protect, is deferred now. They may aim to present it not as a set of inherent attributes but just as a qualifier that modifies the inner essence of the noun "persons."

When it is essential to be politically correct, speakers tend to use phrases that are not taken to be offensive. The more negative the meaning ascribed to a phrase, the less frequently it will be used (e.g., "foreigners"). A change in its original structure can be enough to make addressees elicit new senses. Similarly, a change in a verbal construction made up of positive-laden terms (e.g., "Spaniards") helps see the objective reality we are making reference to from a different light. It is in this way that associations (either positive or negative) are diluted or reinforced. The subtle difference may pass unnoticed. Nonetheless, this usage is curious, to say the least, as is the case of another expression such as "homosexual persons," which is also statistically very rare; in the CREA, there are only six instances of this term in Spanish politics and social-science texts. In my data, the content of which touches on equal rights and dignity claims, I found 141 occurrences. Since the noun "homosexuals" is still loaded with negative connotations, the addition of the word "persons" can have no other function than to emphasize what these speakers are first interested in (i.e., they are people), and to overlook the pejorative connotations with which Spanish society may still associate the most usual term (i.e., "homosexuals").

As might be expected, in this corpus there were no homophobic derogatory terms of the type addressed to females: e.g., "bollera" [dyke/pussy licker], "tortillera" [rug muncher], "marimacho" [butch] or "camionera" [diesel dyke].[13] There is one example, however, in which one of the speakers employs an expression (i.e., "maricón" [faggot]) that, in general, is employed to insult gay men. In this session, an expert on evolutionary psychology is discussing the potential consequences that having been brought up by same-sex couples may have on a child's sexual orientation. She tries to explain that there is no factual evidence to confirm that this situation marks them so that they engage only in homosexual relationships later in life. This professor alludes to the experience of one child who was taken in by a gay couple and had been living with them for ten years. The boy, who is reported to be very happy with his family, calls into doubt the claim that the children raised by same-sex couples will become homosexual themselves: "¿Pué no dicen que vamo a zé maricone tós los que vivimos con homozezuale? Pué a mí me guztan la schavala a morí" [Can you believe people say that everybody living with gays are gonna be fags? Well, not me, I'm just crazy 'bout honeys].[14]

In the CORDE (*Corpus Diacrónico del Español*), however, I came across some examples relevant to this study where terms such as lesbians, gays, or other related expressions were mentioned. This is a diachronic corpus that consists of 236,709,914 tokens. It includes prose and verse texts from the origins of the Spanish language until the latter half of the twentieth century. In 1927, for instance, Eugenio Noel uses for the first time the expression "tortillera," in a novel entitled *Las Siete Cucas* [*The Seven Pussies*].[15] Juan Goytisolo's *Señas de identidad* [*Marks of Identity*], 1966, is the next text in which similar usage can be found.[16] There is only one occurrence of the word "bollera" in the CORDE; it is found again in a novel, in this case *El gran momento de Mary Tribune* [*Mary Tribune's Great Moment*], 1972, by Juan García Hortelano.[17] Sexual orientation is depicted with no negative value judgments in any of these texts. As for "marimacho," this is the preferred option on a rather larger number of occasions (fifty-two occurrences). The first mention to be found in the diachronic corpus of Spanish is in Francisco de Quevedo's *Entremés de la destreza* [*Interlude of Dexterity*], c. 1620.[18] Typical masculine attitude and attire (sometimes respected and on other occasions despised by people and even by the person who is so described) are the outstanding features associated with this form of address: e.g., strength of spirit, self-assurance, roughness and fish-wife-like behavior. Finally, in the CREA there are only two occurrences of the word "camionera" that may fit in a certain way the meaning referred to here. It is interesting to note that in 1990, Spanish rock singer Luz Casal gave an interview in which she acknowledged that her bad language and wearing of leather trousers may have made the public think that she looks like a butch lesbian. In *Todo por la pasta* [*Anything for the Dough*], 1996, actress Pilar Bardem plays the role of a lesbian wearing flip-flops, who drives a truck and smokes cigars.[19] This is the second occurrence of the lemma in this corpus. The director of this tragicomic thriller, Enrique Urbizu, turns to an explicit visual metaphor; this female character embodies the archetype of what would be a diesel dyke. Urbizu, nonetheless, does not use this image as a means of levying harsh criticism; in truth, all the characters embody exaggeration in a way that the public can only laugh at or feel sympathy for: e.g., the typical macho man, the typical he-man, or the typical Spaniard with all his/her virtues and prejudices.

Lesbians in the Spanish language

As Table 1 above shows, in my corpus the lemma "lesbian" is not as common as other sexual-orientation-related terms. In the CREA it was possible to retrieve 414 occurrences, but there is evidence of usage earlier than 1975. In order to check this point, I also performed a search in the CORDE. With its current meaning, the first example in a Spanish text (a novel by Colombian José Asunción Silva entitled *De sobremesa* [*After-Dinner Conversation*]) dates back to around 1896; here a poet makes a melancholic reference to Sappho.[20] From the Iberian Peninsula, Camilo José Cela's *La colmena* [*The Beehive*], 1951, is the first text mentioning lesbians; a female character known under the pseudonym of "the Uruguayan" is criticized for speaking ill not only of other lesbians but also of gay males, prostitutes, and the clients she sleeps with.[21] The language Cela employs romanticizes lesbians and stresses two fundamental ideas: silence and suffering related to this identity. The Nobel Prize winner describes these women as follows: "las tiernas, las amorosas putas del espíritu, dulces, entristecidas, soñadoras y silenciosas como varas de nardo" [the tender, loving whores of the spirit, sweet, saddened, dreaming, and silent like spikenards.]

Table 2 below summarizes the most important data concerning the types of contemporary texts written in Spanish in which the lemma "lesbian" appears. This usage can be compared with that of its counterparts (i.e., "gay" and "homosexual"), which happen to be more frequent. The difference in context of use is obvious: whereas "lesbian" is a word recurrent especially in literature, "gay" is preferred in politics; and "homosexual," just like "heterosexual," is present in texts on health, especially those dealing with AIDS and other sexually transmitted diseases. The word "gay" was used first in Fernando Savater's *Caronte aguarda* [*Caronte Awaits*], a text from 1981,[22] although the daily newspaper *El País* published an article by Juan Cruz Ruiz on August 31, 1977 on the concept of "gay power," which is said to have existed in Europe and America since the Victorian period.[23] The first usage of the term "homosexual," however, is to be found much earlier, in an 1883 text. In a collection of essays by Dominican Emilio Rodríguez Demorizi, in a peculiar dictionary entry, we can read the following: "mover las manos a la altura de los hombros, como si fueran alas: homosexual" (to move the hands at the height of the shoulders, as if they were wings: homosexual).[24] Since any more detailed contextual information is lacking, it is possible to conclude that the meaning of this word here seems to be possibly associated with behavioral traits ascribed to this group of people, who may be identified externally, among other things, through a stereotypically exaggerated movement of their hands.

By examining the contexts of the word "lesbian" in the texts available, it has been possible to decipher aspects other than meaning. I am interested in the denotation of this lexical item, but obviously what attracts my attention still further are the connotations and the potential writer's prejudices (if any) filtered by what is said and by the way in which it is said. Such elements are useful indicators in discerning the nature of society which generates various discourse practices, including the discourse of prejudice. Since it was the Spanish parliament that first passed the controversial same-sex marriage law in June 2005, for the purposes of this study I will only comment on ex-

Table 2. Statistics of usage of sexual-orientation-related terms in Spanish, in the CREA, 1975–2005.

Topic	Lesbian/s		Heterosexual/s		Gay/s		Homosexual/s	
	%	Occurrences (414)	%	Occurrences (559)	%	Occurrences (562)	%	Occurrences (3,093)
Fiction	28.74	119	9.30	52	14.23	80	13.28	411
Social sciences, beliefs, and thought	22.70	94	16.45	92	19.03	107	20.17	624
Politics, economy, commerce, and finance	16.18	67	10.91	61	20.82	117	17.97	556
Health	12.80	53	50.44	282	8.72	49	25.21	780
Arts	9.17	38	4.47	25	18.86	106	11.47	355
Leisure, daily life	6.03	25	2.86	16	13.70	77	6.20	192
Oral texts	3.62	15	4.83	27	1.96	11	4.81	149
Science and technology	0.24	1	0.71	4	1.07	6	0.45	14
Miscellaneous	0.48	2	0.0	0	1.60	9	0.38	12

cerpts of texts written in Spain, which comprise up to 62.25 percent of all the texts in the CREA. As shown in Table 3 below, there are some slight differences as to the main topic of all the documents written in Spanish and those written in Spain in which the term "lesbian" occurs. In the latter case, there are a greater number of examples in the topic area labeled "social sciences, beliefs, and thoughts." Within this subclass it is worth noting that the texts here deal mainly with language, education, ethics and religion, geography and history, sociology, astrology, psychology, philosophy, anthropology and ethnology, mythology and folklore, and, unsurprisingly, eroticism, sexology, and women.

In some of these documents, the word's context sometimes conveys the ideas of ugliness, vice, illness, pathology, immorality, sin, and perversion. As stated in some news items collected in the corpus, by 2001, in some Arab countries women accused of lesbianism were subject to the death penalty. On other occasions, this term is associated with uncontrollable anger, prostitution, and forms of criminal activity. In fact, the so-called pernicious influence of gays and lesbians is compared with that of drug addicts. Doubts about (sexual) normalcy and references to defects abound, as well as mention of issues of conscience and moral dilemma. Further references to the physical appearance of these women are plentiful—suggesting that they are too masculine to be considered women—as well as to a behavior that is described in similar terms (more often than not with an implicit pejorative tone). Some authors mention that lesbians (as a sym-

Table 3. Statistics of usage of the lemma "lesbian" in Spain in the CREA, 1975–2005.

Topic	Lesbian/s	
	%	Occurrences (253)
Fiction	20.16	51
Social sciences, beliefs, and thought	22.53	57
Politics, economy, commerce, and finance	20.55	52
Health	13.83	35
Arts	12.65	32
Leisure, daily life	6.32	16
Oral texts	3.95	10

bol of the rejection of traditional roles ascribed to women) have been regarded as a threat to the capitalist patriarchal family system or even the human race.[25] This is said to be one of the reasons why lesbians have been repressed and persecuted although, paradoxically, not even in the restrictive Victorian era was there anything equal to anti-lesbian legislation, probably because most citizens were not even able to conceptualize the existence of such a person. I would suggest that it is precisely because of this that we very often find the word "lesbian" attached to the words "gays" and "collective." In these cases the implication is clear: in order to reach understanding and social approval through dialogue and action, these individuals have had to create groups in support of their interests and against social injustices.

One outstanding counterexample to the general rule is an excerpt from playwright Fernando Arrabal's *El arquitecto y el emperador de Asiria* [*The Architect and the Emperor of Assyria*], 1966.[26] One of the characters, a nameless doctor, states that one community in which only girls are born will be free of wars, religions, proselytism, and car accidents; that is, it will give birth to a happy humanity, the best of worlds, in which money will be spent on dildos. Another peculiar example, again from the theatre, is taken from a play by Alberto Miralles, *Comisaría especial para mujeres* [*Special Police Headquarters for Women*], 1992.[27] The cleaning lady in an imaginary women-only police station picks up the phone while on duty and very intelligently replies to a father whose query concerns how to deal with his daughter's lesbianism, as if it were an affliction for which pills may provide a cure. In the end, in incredibly direct fashion the cleaning lady tells him that it is the father, not his lesbian daughter, who really needs medication to treat his disease: narrow-mindedness.

In sexology texts, it is possible to read that lesbianism involves a less active sex life and in particular greater emotional stability than that associated with male homosexuality (which is often identified with promiscuity and therefore is judged in negative terms). However, from such texts lesbian sexuality can also be read as something to be ignored, or alternatively, as a sexuality which must be recognized openly, thus enabling lesbians to escape ostracism and secure societal recognition. In medical texts lesbian sexual activity is regarded as harmless. Meanwhile, in the context of psychological research, these practices are described in considerable detail, with no indication of disapproval (indeed the opposite is the case). Nevertheless, as some excerpts show, it was as late as 1973 when the American Psychiatric Association removed homosexuality from the catalog of mental illnesses. From then on, in the United of States lesbians were officially deemed not to suffer from any more psychological diseases than did heterosexual women. At the same time, however, other authors assert that suicide, alcohol abuse, and crimes of passion are more frequent among lesbians. Moreover, in other examples within various categories of texts included in the CREA, we can see that this minority group, together with gay men, are often said to have been victims of threats, moral disapproval, social intolerance, degrading treatment, penal persecution, verbal harassment, physical violence, property damage, and even death.

As expected, there are numerous excerpts where outdated patterns of speech and prejudices are reproduced. One such observation, in an article by Jaime Campmany, a journalist with *ABC*, Spain's right-of-center daily newspaper, was published on May 7, 1985:

> Antes, por las calles principales de nuestros pueblos, aldeas y ciudades, pasaban, como Pedro por su casa, los rebaños de churras y merinas o las recuas de mulos hastíales que decía don Ramón María del Valle-Inclán. Ahora, como estamos en pleno progreso, no sólo pasan hormigueros de coches, oleadas de contestatarios y manifestantes contra la OTAN, huelguistas, sindicalistas, ecologistas antinucleares y pequeñas manadas de lesbianas y mariquitas. Ahora desfilan bajo los balcones las piaras de cerdos contestatarios por el trato de Europa.[28]

This journalist's style is worthy of note, and the mental image his words may conjure up for the reader is somewhat original. The main topic of this news item is the European Union's export ban on pigs from Spain, which may account for his use of so many animal, or animal-related, metaphors. According to Campmany, thanks to previous years' progress in terms of economic growth and social change, the main roads in Spanish cities are no longer filled with the sheep or trains of pack mules that the writer Valle-Inclán spoke about; they are instead swarming with cars and waves of people on strike, anti-NATO demonstrators, rebels, trade unionists, antinuclear ecologists, and small herds of lesbians and faggots. Besides the pejorative tone of this final phrase due to the term he employs in referring to male gays, its interest lies in the collocation of "manadas de lesbianas y mariquitas" [herds of lesbians and faggots]. The writer, who views the past nostalgically, seems to show little sympathy for any of the people he lists as taking to the streets to demonstrate about things that are wrong in Spain after forty years of dictatorship. Some of these antiestablishment individuals are gays and lesbians, whom he compares with animals, either wild or tame. In a more literal reading of this metaphor it seems that, from this writer's viewpoint, the gay and lesbian collective is portrayed as part of the undistinguished masses of society. They may be acting together, that is true, but in all probability not as a result of planning or coordination but rather through imitation or because of fear, which may make them appear irrational and lacking a distinct opinion or moved by outside forces.

In another example from a 1989 article also appearing in *ABC*, once again gays and lesbians are participants in a demonstration, which is described as "picturesque."[29] It is not clear why the word "pintoresca" was chosen to refer to an event of this type, since the goal of the demonstration was to highlight the lack of research on how women can acquire AIDS. Moreover, no other contextual information is available to help enhance the understanding of why something like this could be described in such terms. One could envision a colorful parade, perhaps, a rather positive image. Nonetheless, when the people involved in the event are categorized as a marginal collective, the tone becomes somber, and the reader's perception of this group is influenced accordingly.

There is a further curious description of lesbian sexuality in the 1988 novel by Manuel Hidalgo, *Azucena, que juega al tenis* [*Azucena, Who Plays Tennis*].[30] Speaking about Regina, an independent, older woman, who seems to regard men like him as childish and dependent, a young man wonders whether she herself is a lesbian. She may seem to be so, firstly, on the grounds of her degree of independence and experience. Secondly, she suggests that there is surely no other option for her since it is becoming more and more common for women of her age, bored with previous heterosexual partners, to embark upon relationships with other women. The young man adds (and perhaps this is the aspect most worthy of comment) that, in his opinion, the excuses for this change in sexual orientation are questionable. They are as follows: the familiar story of tenderness between women; the rejection of male chauvinism; and male-female penetration as a means of control. His portrayal of lesbians, and their personal traits, is provocatively stereotypical, implying the acceptance of simplistic distinctions such as those between weak and strong women, or princesses and dykes. Through such views this fictional character explains away lesbianism as a consequence of unsuccessful heterosexual relationships. In doing so he may be not only calling into question the genuineness of these women's feelings but also denying the possibility of the essential nature of such sexual orientation. It is curious to note, however, that a 1997 article on sociology published in the daily newspaper *El Mundo* is more critical about the authenticity of heterosexual women's sexual choices, claiming that in their relationships they look for wealth and social status, whereas lesbians do not.[31] This attitude is reminiscent of how lesbian characters are occasionally depicted in some literary texts as the very incarnation of real and pure love. This, however, is not always the case; in his poem "Femmes Damnées" [Damned Women] (banned from 1857 until 1949), Charles Baudelaire referred to lesbians as "virgins," "martyrs," "devotees," "demons," "monsters," "she-satyrs," "spirits filled with contempt for reality," and "seekers of infinity."[32] As can be appreciated in other texts taken from the *Corpus de Referencia del Español Actual*, the man and woman in the street have added other less poetic terms to this subject. The expressions used are the following: "seres anormales" [abnormal], "monstruos enfermos con cuerpos y mentes taradas" [sick monsters, crippled in both body and mind], "traición a la feminidad" [traitors to femininity], or "de segunda categoría" [second-rate citizens].

Lesbians in the Spanish Parliament

The data described above show the linguistic representation of lesbians in different contexts where speakers and writers are not necessarily aware of the need to resort to verbal hygiene as a means of avoiding offense to members of various social groups generally included within the umbrella term "minority." In the cases cited previously the tone with which these expressions are employed, and therefore the implicit connotations carried by these terms, can be regarded as sexist, racist, and homophobic. These findings offer a bleak portrayal of contemporary Spanish society. Nevertheless, it is possible that change may occur in public discourse, especially when important matters concerning the rights of all individuals (irrespective of their sexual orientation) are being discussed. My aim, therefore, is to confirm the extent to which this holds true in the texts collected from the minutes taken at sessions of the Spanish parliament. For this purpose, as was suggested earlier, I have studied the collocates of the lemma "lesbian," what may be inferred from the potential set of choices at the speakers' disposal, the implications derived from verbal presences and absences, and the features ascribed to these women through the syntactic processes they are involved in as subjects or objects. Thus it will be possible to draw conclusions on the type of public image that Spanish parliamentarians have been creating for the lesbian community during this time. Subsequently, my observation of the way such speakers may have been promoting a more correct version of this image in the context of the political arena will lead me to revisit how Spanish society is perceived by others.

Returning to the raw data of the corpus under discussion (see Table 1 above), it is possible to notice the high frequency with which speakers use the term "homosexual," which in theory refers to both male and female gays. Grammatical gender in Spanish can work sometimes as a subtle mechanism that confounds and veils sexual differences under an accepted, albeit somewhat controversial, generic masculine plural. This means that "homosexuales" may embody only men, or both men and women together. In contrast, "gays," a referent that is generally male, can also in some cases refer to both men and women as well. That is why it was necessary to analyze all the examples in which I found not only expressions such as "lesbiana" and "lesbianas," which are the most recurrent pattern, but also "mujer homosexual" and "mujeres homosexuales." As for "mujer gay" and "mujeres gays," although these are acceptable labels searchable in Google, there were no such occurrences of this phrase in the corpus studied. Since my aim was to examine the linguistic construction of women with this particular sexual orientation, the denotation had to be unequivocal and unambiguous. As the figures in Table 1 above suggest, it may seem that the actual presence of lesbians in all the parliamentary discussions is not as significant as that of male gays or heterosexuals; nonetheless, the frequency of the lemma itself is relevant for this type of corpus, in view of the dual grammatical gender of the word "homosexuals."

Some of the ideas that are dealt with directly when the term "lesbian" is mentioned are useful to describe Spain, or rather Spaniards, and their prejudices. Other ideas are entailed and, like the previous ones, are key to understanding this and other facts about the country's ideological and political thinking. Speakers

are interested in several conceptual areas that the following semantically related words encapsulate: marriage and couples;
people, women, and men; mothers, parents and children; gays,
lesbians, homosexuals, transsexuals, and bisexuals; rights, discrimination, and equality; movements, associations, and struggle; and restrictions and obstacles. The lexical fields of these
terms are indicative of the main concerns of the texts in which
the lemma "lesbian" is present. Taboos such as same-sex marriage and the new type of family relationships this may imply
are not overlooked. The main participants are all individuals
whose non-standard sexual orientation is foregrounded. Liberal
politicians refer to nonstandard sexualities as normal, in contrast to the views expressed by more conservative political
voices. Thus the former consider that all citizens should have
the same rights, especially in matters concerning marriage,
equality, and intimacy. This may entail two different implications: firstly, that this has not been the case previously; secondly, that there are still social groups (e.g., gays, children,
women, and workers) who are identified as minorities and regarded as existing in inferior conditions and at the mercy of the
goodwill of the state and the authorities. It is worth noting the
most frequent type of time references made during these interventions: the temporal framework referred to is now ("ahora");
it is currently ("actualmente") that actions are being taken, or
rather have to be taken. The contrast between the past and the
present seems to be clear, and so does the urgency to bring about
some (positive) changes in society. Some MPs insist on defending the dignity of gays and lesbians and resort to the use of a
modal verb such as "debemos" [we must], which epitomizes the
notion of a strong internal moral obligation. In this case the inclusive first-person plural pronoun encapsulates the speakers
themselves, their party, all others across the political spectrum,
the government of the moment, and of course Spanish society.
These MPs may understand that, since they serve as elected representatives, it is their responsibility to act on behalf of a community that has long been deprived of liberty and public respect.
It is no surprise therefore that there are many references to the
span of time during which this situation has been so, the preferred choice being the word "años" [years]. What must be done
by this "we" involves intentional material processes constraining human action that mainly consist of either making the best
of current conditions; modifying the existing state of affairs
(which may be intolerable); or setting up a new situation (e.g.,

"to work," "to do," "to face," "to get," "to go on," "to finish,"
"to commence," "to try," "to make an effort," "to amend," "to
move forward," "to eradicate").[33] Other processes (mental,
verbal, and relational) are instrumental in mapping out the complete scenario in which these politicians are primary participants. They state that they must be efficient, cautious, ready,
sensitive, consistent, or rigorous, all of which, on being made explicit, might lead to the idea that matters concerning lesbians in
particular, or homosexuality in general, were not taken as seri-
ously at an earlier point in time. The overall picture of the ideal
spokesperson is that of someone who feels that they must be
able to explain their own decisions and demand that others act,
someone who needs to speak and reveal how events are developing, and who must doggedly pursue and debate key issues when
necessary. They also know that it is essential to find agreement,
not to forget, and to take time to reflect. Furthermore, the recurrent allusion to the "acceptance of the obvious" makes the audience aware of the gap that exists between the law and reality,
that is, between old social constraints and new behavioral models that are no longer going to be subject to punishment. From
my reading of the corpus, I deduce that politicians admit that
the state must play an important role in a process during which
various obstacles will be eradicated. These problems, of which
they are now conscious, have made individuals—especially gays
and lesbians—suffer; this is a further idea recurrent in parliamentary speeches. Unsurprisingly, each political persuasion
suggests that the distress these individuals have had to endure
can be divided into very different categories. Conservative
voices refer to the psychological pain caused by identity crises
and lack of self-respect and to the physical pain provoked by various kinds of sexually transmitted diseases. These right-wing
MPs also point out how children brought up by homosexual couples are more often reported to experience sexual aggression and
rape. On the other hand, left-to-center MPs talk about a different
type of suffering: marginalization and social and legal discrimination, as well as discrimination in the work place. From the
perspective of the former speakers (the Conservatives), much of
the explanation of this discontent lies in a factor inherent to
gays (doubtlessly, their sexual orientation itself), which happens
to affect not only themselves but also those around them and
contributes to their painful emotional state, and even their lack
of good health. Furthermore it can be inferred that the speakers,
by expressing a sentiment of empathy for the terrible situation

in which gays and lesbians find themselves, may enhance their own reputation. However, these sentiments may also be read as an indication of the moral superiority the speakers claim for themselves in expressing sympathy for the suffering of others. Yet these speakers see fit not only to make negative pronouncements about what is essentially a private matter—one's sexuality—but also to seek to link nonnormative sexuality to public crime, e.g., child sex abuse. Nonetheless, for the center-left politicians, the opposite holds true. For them, it is something external to homosexuals that causes them pain—that is, societal rejection because of their sexuality. People's twisted perceptions of the homosexual way of life and traditional standards of social conduct and mores—in a word, other people's prejudice—hamper homosexuals from having the same rights as other citizens. Here, the source of guilt is not the object of suffering, as suggested in the previous case. In fact, the reverse holds true, it being possible to identify the agent responsible for this affliction through the traditions, bigotry, and conservatism apparent in certain sectors of Spanish society. Therefore, such suffering is not the fault of the gay and lesbian community but rather that of a dysfunctional society, which demonizes them, even though they have not committed any crime.

From the minutes of the sessions, women are seen as the victims of violence, either domestic or otherwise. It is also shown that they have more difficulty in finding employment. An additional type of distress to which they may be subject is emotional blackmail, especially if they are mothers and if they are divorced. Moreover, society may find lesbianism and motherhood incompatible notions. Lesbians, as women and as homosexuals, are doubly marginalized. This notion is reinforced when some experts claim that such women are invisible due to their double condition of being female and being homosexual. The word "invisibility" and all the other lemmas semantically related to it are used when speakers refer to minorities or to what may be considered to be underprivileged social groups. Unsurprisingly, in the texts analyzed, this category includes children, the handicapped, women, handicapped women, battered women, handicapped and battered women, poor women, female immigrants, female prostitutes, male gays, and finally, lesbians.[34] This invisibility has two clear implications: on the one hand, people act as if these individuals did not exist because they cannot actually acknowledge their existence, mainly on the grounds of their sense of morality. On the other hand, and as a consequence of this attitude, these nonexistent, invisible individuals cannot possibly be entitled to any rights that citizens have because they are not like the majority, or rather, they are not the majority. In this state of marginality and exclusion by dominant groups, minority groups are disempowered, lacking a voice to be heard in society. That is why they frequently depend on the capacity and desire of others to "see" them, and thus make them visible to all sectors of society. Public recognition of the past twenty-five years of discrimination endured by gays and lesbians comes first in the shape of a general apology, from the government and some sectors of society, for not having treated them equally as Spaniards, this approach embracing civic standards of equality, rather than emotional value judgments. The matters dealt with in the parliament have to do with social justice and equality for all those whom politicians represent; it is not simply a question of human feelings or ethics—it is a question of effecting legislative changes in order to comply with the main principles of the Spanish constitution:

> No sé, señorías, si es necesario recordar que la propia Constitución española, en sus artículos 1.1, 9.2, 10.1 y 14 recoge que el libre desarrollo de la personalidad y la igualdad ante la ley, que constituyen principios fundamentales de nuestro ordenamiento jurídico y social, demandan de todos los poderes públicos la promoción de las condiciones para que esa libertad e igualdad de los ciudadanos y de los grupos que se integran sean reales y efectivas, debiendo ser removidos los obstáculos que impidan o dificulten su plenitud. Asimismo, en el artículo 39 de la Constitución se dice: Todo hombre y toda mujer, en el libre ejercicio de su autonomía personal, tiene derecho a constituir, mediante una unión afectiva y estable, una comunidad de vida que completada o no con hijos dé lugar a la creación de una familia, cuya protección social, económica y jurídica deben asegurar los poderes públicos. (María Olaia Fernández Dávila—*Grupo Mixto*)

> [I don't know, honorable members, whether it is necessary to remind you of the provisions of the Spanish Constitution, whose sections 1.1, 9.2, 10.1, and 14 assert that two key founding principles of our legal and social systems—the free development of people's personality and the equal treatment of individuals before the law—demand from the public powers the promotion of conditions to encourage the freedom and equality of citizens, and the freedom and equality of the communities they belong to, so that all obstacles preventing this must be removed. Likewise, in section 39 we can read: in the exercise of their individual freedoms, all men and women have the right to create, by means of a stable loving relationship, a commu-

nity of life, which, with or without children, can become a family. The public powers must ensure its social, economic, and legal protection

As explained above, the primary aim of this study was to analyze the contexts within which the most typical sexual orientation-related term used in Spanish to name female gays, that is the word "lesbianas" [lesbians], was found. In the corpus, however, they are sometimes also referred to as "mujeres homosexuales" [homosexual women], "mujeres lesbianas" [lesbian women], "mujeres que tienen una orientación homosexual" [women with a homosexual orientation], "mujeres con conducta homosexual" [women of homosexual conduct], and even just "mujeres" [women]. Two examples here are perhaps of particular interest. In one case (i.e., lesbian women), the speaker reiterates the idea of femaleness by adding a noun that is redundant with regard to finding out who the referent is. The cotexts in the instances pinpointed may explain the avoidance of the standard term "lesbianas." By and large, when this is the preferred phrase one notes that it is because there is a need to stress the gender of the people being spoken about, in contrast to that of the other subjects of discussion; that is, they are first women and later lesbians, or even something else. In fact, in certain instances, lesbians are not only women with a particular sexual orientation, their marital status (generally, divorced) is also mentioned. Furthermore, because of their biology, they can become mothers, which is the other feature MPs focus on at times. In short, parliamentary speakers will use the expression "lesbian women" if sexuality is not at stake as much as other characteristics which these individuals may possess.

I made comments above on what is apparently a redundant expression, "lesbian women"; now I will refer to the opposite, where speakers seem to fail to notice the obvious: that is, why there still exists so much opposition to the question under discussion. According to one Catalan politician:

> La realidad social en el Estado español y en el resto del mundo es que existen miles de personas, miles de hombres y de mujeres, que son hombres que aman a hombres y mujeres que aman a mujeres. (Joan Saura Labordeta, *Iniciativa—Verds, Grupo Mixto*)

> [In present-day society in Spain and the rest of the world, there are thousands of people, thousands of men and women, who are men who love men and women who love women.]

As these words demonstrate, the left-of-center representatives find it hard to accept that other politicians choose to support a biased law by which same-sex couples might be prevented, for instance, from adopting children. They are astonished at the idea suggested by the conservatives that sexual orientation may prevent gays and lesbians from being able to show affection towards others in an unselfish, loyal, and benevolent way, or that they are incapable of showing affection for another out of kinship or through personal ties. In the excerpt selected, any reference to sex is explicitly avoided, because sex is seen as a matter of private choice on which judgment must not be passed. Given that, for the right-of-center, the nature of the problem is essentially moral: by overlooking the type of sexual relationship people have and by stressing, by way of contrast, the loving nature of such relationships, it is hoped that objections on the grounds of morality will be silenced. As the quotation shows, what is important is that everywhere thousands of people, thousands of men and women exist, who happen to be men who love men and women who love women, respectively. In such statements affection is regarded as more important than the sexual aspect of the relationship—which continues to provoke controversial views—that is, love being emphasized over sex.

It is possible to detect an echo of the same idea in other parliamentary sessions. In an attempt to naturalize all types of (sexual) relationships and, subsequently, to regulate marriage, adoption, widow's/widower's pensions, inheritance rights, access to Social Security benefits, and other legal matters on equal terms, these liberal politicians prefer to deal with feelings. This approach, of assimilation to the conventional, is rather astute, given that the conservative politicians had tried to debunk the arguments of those supporting the same-sex marriage law by pointing out gays' promiscuousness, emotional instability, and inability to love others unselfishly. The liberal politicians maintain that love is something natural, irrespective of the sexual orientation of the subjects involved, and that it is something to which every citizen has the right; and that if parliament were to fail to endorse this, the legal system in Spain would be rendered defective and discriminatory. One of the grounds on which those in favor of the new law had to establish their defense may appear sentimental, but in the end it was effective. Their claim was that love equals happiness and that, by not giving everybody a chance to be happy, the then-current Spanish law stood in the way of equality, and thus democracy was also called into question. The

following statements by a number of MPs defending the introduction of the new legislation sum up this sentiment:

> Tan natural es que dos hombres se amen y que dos mujeres se amen
> como que se amen un hombre y una mujer. [Love between two men,
> or two women, is as natural as love between a man and a woman.]
> (Marisa Castro Fonseca—*Izquierda Unida*)

> ¿Dónde está escrito que un hombre por ser homosexual o una mujer
> por ser lesbiana no pueda dar amor? [Where is it written that a gay
> man or a lesbian by simple reason of being homosexual does not
> have the ability to give love to others?] (Marisa Castro Fonseca—
> *Izquierda Unida*)

> Heterosexuales, gays, lesbianas y bisexuales, todas las personas son
> iguales, con la misma capacidad de amar, con el mismo derecho a ser
> amados, a fundar una familia, a obtener la protección de la sociedad,
> del ordenamiento y, en definitiva, a ser felices. [Heterosexuals, gays,
> lesbians and bisexuals, everybody is the same, everybody has the
> same capacity for love, the same right to be loved, to make a family,
> to be protected by society and the law; in short, to be happy.] (José
> María Gonzalo Casal, Coordinator of the "Servicio Vasco de aten-
> ción jurídica y psicológica a los colectivos de Gays, Lesbianas y
> Transexuales" [Basque Legal and Psychological Services for Gays,
> Lesbians and Transsexuals])

> Nuestro empeño de contribuir a construir una sociedad donde la
> forma de amar no sea motivo de discriminación. [Our effort to con-
> tribute to building a society where people cannot be discriminated
> against on the grounds of the way in which they love others.] (Leire
> Pajín Iraola—*PSOE*)

The comment below made by Victoria, a young woman of
twenty-two, encapsulates the above declarations. This statement was uttered during a research project carried out by Professor González Rodríguez at the University of Seville and
presented before the parliament's Comisión de Justicia [Justice
Commission] on June 20, 2005. Victoria recollects her impres-
sions of her family and compares how she perceived it when she
was a child with how she sees it now in adulthood. For her, true
love is what matters, echoing one of the strategies employed in
the parliament that may have influenced the final voting session:

> A lo mejor antes decía: ¡Ah!, mamá y mamá, qué bien. No sé qué,
> mis madres se quieren, no sé cuántos. Pero después llega un mo-

mento en que ves la vida realmente y tú dices: Realmente se quieren. [Perhaps, before I said: "Oh! Mummy and Mummy, good! You know, my moms love each other, whatever." Later on there comes a time when you see how life is and you say: "Well they truly love each other."]

CONCLUSION

From June 20 to June 30, 2005, the debates over same-sex marriage raged between Spain's political parties, each side defending its own position by following a clearly different line of reasoning. As has been suggested above, in the Spanish parliament there were two conflicting views on the law that ultimately was passed and on the people who would benefit most from its implementation. No anomalies arose when looking at the data; indeed it was possible to observe an evident divide between a reactionary Spain and the more socially liberal majority; between those who apparently regard themselves as more worthy of respect than others and those who are determined to respect all; those who seem to ignore fundamental sections of the constitution and those who seek to ensure that it is followed to the letter; those who seek to perpetuate traditional values and those who simply accept social realities; conventional religion versus open-mindedness and solidarity.

The right was accused of veiled homophobia, their arguments being poles apart from those put forward by the left. The former showed their disgust at gays and lesbians' showy demonstrations and openly expressed a preference for gay and lesbians to remain imperceptible in society. The left expected the gay community, especially lesbians, to "come out of the closet" so as to put an end to their being invisible. On the other hand, prejudice or ignorance seems to have motivated the decisions taken by most conservative politicians, their fear of disease, immorality, or emotional and psychological instability being key themes in their speeches. Heteronormativity stigmatized the idea of a family different from the traditional heterosexual nuclear family, right-wing rhetoric maintaining that the sanctity of marriage must be between a man and a woman. In contrast left-wing politicians repeatedly invoked the notion of normalcy—this being one of the reasons they tried to show how similar lesbians are to "us." In the excerpt below, we are reminded that such a woman can be our neighbor, our doctor, a waitress, a cleaning lady, our favorite author, an actress in a sitcom, our colleague at the office, a childhood friend, in short, anyone we know:

> Las lesbianas son la vecina del segundo, la camarera del bar donde tomamos café, la médico del ambulatorio, la escritora que les gusta tanto, la mujer que hace el trabajo doméstico, la mujer que se sienta a nuestro lado en el autobús, la okupa que acaban de desalojar, la actriz de telenovela, la alcaldesa, la compañera de oficina, la amiga de la infancia . . . (Rosa María Bonàs—*Esquerra Republicana de Catalunya*)

In contrast to this notion of acceptance, an example of enduring prejudice against lesbians can be observed in a case that appeared in the press at the turn of the millennium. Dolores Vázquez was accused of having murdered a young woman, Rocío Wanninkhof, and was convicted and sent to prison on September 7, 2000. Her conviction was based on conjecture, a psychological report describing her as "cold, hard, distant and lesbian." I understand how the first three adjectives are helpful forensically speaking, murderers being often depicted in all or some of these terms. In criminal psychology killers are portrayed as having a ruthless streak, abnormal motivations, lower levels of intelligence, and aggressive, fearless, assertive, and impulsive personalities. They have poor social skills and no regard for the feelings of others.[35] However, the fourth word in the description (i.e., relating to the woman's sexual orientation) appears superfluous, since it adds no relevant information that might be useful in a police investigation. To return to data in the corpus, conservative psychologists represent lesbians as a marginal sector of the populace, who tend to separate from their partners more often than heterosexuals or even gay men; and who, as mothers, are portrayed as being very demanding, lacking in affection, and insensitive. More liberal-minded reports state just the opposite, affirming that such women can be tender and loving, can establish norms effectively, and rather than hindering their development, can raise children who are open-minded and free of prejudice.

Most texts produced by ideologically committed people on the left reinforce the idea that gays still lack freedom and deserve to be treated with tolerance, respect and dignity, which means that they have previously been deprived of these. They are also said to require information, support, and psychosocial attention, which might make them appear weak and powerless, but at the same time acknowledged and supported. Most conservatives attribute the source of homosexuals' physical, mental, and spiritual ills to their sexual orientation. More liberal commentators would add, however, that if the homosexual community had not been rejected as it has been, it would never have been metaphorically "ill." Further, the data studied indicates that many sectors of Spanish society consider that, had heterosexuals been discriminated against by society in the way that homosexuals have been, they too would have suffered in this way.

Nevertheless, for the most part the representation of gays and lesbians can be seen as optimistic. They are said to have been patient, exemplary, and persistent in their indefatigable fight for equal rights. From the data studied, according to politicians from the center-left, the homosexual community is reported to have worked hard to change societal views, in a context that had transformed them into objects of violence, mockery, contempt, defamation, insult, and persecution in a country that had regarded them as harmful and had prosecuted them as a danger to society.[36] Common sense and justice prevailed in the end, with the passing of antidiscrimination legislation. However, this change did not mean an end to victimization of the homosexual community. Changes in society forced politicians to change an outdated system; the next step must be to foster respect for difference within society as a whole.

I would like to conclude by quoting some lines from a speech delivered by the young socialist MP Carmen Montón Giménez on June 30, 2005, an historic date for same-sex couples and Spanish society in general. In a few phrases she describes the past and the present of a country that on that date took a giant step forward in securing equal rights for gays and lesbians. Previously, this sector of society had been thought to be lazy, criminal, and degenerate. Norms and institutions had been homophobic so far; most sections of the population now were not. The new law, which was able to change this unjust picture, made this female politician, and also many others, proud of the time in which they were fortunate to live:

> Yo nací en 1976 y en una generación hemos pasado de una ley de vagos y maleantes que consideraba al homosexual peligroso *per se*, le privaba de libertad y le sometía a vigilancia para salvaguardarle de sus instintos degenerados, a la plena equiparación de derechos para gays y lesbianas con la reforma del Código Civil que hoy vamos a aprobar. Por ello me siento orgullosa de vivir en este país y en este tiempo. Hoy demostramos la madurez de nuestra sociedad y que

somos muchos los que no estamos dispuestos a soportar y consentir más la injusticia.

[I was born in 1976. In the span of a generation, and thanks to the new Civil Code we are about to pass today, we have turned from a law against lazy people and thugs, which regarded homosexuals as dangerous *per se*, which deprived them of freedom, and watched over them to rescue them from their degenerate instincts, to full equality of rights for gays and lesbians. That is why I feel proud of living in this country and living here now. Today this proves the maturity of our society; today we show that there are many people like us who are no longer going to tolerate injustice.]

Notes

My thanks to Prof. Andrew Blake for his helpful comments on the draft version of this paper.

1. Norman Fairclough, *Analysing Discourse: Textual Analysis for Social Research* (London: Routledge, 2003), 47.

2. Norman Fairclough, *Critical Discourse Analysis: The Critical Study of Language* (Harlow: Longman, 1995), 11.

3. Roger Fowler, *Linguistic Criticism* (Oxford: Oxford University Press, 1986); Roger Fowler, *Language in the News: Discourse and Ideology in the Press* (London: Routledge, 1991); Robin Tolmach Lakoff, *The Language War* (Berkeley: University of California Press, 2000); and Fairclough, ibid.

4. Henry G. Widdowson, *Text, Context, Pretext: Critical Issues in Discourse Analysis* (Oxford: Blackwell, 2004).

5. See http://www.senado.es/buscador/.

6. Michael Scott, *WordSmith Tools 3.0.* (Oxford: Oxford University Press, 1999).

7. Charles F. Meyer, *English Corpus Linguistics: An Introduction* (Cambridge: Cambridge University Press, 2002).

8. Encarnación Hidalgo Tenorio, " 'I Want to Be a Prime Minister,' or What Linguistic Choice Can Do for Campaigning Politicians," *Language and Literature* 11/3 (2002): 243–62.

9. Keiran O'Halloran, *Critical Discourse Analysis and Language Cognition* (Edinburgh: Edinburgh University Press, 2003).

10. Deborah Cameron, *Verbal Hygiene* (London: Routledge, 1995).

11. Douglas Biber, Susan Conrad, and Randi Reppen, *Corpus Linguistics: Investigating Language Structure and Use* (Cambridge: Cambridge University Press, 1998).

12. REAL ACADEMIA ESPAÑOLA: Banco de Datos (CREA) (en línea), *Corpus de Referencia del Español Actual.* http://www.rae.es.

13. Some other terms and the explanation of their origin can be found at http://www.lesbianas.tv/.

14. The boy comes from an area in Spain where (s) is pronounced as (□), and the psychologist has tried to imitate his accent, which is finely rendered. I won't dare to do so in my translation.

15. Eugenio Noel, *Las Siete Cucas* (Madrid: Cátedra, 1992). "Cucas" is the nickname of the main characters of this novel, the widow and the daughters of "Coquiles," a man who killed his master's wife and servant when he broke into their house to rob them. In vulgar Spanish, the word "cuca" can also refer to a woman's vagina.

16. Juan Goytisolo, *Señas de identidad* (Barcelona: Mondadori, 1996).

17. Juan García Hortelano, *El gran momento de Mary Tribune* (Barcelona: Grupo Zeta, 1999).

18. Francisco de Quevedo y Villegas, *Entremés de la destreza* (Madrid: Gredos, 1971).

19. *Todo por la pasta* dir. Enrique Urbizu (Creativideo, 1996).

20. José Asunción Silva, *De sobremesa* (Colombia: Presidencia de la República, S.L., 1996).

21. Camilo José Cela, *La colmena* (Barcelona: Noguer, 1986).

22. Fernando Savater, *Caronte aguarda* (Madrid: Cátedra, 1981).

23. Juan Cruz Ruiz, "Más de doscientos espectáculos en el Festival Internacional de Edimburgo," *El País*3 (August 31, 1977). http://www.elpais.com/articulo/cultura/FESTIVAL_INTERNACIONAL_DE_EDIMBURGO_/ESCOCIA/doscientos/espectaculos/Festival/Internacional/Edimburgo/elpepicul/19770831elpepicul_4/Tes/.

24. Emilio Rodríguez Demorizi, *Apuntes diversos (Informes y articulos sobre lengua y folklore de Santo Domingo)* (Santo Domingo: Universidad Católeca, 1975).

25. Esther Ferrer, "Encuentro Internacional del Movimiento Feminista en Vincennes (París)," *El País* (June 21, 1977). http://www.elpais.com/articulo/sociedad/FRANCIA/feminismo/autonom ia/lucha/clas es/elpepisoc/19770621elpepisoc_1/Tes/.

26. Fernando Arrabal, *El arquitecto y el emperador de Asiria* (Madrid: Cátedra, 1966).

27. Alberto Miralles, *Comisaría especial para mujeres* (Madrid: SGAE, 1994).

28. Jaime Campmany, "Escenas políticas," *ABC* (May 7, 1985).

29. José María Fernández Rúa, "Inmunólogos norteamericanos aportan nuevos datos sobre el virus del Sida," *ABC* (June 8, 1989).

30. Manuel Hidalgo, *Azucena, que juega al tenis* (Madrid: Mondadori, 1988).

31. Myriam López Blanco, "Corazones solitarios: Diversos análisis de los anuncios de contactos publicados en varios países han desvelado la evolución en las preferencias de pareja," *El Mundo—Salud (Suplemento)* (February 13, 1997). http://www.elmundo.es/salud/1997/234/01680.html.

32. Translation available at http://www.piranesia.net/baudelaire/fleurs/index.php?poeme = 144&lang = en.

33. For further detail about the systemic-functional conception of semantic roles, processes, participants, and circumstances, see Michael A. K. Halliday and Christian M.I.M. Matthiessen, *An Introduction to Functional Grammar* (London: Arnold, 2004).

34. See Richard D. Mohr's notion of "invisible minority" in *Gays/Justice: A Study of Ethics, Society, and Law* (New York: Columbia University Press, 1988).

35. Eric Gartman, "A Very Important Breakthrough in Understanding

Crime," May 6, 2000. http://www.amazon.com/gp/product/0684852667/103–1092027–3477406?v = glance& n = 283155.
    36. See the 1954 *Modificación de la Ley de Vagos y Maleantes*.

REFERENCES

Arrabal, Fernando. *El arquitecto y el emperador de Asiria*. Madrid: Cátedra, 1966.

Asunción Silva, José. *De sobremesa*. Colombia: Presidencia de la República, S.L., 1996.

Biber, Douglas, Susan Conrad, and Randi Reppen. *Corpus Linguistics: Investigating Language Structure and Use*. Cambridge: Cambridge University Press, 1998.

Cameron, Deborah. *Verbal Hygiene*. London: Routledge, 1995.

Campmany, Jaime. "Escenas políticas." *ABC* (May 7, 1985).

Cela, Camilo José. *La colmena*. Barcelona: Noguer, 1986.

Cruz Ruiz, Juan. "Más de doscientos espectáculos en el Festival Internacional de Edimburgo." *El País* (August 31, 1977). http://www.elpais.com/articulo/cultura/FESTIVAL_INTERNACIONAL_DE_EDIMBURGO_/ESCOCIA/dos cientos/espectaculos/Festival/Internacional/Edimburgo/elpepicul/19770831 elpepicul_4/Tes/.

Fairclough, Norman. *Analysing Discourse: Textual Analysis for Social Research*. London: Routledge, 2003.

———. *Critical Discourse Analysis: The Critical Study of Language*. Harlow: Longman, 1995.

Fernández Rúa, José María. "Inmunólogos norteamericanos aportan nuevos datos sobre el virus del Sida." *ABC* (June 8, 1989).

Ferrer, Esther. "Eucuentro Internacional del Movimíento Feminista en Vincennes (Paris)." *El País* (June 21, 1977). http://www.elpais.com/articulo/socie dad/FRANCIA/feminismo/autonomia/lucha/clases/elpepisoc/19770621el pepisoc_1/Tes/.

Fowler, Roger. *Language in the News: Discourse and Ideology in the Press*. London: Routledge, 1991.

———. *Linguistic Criticism*. Oxford: Oxford University Press, 1986.

García Hortelano, Juan. *El gran momento de Mary Tribune*. Barcelona: Grupo Zeta, 1999.

Gartman, Eric. "A Very Important Breakthrough in Understanding Crime," May 6, 2000 http://www.amazon.com/gp/product/0684852667/103-1092 027-3477406?v = glance&n = 283155.

Goytisolo, Juan. *Señas de identidad*. Barcelona: Mondadori, 1996.

Halliday, Michael A. K. and Christian M.I.M. Matthiessen. *An Introduction to Functional Grammar*. London: Arnold, 2004.

Hidalgo, Manuel. *Azucena, que juega al tenis*. Madrid: Mondadori, 1988.

Hidalgo Tenorio, Encarnación. "'I Want to Be a Prime Minister,' or What Linguistic Choice Can Do for Campaigning Politicians." *Language and Literature* 11/3 (2002): 243–62.

López Blanco, Myriam. "Corazones solitarios: Diversos análisis de los anuncios de contactos publicados en varios países han desvelado la evolución en las preferencias de pareja." *El Mundo–Salud (Suplemento)* (February 13, 1997). http://www.elmundo.es/salud/1997/234/01680.html.

Meyer, Charles F. *English Corpus Linguistics: An Introduction*. Cambridge: Cambridge University Press, 2002.

Miralles, Alberto. *Comisaría especial para mujeres*. Madrid: SGAE, 1994.

Mohr, Richard. *Gays/Justice: A Study of Ethics, Society, and Law*. New York: Columbia University Press, 1988.

Noel, Eugenio. *Las Siete Cucas*. Madrid: Cátedra. 1992.

O'Halloran, Keiran. *Critical Discourse Analysis and Language Cognition*. Edinburgh: Edinburgh University Press, 2003.

Quevedo y Villegas, Francisco de. *Entremés de la destreza*. Madrid: Gredos, 1971.

Rodríguez Demorizi, Emilio. *Apuntes diversos (Informes y artículos sobre lengua y folklore de Santo Domingo)*. Santo Domingo: Universidad Católica, 1975.

Savater, Fernando. *Caronte aguarda*. Madrid: Cátedra, 1981.

Scott, Michael. *WordSmith Tools 3.0*. Oxford: Oxford University Press, 1999.

Todo por la pasta. Directed by Enrique Urbizu, with Pilar Bardem. Creativideo, 1996.

Tolmach Lakoff, Robin. *The Language War*. Berkeley: University of California Press, 2000.

Widdowson, Henry G. *Text, Context, Pretext: Critical Issues in Discourse Analysis*. Oxford: Blackwell, 2004.

Lesbian Literary Identities in the Chueca Book Business

Jill Robbins

QUEER THEORISTS HAVE BUILT ON HENRI LEFEBVRE'S *THE PRODUC-tion of Space* in order to elaborate concepts of queer space tied to social and cultural practices across time, which, as Lefebvre explains, intersect with the designs and intended uses of architecture so that "an already produced space can be decoded, can be *read* [because] such a space implies a process of signification" (17).[1] "Codes," he continues, "will be seen as part of a practical relationship, as part of an interaction between 'subjects' and their space and surroundings" (18). Lefebvre conceives of a conceptual triad consisting of spatial practice, representations of space, and representational spaces. These are linked to each other and to other cultural spaces through a variety of networks, some of them physical (streets, metros, buses, trains, airplanes, pedestrian footsteps, freeways), some of them electronic (phones, internet), some of them historical, some of them linguistic, some of them economic, some of them symbolic. Michel de Certeau figures these networks as pedestrian steps in *The Practice of Everyday Life,* which allows him to trace relationships between people, and between people and spaces, including those spaces that are hidden from the planned grid of the city because they are informal and underground spots of congregation.[2] He likens those footsteps—their spatialization of the abstract city design and their subversion of panoptic and consumerist intentions—to the rhetoric meanderings of figurative language, which defy normative grammars.

Both Lefebvre and de Certeau associate the social and symbolic construction of urban life with art and, in the case of de Certeau, specifically with literature, making their theories particularly apt for my purpose here of examining the image of lesbian Madrid that emerges where networks linking Spain's imperial past and neoliberal present intersect with gender, race, and sexuality in literary spaces. These cross-sections do not play themselves out solely in sites explicitly associated with sexual interchange. They are also implicit in the clash of economic, political, and aesthetic values in gay/lesbian bookstores, which manifest themselves in their layout, stock, location, and functions, as well as their publishing policies, all of which have tended to maintain a homogeneous image of lesbianism, to eliminate bisexuality, and to marginalize women in relation to gay men.

This article will explore the role of a particular gay/lesbian bookstore, Berkana, in the construction of Madrid's "queer literary spaces," those areas of the city—the Chueca neighborhood, in particular—that have transformed and been transformed by queer social and cultural practices, including literary writing and reading.

CHUECA HETEROTOPIAS: THE HIDDEN HISTORIES OF GENDER, CLASS, DISABILITY, AND NATIONALITY

The Chueca neighborhood is now synonymous with the gay life of Madrid, but it is a fascinating heterotopia whose histories intersect in complex ways with those of the capital in general. It is part of the Justicia (Justice) division of the city; the name "Chueca" comes from the Plaza, which is an important metro stop. Bernardo Veksler points out that:

> Su denominación actual es reciente. Antes, lució el nombre de las pequeñas barriadas del Barquillo, de las Salesas, de las Maravillas, del Refugio o el Hospicio. Luego, pasó a ser parte del distrito Centro e institucionalmente conocido como Justicia. Pero, su transformación de los últimos años impuso a Chueca y los madrileños paulatinamente fueron identificando al lugar con el nombre de esa plaza.[3]

> [Its current denomination is recent. Before, it bore the names of the small neighborhoods of Barquillo, Salesas, Maravillas, Refugio, and Hospicio. Later, it came to be part of the Central district institutionally known as Justicia. But its transformation in the past few years imposed the name of Chueca, and the people of Madrid gradually began identifying the area with the name of that plaza.]

According to Veksler, the Justicia division, traditionally the home of the poor working classes and those living on the wrong side of the law, began to represent marginality during the reign

of Philip II, who exiled the ironworks to the Barquillo neighborhood (32), and it began to embody resistance to state authority
during the reign of Carlos III in the late eighteenth century (33,
43–44). In the nineteenth century it was the site of cafés, whore-
houses, and theaters (60–64), to which were added a circus and
movie theaters in the early twentieth century (66–67). Some as-
sassinations and skirmishes took place in the area during the
Spanish Civil War (78–82), and during the Franco years the
neighborhood was a stronghold of the working class and working-class prostitutes. The headquarters of the labor union,
UGT—Unión General de Trabajadores—is still located on Hortaleza Street.

In the late 1970s and 1980s Chueca was, along with the Malasaña neighborhood, one of the main areas of the artists associated with the *movida madrileña,* who populated its bars, dives,
dark rooms, galleries, theaters, and terrazas, and even the metro
entrance of the Chueca Plaza, which was a prime spot to score
and use heroin. The headquarters of the ONCE [National Organization for Blind (Disabled) Spaniards][4] is also in the neighborhood, on Prim Street. All of this means that the people crossing
through the Chueca Plaza could be characterized—that is, stigmatized and/or empowered—not only by their sexual orientation but also by their labor membership, artistic interests, or
physical disability.

For the most part, however, Chueca has been, since the late
1970s and 1980s, one of the key sites of Madrid's "queer city,"
which Dianne Chisholm defines as "a city of queer sites—
buildings, streets, quarters, and neighborhoods that have a history of gay and/or lesbian occupation and that historians cite
from city archives and sources not yet archived."[5] These would
include the headquarters of COGAM (the Madrid LGBT Collective), gay travel agencies, gay bars, and drag shows, all of which
have subsequently appeared in gay literature and film and are
still listed in the Shanguide, the Zero guide, and gay tourbooks.

From the 1990s on, the combined effects of globalization, neo-
liberalism, wealth accumulated from investments in Latin
America, and the euro transformed the city in general, and
Chueca in particular, from an anarchic bohemian utopia into
more of a postutopian destination for well-to-do consumers. Fernando Villaamil has commented on the effect these changes
have had on the constituent population of Chueca. As he explains, the neighborhood provided a refuge and a social ambi-
ence that permitted the formation of a gay community in the

early post-Franco years. Now, he claims, it is a gathering place for young, HIV-negative men who rarely mix with the older generation save in dark rooms or in prostitution.[6] These changes have allowed the neighborhood to market itself as a mecca for gay tourists, in what Chisholm calls the "phantasmagoric homogenization and totalization of queer city space, its trendy circulation and abstraction in the (circuit-party's) nonplace" (17).[7]

The 1990s also saw an increase in immigrant populations (economic exiles) from Africa, Eastern Europe, and Latin America, with the result that Spaniards, who had been exoticized as passionate, irrational Mediterraneans by their European neighbors, sometimes applied the same racist stereotypes to a significant portion of the people living within their borders. It is notable, then, that the immigrant population has been markedly absent from Chueca, except for young men making their living by prostituting themselves or performing in drag or strip shows. With the exception of that group of non-Spaniards, the vast majority of foreign-born men and women who socialize in the plaza are tourists rather than immigrants.

The majority of the business establishments in Chueca—including bars, clothing stores, and gyms—also mark a gender divide in that they cater primarily to the perceived tastes of globalized gay *male* consumers. This does not mean necessarily that they exclude women altogether, although the dark rooms and saunas—once open to men and women—now do. But even the advertisements in the free circulars like *Shangay* and *Odisea*, which are distributed in bookstores and other businesses throughout Chueca, are devoted almost exclusively to the needs and desires of gay men and specifically to a globalized image of gay sexuality that emphasizes youth, muscles, and a very recognizable fashion sense, a trend that Leopoldo Alas and Luis Antonio de Villena lament at length in the former's *Ojo de loca no se equivoca: Una irónica y lúcida reflexión sobre el ambiente* and that Alberto Mira defends in *De Sodoma a Chueca: Una historia cultural de la homosexualidad en España en el siglo XX.*[8]

In marketing primarily to men, the gay establishments of the Spanish capital mirror globalized gay businesses. Suzanna Danuta Walters explains:

> Not only is the new campaign to get gays shopping . . . motivated by a more general trend in niche marketing, it is obviously emerging in the context of increasing gay visibility, political power, and social inclusion. . . . Given this truth—that marketing to gays is a business

decision (with confusing political ramifications), it should come as no surprise that the world of the marketplace promotes a view of gays as largely male, extremely wealthy, overwhelmingly white, and ready to spend their disposable wealth with admirable brand loyalty.[9]

Ricardo Llamas and Francisco Javier Vidarte comment on a similar increase in gay marketing throughout Chueca in *Homografías* (214–17), which tips the balance of power in favor of the wealthier patrons of Chueca establishments: "Las selecciones de clientelas que se establecen en función de unos u otros criterios son el factor de control más evidente. De éstas, la más patente [. . .] es la selección impuesta por el poderío económico, que deja un tanto fuera de onda, sobre todo, a los más jóvenes" [The selections of clientele established according to a variety of criteria are evident factors of control. Of these, the most obvious is the selection imposed by economic power, which leaves the youngest, above all, out of the loop].[10] Women are also left out in greater numbers because they tend to earn less than men (Walters 243). In Chueca, the same assumptions about and the realities of the income disparity between men and women appear in the dearth of businesses catering to lesbians.

This subtle form of gender discrimination applies to Chueca's social environment as well. The overwhelming majority of gay and lesbian bars and discos in Madrid are located in Chueca, but women have few options, and even lesbian bars are never exclusively lesbian, or even exclusively homosexual, so that women often have to contend with unwanted advances from straight men. Still, it is in Chueca that most lesbians congregate for romantic and/or sexual encounters. After all, it is more convenient and economical to walk from one place to another than to travel by car, bus, metro, or taxi to another spot if one chooses to leave the first. Chueca, then, is an ambiguous meeting place for Spanish lesbians because its parameters conform much less to those of lesbian identity in Madrid, than they do to those of gay male identity. These conditions have repercussions, not only for the sale of books and other merchandise to lesbians but, more significantly, for lesbian politics and female equality in general.

Berkana

The most important gay/lesbian bookstore in Madrid, Berkana, was founded in 1993 by Mili Hernández, a leading lesbian activist. Although it is now an icon of Chueca, Berkana's first location was not in the neighborhood at all but hidden not far away on the Calle de la Palma in Malasaña. Despite the post-Franco hipness of that neighborhood, especially in the years when it was associated with the gay-friendly *movida*, the store was bracketed there among establishments that were not gay, and it was not especially visible to local, national, or international communities. It was a location that one found by chance or through word-of-mouth from other gay or gay-friendly people. Berkana's next location was almost literally in the Chueca Plaza on Gravina Street, clearly visible as one left the metro stop or sat at one of the outdoor terrazas in the plaza. In 2001 it moved to its current location, on a busy thoroughfare on the outer fringe of the Chueca neighborhood, nearly at the border with Malasaña, on Hortaleza Street, in plain sight of considerably more passersby of all orientations than either of the previous locales. (Indeed the tattoos, piercings, clothing and hairstyle of most pedestrians on Hortaleza and Fuencarral Streets are definitively queer, even when not gay or lesbian). The nearby shops on Hortaleza Street are a mixture of globalized gay businesses—cafés with plasma screens and trance music, cabarets, clothing stores and gyms—and traditional Spanish locales, including old-style cafes, lighting fixture stores, pet shops, and closer to Gran Vía, the Pérez Galdós bookstore, which specializes in used books. We could say, then, that the passages of the Berkana bookstore trace a change in gay visibility from the rigid closet of the Franco days to a semi-closet in Malasaña, to an openness within a larger, wholly gay *"gueto"* (enclave or community) in the Chueca Plaza, and finally to a borderland where LGBT identities mingle with a variety of others. The moves have been, in other words, not only physical but also symbolic and historical, in consonance with the broader changes in the politics and economics of post-Franco Spain.

These relocations have been accompanied by changes in the marketing strategies and relative prosperity of the bookstore. Gay and lesbian bookstores have traditionally been not only business establishments but also spaces in which people could congregate for political or purely social purposes, and Berkana has certainly served this purpose. This particular bookstore, however, became a political literary space in a symbolic, as well as material, sense when it took the activist role literally into the book trade in 1995. In that year the store ceased to be just a seller of books and branched out into the publishing business with the foundation of Egales, dedicated to publishing gay and lesbian literature, particularly essays, anthologies, and entertaining, easy novels that normalized and legitimized homosexuality for gay and lesbian readers and thereby eased the coming-out process.

Lesbian Books in Gay/Lesbian Bookstores, or The Sexual Politics of the Book Business

Although Berkana and Egales were founded by a woman, lesbians have remained less visible than gay men in the bookstore and in books themselves. The rationale for this disparity has often been explained in economic terms: as the founder of Berkana, Mili Hernández, told me in 1999, books for and about lesbians just do not sell (at least not in the gay bookstores), a view that was corroborated by Oscar Pérez, the founder of Odisea—a publisher that, like Egales, markets to gays—in a newspaper interview in 2003.[11] This reasoning, however, seems faulty on several grounds. It does not, for example, take into account the general gender disparity in book publications and sales in the Spanish-language market. Laura Freixas discusses this very issue in *Literatura y mujeres: Escritoras, público y crítica en la España actual* [*Literature and Women: Women Writers, Public and Criticism in Spain Today*], where she also notes that books by and for women *sell less* than those by and for men because they are *published less*.[12] Current book sales, in other words, are rather unreliable indicators of future market trends, since they only reflect the status quo, which in itself may be determined by factors extraneous to the market, such as the assumption by publishers that women write less well than men (72–74), and that women's books will only be of interest to women (70).

Freixas has also noted that women actually read *more* than men in Spain (38). How, then, can gay and lesbian booksellers and publishers claim that lesbians read less? This assertion assumes that it is possible to identify the sexual identity of book buyers in Berkana and in the broader book market according to the books they buy. The majority of Spanish bookstores, which represent a far higher percentage of total book sales in Spain than their gay/lesbian counterparts, cannot make assumptions about the sexual identity of their customers, so such a claim is impossible to verify.

Berkana also limits the possible sales to lesbians by the "women's books" it chooses *not* to stock. For example, there are no books of generic interest to women, such as those dealing with maternity or menopause, and none that address generic social and economic inequality for women, books that the feminist bookstore, Librería Mujeres, carries in abundance.[13] It is also surprising to find that, although Berkana carries many books in translation, and particularly in translation from English, there are no books by Chicana or U.S. Latina writers. Another limitation that has more to do with the mechanisms of globalized publishing than with the politics of the bookstore per se is the dearth of books—fiction, poetry, or essay—by Latin American women. I have discussed elsewhere the difficulty experienced by Latin American writers in penetrating the market for literature in Spain, a problem complicated by the fact that Spanish publishing firms, themselves the victims of globalization, have bought many of the important Latin American firms and thus control the distribution of Latin American literature, not only in Spain, but also in Latin America itself.[14] It is not surprising, then, that most of the Latin American writers familiar to Spanish readers have either lived in Spain for many years or have been published by firms owned by Spanish interests. In Berkana, the majority of the books by Latin American women authors were either written by those living in Spain (Cristina Peri Rossi, for example) or have been published by Egales or Odisea.[15]

The assertions by Mili Hernández and Oscar Pérez regarding sales to women are also based upon the false assumption that lesbian readers buy books exclusively in gay and lesbian bookstores. Luis Antonio de Villena has noted that cultured gay men do not: "El público gay muy culto está en el armario, y son los que compran toda esa literatura en cualquier librería normal, no en Berkana" [cultured gay readers are in the closet, and they buy gay literature in any normal bookstore, not in Berkana] (Alas, Ojo 112). Whether they be male or female, cultured book buyers—like lesbians in general—shop outside Chueca and thus extend literary queerness to bookstores and publishers that deal in literature that could be considered queer but is not explicitly so. The bookstores in Madrid are quite varied, from the small, traditional kind like La Celestina or the Pérez Galdós that specialize in used and rare books, to those with a political history like the Librería Mujeres, to those associated with publishing houses like Hiperión, to those that serve as an extension of cultural establishments like the Reina Sofía museum or the Círculo de Bellas Artes, to large commercial establishments like the bookstore of the Corte Inglés department store or the Casa del Libro (the

Barnes and Noble of Madrid), to those somewhere in-between, like Crisol. None of these is in Chueca proper, although the Pérez Galdós is just a few blocks from Berkana on Hortaleza Street, and the Casa del Libro, a few blocks further, on the Gran Vía. These bookstores do not market exclusively to gays and lesbians but to a variety of niches, from the scholar to the student to the casual or nostalgic reader, male or female, Spanish or not, gay or straight, of any age. To the extent that gays and lesbians buy books there, and that these stores stock books of interest to gays and lesbians, including books published by Egales, the publishing house that came out of the Berkana bookstore, they may be included in the network of queer spaces in Madrid.

LAYOUT

A few years after moving to Chueca, Berkana entered the business of selling nonprint items, which it stocked in a sister store near the Gravina Street location. These items were incorporated into the bookstore proper when it moved to its current location on Hortaleza Street. As Mili Hernández explains: "Somos una de las mayores de nuestro tipo del mundo, con librería, videoteca, cafetería, venta de ropa, complementos, regalos, y secciones de revistas y libros en inglés y francés repartidos en dos plantas" [We're one of the largest of our kind in the world, with a bookstore, video store, café, clothing sales, miscellaneous items, gifts and sections with magazines and books in English and French spread over two floors]. The store, in other words, is not just a bookstore now but part of a growing sector of businesses that market to the particular niche of gay people.[16]

This type of transformation is not exclusive to Spain, of course. Walters also comments on the phenomenon in *All the Rage:*

> When I came out in Philadelphia in the late '70's, the gay bookstore, along with the gay bar, were my places of reference and often my places of reverence as well. Going to the bookstore seemed less like an act of financial support than a search for a place of affirmation and information. . . . Now, as it becomes increasingly hard to discern the difference between buying gay and being gay, the gay entrepreneur emerges as a figure to be reckoned with and gay bookstores face an increasingly uncertain future (273).

Walters describes the loss of these noncommercial functions of the bookstores and indeed of the bookstores themselves, with a melancholy similar to that which I noted in an earlier article regarding the disappearance of small Spanish bookstores that were sites of resistance under Franco ("Globalization"). Berkana, however, has branched quite profitably into pride-related items and erotica—porn videos, dildos, comics, beefcake calendars, magazines, and the like—while remaining a meeting place for activists. And, unlike similar establishments elsewhere in Spain,[17] it is prospering—that is, it is not disappearing at all— thanks in large part to the diversification of its stock and its niche marketing to gay consumers, in Madrid and elsewhere in Spain, as well as tourists and other non-Spaniards who buy materials in the store and on its website.

Although Berkana itself does not exclude women, the layout of the store has at times favored the male consumer, to the extent that some women have told me that they are reluctant to enter the store at all. This is because the first images that they see upon entering are those of the erotic postcards and comics designed almost exclusively for men. Recent releases—both gay and lesbian—are arranged on tables in the middle of the store, and the materials on the shelves are divided into "narrativa masculina" [literally, "masculine narrative," but generally meaning "fiction by and for men"], located nearest to the door, then a large display case with gay and lesbian mugs, magnets, flags, and the like, followed by essays in Spanish, then poetry, and only then, "narrativa femenina" ["feminine narrative," or fiction by and for women], with works in translation in the furthest corner. The women's narrative section, ironically, is located in front of the display table holding books of photography featuring male nudes. Farther back to the left, two sections of films— commercial and porn—frame the café, where social gatherings and informal political meetings are held and through which one passes to reach the stairway to the lower level. There, after passing a section with T-shirts, one used to find the hard-porn books and films for men, and at the very back, under lock and key and the vigilance of a male clerk, the dildos, condoms (for penis, dildo, and fingers), and lubricants.[18] This layout made it highly unlikely that a lesbian would buy a dildo at Berkana: in other words, the setup of the store seems to imply that sex toys and condoms are for men only. Indeed, the sex shops in Chueca that cater explicitly to men make these objects much more accessible to lesbians than does Berkana, as does a new store for women, La Juguetería, which, like Good Vibrations in San Francisco, also instructs customers on safe sex and on the proper use and care of sex toys.[19] In the summer of 2004, Berkana advertised with enormous posters a new book, with a prologue by Mili Hernández, on the *Kama-sutra lésbico: Para vivir la sexualidad en libertad* [*The Lesbian Kama Sutra: How to Live Sexuality in Freedom*], so it is ironic that the bookstore did not at that time take a more active role in promoting safe sex among lesbians by making it easier for women, as well as men, to buy dildos and condoms in the store, an apt location for pedagogy regarding their uses.

LESBIANS IN ANTHOLOGIES AND HISTORIES IN THE BOOKSTORE

The invisibility of lesbians extends to literary histories and anthologies as well, even when these are purportedly dedicated to gay and lesbian literature. Sympathetic anthologists abide by a "gentleman's agreement" in not outing authors, as Connie, the co-owner of the Barcelona bookstore Cómplices explained to me in July 2000. Julia Cela confirmed this pact when I asked her why she did not include Spanish women in her *Galería de retratos: Personajes homosexuales de la cultura contemporánea* [*Portrait Gallery: Homosexual Figures in Contemporary Culture*].[20] This could also explain why, among the 126 poets in Luis Antonio de Villena's *Amores iguales: Antología de la poesía gay y lésbica* [*Same Loves: Anthology of Gay and Lesbian Poetry*], only three are Spanish women (Gloria Fuertes, María Mercè Marçal, and Andrea Luca), and these were already out of the closet when the book was published.[21] Alberto Mira's *Para entendernos: Diccionario de cultura homosexual, gay y lésbica* [*Towards Understanding Ourselves: Dictionary of Homosexual, Gay and Lesbian Culture*] does not even include those three poets, though it does have entries on Ana María Moix, a poet/novelist who is out but whom Villena did not include in his collection, and Esther Tusquets, whose numerous novelistic portrayals of lesbianism defy her attachment to the closet.[22] Likewise, Mira's exhaustive study (615 pages), *De Sodoma a Chueca: Una historia cultural de la homosexualidad en España en el siglo XX* [*From Sodom to Chueca: A Cultural History of Homosexuality in Twentieth-Century Century Spain*] does not include the literary work of a single lesbian, although there are occasional references to their critical work.

Spanish women are not the only figures under represented in the texts I have mentioned: Latin Americans in general, and Latin American women in particular, are strikingly absent. In the case of the anthologies mentioned above, it is interesting to note how few Latin American figures are included, despite Villena's claim that: "*Amores iguales* quiere ser una antología general, panorámica, pero prestando mayor atención a la poesía escrita en español, en España y América, aunque sin llegar al exclusivismo pobre que suelen ostentar al respecto las antologías anglosajonas" [*Amores iguales* is intended as a general, panoramic anthology but one that pays greater attention to poetry written in Spanish, in Spain and Latin America, but without the poor exclusionism that tends to characterize Anglo-Saxon anthologies] (24). More shocking, however, is the fact that, with the exception of Cristina Peri Rossi, who, after all, has lived in Spain since 1973, and Sor Juana Inés de la Cruz, who lived when Mexico was still considered to be part of Spain, Villena seems to have eyes only for Latin American and Latino *men*, and mainly for Mexicans and Cubans. Even there we find odd omissions: for example, he does not mention Xavier Villarrutia or even the most famous gay writer and arguably the greatest poet ever to come from Cuba, José Lezama Lima. The Spanish male anthologist's selections, in other words, highlight certain blind spots that belie the image of tolerance that contemporary Spaniards seek to project on the global stage. Julia Cela's book is a bit more evenhanded, allowing three Latin American artists (Frida Kahlo, Manuel Puig, and José Lezama Lima) to Spain's seven (Federico García Lorca, Salvador Dalí, Luis Cernuda, Luis Antonio de Villena, Eduardo Mendicutti, Jaime Gil de Biedma, and Terenci Moix).

Mira's *De Sodoma a Chueca* is equally problematic. The subtitle—*A Cultural History of Homosexuality in Twentieth-Century Spain*—implies that the book will include not only Spanish authors but also foreign authors who came to form part of the Spanish cultural world in the twentieth century, given that "in Spain" is not synonymous with "Spanish." Again, however, the offerings are uneven, with the majority of references limited to French, British, and U.S. authors and a one-paragraph treatment of key Latin American authors of the early twentieth century that is not entirely accurate. Again, women like Victoria Ocampo, Alfonsina Storni, Gabriela Mistral, Frida Kahlo, and

Alejandra Pizarnik are completely absent, despite their contact with Spanish women authors and their considerable influence on the refiguration of female sexuality in the twentieth century. Later on in Mira's study, Puig merits a few pages, and Severo Sarduy appears on one, but there is no mention of José Lezama Lima, Luis Rafael Sánchez, César Aira, Fernando Vallejo, or Jaime Bayly. The omission of the latter two is particularly surprising, given that their novels—*La virgin de los sicarios* [*Our Lady of the Assassins*] and *No se lo digas a nadie* [*Don't Tell Anyone*] respectively—are sold in Berkana and have been made into films that have circulated throughout the world, including Spain.

THE LESBIAN CITY IN A LESBIAN BOOK

I have spoken briefly about the circulation of lesbian bookstores, lesbians in bookstores, lesbian book sales, and foreign lesbians in books and bookstores. Now I would like to turn briefly to the ways in which these movements and crossings are represented in literature, specifically in a novel, *Donde comienza tu nombre* [*Where Your Name Begins*], which was published by Mabel Galán in the Safo collection of Odisea in 2004.[23] This book, unlike most of the books published by gay/lesbian publishers, successfully crossed over in Summer 2004 to the Barnes and Noble of Spain, the Casa del Libro, a mainstream bookstore operated by the Espasa-Calpe publishing house, where it was prominently displayed on the "new book" table and in the front window. Odisea, like its sister publisher Egales, was founded by activists to provide a venue for narrative designed specifically for the Spanish gay and lesbian reading public, and for many years their books were stocked exclusively by gay/lesbian bookstores. Needless to say, before this novel, they were rarely carried by the Casa del Libro, where even queer theory has remained largely taboo. *Donde comienza tu nombre*, however, became a crossover hit, giving sudden visibility to lesbian relationships. In the following pages, I will suggest some reasons for its success among mainstream readers and some of the red flags such acceptance should raise in this case.

In *Virtuous Vice: Homoeroticism and the Public Sphere*, Eric O. Clarke explains some of the ways in which mainstream culture deforms queer culture by mediating its values:

In the first mode, queer interests are bestowed value only insofar as they conform to the heteronormative standards retained within publicity's supposedly universal moral-political principles. In mode two, this bestowal becomes the alibi for, and thus is overlapped by, the mediation of homoeroticism through the extraction of commercial value.[24]

Indeed, although it could be argued that the more tolerant attitude of the Zapatero government has helped move gay and lesbian issues out of the closet, the decision to put *Donde comienza tu nombre* prominently on display in the Casa del Libro was based primarily on economic motives, not moral, political, or aesthetic ones. The bookstore markets this book aggressively because promoters understand the desire of contemporary Spaniards to see themselves and be seen by others as modern and sophisticated, an image that implies an acceptance of alternate lifestyles and even the emulation of a certain globalized, metrosexual cool.[25] As Walters puts it in *All the Rage*, "Homoerotic imagery . . . speaks to the more legitimized public engagement of *straights* with gays, as if the new visibility of gays makes them more available for the displays of public desire that permeate advertising imagery. Connecting with homosexuals through gay-themed imagery allows heterosexuals access to the (media-constructed) hipness factor" (245–47). The cover of *Donde comienza tu nombre,* adorned with Roy Lichenstein's *Girl with Hair Ribbon,* provides a visual shorthand for this association by adopting a postmodern "high-art" American image of a female that itself references the pop comic-book culture, and refiguring it as a lesbian: it is a wink within a wink that seems to suggest a queer subtext. This image, and the public display of Sapphism (the book is in the Safo collection), would confirm to passersby on the Gran Vía that Spain had indeed become a modern European nation, that it was in on the globalized postmodern game, and that it had definitively left behind the radical moral conservatism of the Franco years.

The trendy metaliterary narrative of the novel itself also allows Spaniards who actually buy and read it to feel that they are painlessly participating in the postmodern experience. *Donde comienza tu nombre* features several plot lines, all linked to a single figure, Isabel, who is simultaneously the author of the story about Rosalía and Irene, the subject of the plot about writing that story, and a tangential love interest in the story about Silvia and Ana. The styles of these different narrative lines recall a variety of literary genres and styles: the romantic melodrama, the cyberchat, the trashy tale of modern chicks in search of sex, the romance of maternal love, and, of course, the postmodern novel. The coexistence of these various styles and the interweaving of multiple plot lines suggest complexity and thereby allow readers who might otherwise have to explain their choice of a novel about the love lives of lesbians to justify their interest on purely literary grounds. Here, however, the multiple diegetic narrative levels are easily identified and neatly resolved at the end. It is pomo light that gives readers the illusion of sophistication without the philosophical premises, the difficulty, and the challenges of works by authors such as Ana María Moix, Juan and Luis Goytisolo, or the *novísimo* poets.

The characteristics of those lesbians and their relationships, and the narrative styles in which they are recounted, appeal simultaneously to the need to heteronormatize homosexuality and the desire to participate in a kinky sexuality associated more with Pat Califia or the *Kama sutra lésbico* than with straight Spanish sexual mores. In one plot line, we follow two young hipsters, Silvia and Ana, from their apartment, where they discuss their failure to pick up women in Chueca, to the chat room (chueca.com) where they next turn to search for lovers, to the headquarters of COGAM, which is hosting a lesbian literary night and where they finally locate potential lovers, including Isabel, the author of the novel within this novel, who happens to be the featured author at the COGAM literary function.

Isabel tries to seduce Ana by inviting her to watch the film *Frida,* starring Salma Hayek as Frida Kahlo, at her apartment. The film has become a lesbian favorite because it presents very clearly the famous bisexuality of the Mexican painter, splendidly embodied by Salma Hayek in several nude scenes, such as the one in which she lies on a bed entwined with the equally nude body of Karine Plantadit-Bageot, the dancer/actress portraying Josephine Baker. This vision is titillating, of course, but problematically so because the Latina and African American actresses' racialized naked bodies, locked in lesbian embrace, are exposed for the benefit of the general public in a manner that corresponds to the Orientalist eroticization of racial others and the heterosexual appropriation of female homoeroticism in pornography, which is played for the pleasure of the male voyeur. By attempting to use this film to arouse her date, Isabel places herself unquestioningly in the position of the straight male viewer, thereby buttressing rather than questioning a sexual-economic order in which the female body serves as a ground.

Apart from her brief interlude at COGAM, Isabel spends most of her time in a gay/lesbian bar eyeing a woman named Mar, reminiscing about her lost love, Marta, fending off a hetero couple looking for a threesome, and finishing her novel about Rosalía and Irene, whose romantic tale echoes, except in its ending, her own relationship with her ex, Marta. The happy ending comes for Isabel, however, when she successfully begins a new relationship with Mar, whose name is a shortened version of Marta, and who promises to incarnate the ideal love that Isabel lost when Marta abandoned her. This resolution—the reincorporation of Isabel into happy coupledom—coincides temporally with the moment when Isabel finishes penning the ending of her novel, which takes place in the very same bar where she herself is writing.

The novel that Isabel is writing falls into two genres: the tale of maternal love and the romance, replete with mystery, surprise plot twists, and, of course, a happy ending. It recounts the love story of Rosalía, a young Spanish lesbian with a queer tattooed, pierced aesthetic, and a conventionally beautiful, sophisticated older woman—Irene. Rosalía first spots Irene on a city bus while on vacation in Lisbon, but the older woman's style and behavior lead Rosalía to believe she is straight. Nonetheless, she follows her, meets her, and finally begins a relationship with her. There is, however, a third mystery woman involved, one whom Irene herself is desperately seeking and with whom she must resolve certain issues that eventually force her to abandon Rosalía in Lisbon without further explanation. As it turns out, the third woman is Irene's straight daughter, Sandra, who had run away from home in anguish after her father forbade Irene from having any contact with her once she came out as lesbian. After abandoning Rosalía and searching the entire city of Lisbon, Irene miraculously finds her daughter in a drug den that represents the decadence of the sixties ideals, or even those of the *movida madrileña* of the 1980s: it is "okupada," meaning that it has been taken over and inhabited by squatters living communally as a form of political protest against the rising cost of living. In the novel, however, the "okupants" are not represented as political activists, or even anarchists, but, rather, as strung-out addicts. As befits the romantic novel, Irene arrives just in time to save her daughter. Rosalía, meanwhile, returns to Madrid, where she reminisces about Irene until the latter returns and finds her in the gay/lesbian bar, and they all live happily ever after.

Despite nods to a globalized queer aesthetic and dating practices, we find in the specific sites described by Isabel in her novel a rhetorical normalization of the "white" heteronormalized Spanish lesbian by contrast to an exotic, erotic other, evident in the descriptions of Lisbon and of Middle Eastern women working in restaurants in Lisbon and Madrid, as well as the image of Frida, which I mentioned above. The sexualized Arab, Portuguese, and Latin American women embody in *Donde comienza tu nombre*, respectively, the latent homosexual Middle Eastern origins of contemporary Iberia and the "pagan" sexuality of the colonial tropics, a move that alludes to what Ana Paula Ferreira has called the phantasms of empire, the ghosts of Iberia's medieval and imperial past in its centuries-long occupation by Arabs and the reconquest of its territory, which culminated in the separation of Portugal from the rest of Iberia, the unification of the remaining territories into the Spanish, the expulsion of Arabs and Jews, the conquest of Latin America, and the enslavement of Africans and indigenous people.[26] The latter dehumanization was justified by the "hedonistic paganism" of those people, which allegedly required the intervention of the Catholicizing Spaniards. By alluding primarily to that distant imperial past, the romantic exoticizing of those cultures in this particular novel ignores the economic impetus for recent Arab, African, and Latin American immigration into Europe, preferring to turn those cultures into providers of recreational space and implicit sexual difference. The representation of Portugal is also problematic: whereas the novel highlights the thoroughly modern gay sites of Madrid—from the bar to the Internet to COGAM headquarters—Lisbon appears still as a city of medieval labyrinthine streets, with hidden pockets of forbidden pleasure and anachronistic hippie hangouts, the latter of which conveniently ignores Madrid's own history of "okupations" in the Lavapiés neighborhood in the 1980s and 1990s before it became an enclave for immigrants, particularly Arabs.

These phantasms are brought together in a crucial scene when Rosalía, who has returned to Madrid without Irene, tries to recapture a particularly poignant moment in their relationship by eating in a Syrian restaurant in the Spanish capital. The image she recalls is that of a belly dancer who performed for Rosalía and Irene in a restaurant in Lisbon on the last night they spent together:

En el semisótano que ocupa un pequeño restaurante sirio asentado en una transitada calle de Lavapiés, una mujer árabe de cabello anaranjado por la henna baila la danza del vientre para un reducido número de personas. Rosalía, entregada a sus movimientos y a la música, se deja llevar libremente por el ritmo sensual de la danza que mece las caderas de la egipcia de un modo inigualable. [. . .]

La egipcia danza meciendo rítmicamente sus caderas y Rosalía no puede sacarse de la cabeza una escena de aquella noche en la que Irene, en un gesto invisible para los presentes, le pasaba sus uñas delicadamente por la base del cuello, mientras una preciosa muchacha libanesa de no más de diecisiete años bailaba al ritmo sensual de la música norteafricana. Sus ojos eran tan verdes y su piel tan morena, que resaltaban de su rostro tanto como los pañuelos multicolores que a modo de falda rodeaban sus caderas y de los que más tarde se despojaría de uno en uno, jaleada por los habituales en la sala. [. . .] No era un lugar de ambiente como los anteriores que habían visitado aquella noche, estaba lleno de extranjeros, árabes en su mayoría, pero la mujer danzó para ellas especialmente, dedicándoles el baile, deteniendo el tiempo delante de su mesa, como si deseara que su danza bautizara sensualmente la relación que acababa de comenzar (143–45).

[In the half-basement occupied by a small Syrian restaurant located on a busy street in Lavapiés, an Arab woman with henna-tinted hair performs a belly dance for a small group of people. Rosalía, bewitched by her movements and the music, lets herself be taken away by the sensual rhythm of the dance that sways the Egyptian woman's hips in a singular way. . . .

The Egyptian woman sways her hips rhythmically, and Rosalía can't get out of her head a scene from that last night, when Irene, in a gesture hidden to the rest, stroked the base of her neck with her fingernails while a lovely Lebanese girl of no more than seventeen danced to the sensual rhythm of North African music. Her eyes were so green, against a skin so dark, that they leapt from her face like the multicolor handkerchiefs that covered her hips like a skirt and which would later be removed one by one by the customers in the room. . . . It wasn't a gay place like the ones they had visited earlier that night; it was full of foreigners, most of them Arabic, but the woman danced especially for them, dedicating the dance to them, staying before their table, as if she wanted her dance to sensually baptize the relationship that had just begun.]

Rosalía and Irene take the dancer's sensuality as a sign of her "natural" lesbian desire, one that justifies their own, given the partially Arabic origins of Spanish culture. By eroticizing the Arab districts and making them part of the lesbian story, then, the novel inverts the more unpleasant Franco-era connotations of "the Arab within," that is, the impure heretic that Spain had excised centuries earlier but which represented a constant threat to the morals of the Catholic nation ideated by the dictatorship.

These signs of Arab culture in Madrid and Lisbon, and others of Latin America (*Frida*), are designed to titillate rather than discomfort the mainstream Spanish reader, and this could explain why the novel was able to attract a large mainstream readership. It poses as a postmodern novel about people who are seen as radical others, but it forges an implicit alliance with mainstream readers that allows them to see queer aesthetics and postmodern sensibilities as exciting, exotic, and perhaps even "normal." It also helps them to see lesbians as Spaniards like themselves, and as a nonthreatening source of pleasure. As an added benefit, by accepting the legitimacy of sexual others, they can see themselves as open-minded, modern, and tolerant global citizens.

CONCLUSION

The diverse sections of this article have sought to reproduce the function of the pedestrian footsteps that Michel de Certeau imagines, which rhetorically recreate the urban landscape:

> The long poem of walking manipulates spatial organizations, no matter how panoptic they may be: it is neither foreign to them (it can take place only within them) nor in conformity with them (it does not receive its identity from them). It creates shadows and ambiguities within them. It inserts its multitudinous references and citations into them (social models, cultural mores, personal factors).[27]

When exploring the queer spaces of Madrid, and the ways in which nonstraight female identities cross through them and become visible, it is important to keep in mind their intersections with other spaces and identifications—such as those associated with race, class, politics, gender, disability, and/or nationality, which have been derived from national, imperialist, and neoimperialist fantasies, the trauma of the Civil War, the repressions of the Franco dictatorship. As we cross through the literary spaces of queer Madrid, Chueca's image as a trendy, globalized gay mecca, or party paradise, or prejudice-free zone, disappears, and we find in its place exchanges, tensions, contradictions, exclusions, and prejudices that resonate across space and time.

Notes

1. Henri Lefebvre, *The Production of Space* (1974), trans. Donald Nicholson-Smith (Oxford: Blackwell, 1991).

Here is the detailed description of the three spaces:

Spatial practice, which embraces production and reproduction, and the particular locations and spatial sets characteristic of each social formation. Spatial practice ensures continuity and some degree of cohesion. In terms of social space, and of each member of a given society's relationship to that space, this cohesion implies a guaranteed level of *competence* and a specific level of *performance.*

Representations of space, which are tied to the relations of production and to the "order" which those relations impose, and hence to knowledge, to signs, to codes, and to "frontal" relations.

Representational spaces, embodying complex symbolisms, sometimes codes, sometimes not, linked to the clandestine or underground side of social life, as also to art (which may come eventually to be defined less as a code of space than as a code of representational spaces) (33).

2. Michel de Certeau, *The Practice of Everyday Life,* trans. Steven Randall (Berkeley: University of California Press, 1984).

3. Bernardo Veksler, *Del Barquillo a Chueca: Transformaciones y glamour de un barrio madrileño* [*From Barquillo to Chueca: Transformations and Glamour in a Madrid Neighborhood*] (Madrid: Vision Net, 2005), Prologue, n.p.

4. Founded in 1938 but inactive during the Franco dictatorship (1939–1975), ONCE was revitalized in the 1980s, under the PSOE, the socialist government, which granted it the right to conduct a national lottery to raise funds. The blind ceased to be invisible but were initially seen largely in connection with the sale of lottery tickets. The success of this operation allowed ONCE to diversify its economic holdings so that, even though it continues to operate the lottery, it is financially independent. The organization was originally dedicated only to the blind, but, through the ONCE foundation, it expanded its activities to promote solidarity between the blind and other disabled people in Spain in 1988, and it continues to exert political influence in an effort to improve accessibility for disabled people in Spain.

5. Dianne Chisholm, *Queer Constellations: Subcultural Space in the Wake of the City* (Minneapolis: University of Minnesota Press, 2005), 10.

6. Fernando Villaamil, *La transformación de la identidad gay en España* [*Transformation of the Gay Identity in Spain*] (Madrid: Los Libros de la Catarata, 2004), 70.

7. Gabriel Giorgi, "Madrid en tránsito: Travelers, visibility, and gay identity," *GLQ* 8.1–2 (2002): 57–79. In his article Giorgi examines how codes of modernity, globalization, democracy, and queerness intersect in tourist literature about Chueca, Madrid's gay barrio. "In making gay people visible," he claims, "Chueca epitomizes the new democratic Spain" (60). That is, "in a democracy that still needs to demonstrate its strength and its resemblance to the older, so-called advanced democracies of the United States and northern Europe, gay visibility stands out as a symbol, a token of social tolerance and achieved freedom" (61). Giorgi notes, however, that this visibility does not extend to lesbians, who are relegated to a footnote in most gay travel guides,

where they constitute "a supplement, a formally corrective addendum to discourses and information produced by and for gay male tourists" (67).

8. Leopoldo Alas, *Ojo de Roca no se equivoca: Una irónica y lúcida reflexión sobre el ambiente* (Barcelona: Planeta, 2002); Alberto Nuira, *De Sodoma a Chueca: Una historia cultural de la homosexualidad en España en el siglo XX* (Madrid: Egales, 2004).

9. Suzanna DanutaWalters, *All the Rage: The Story of Gay Visibility in America* (Chicago: University of Chicago Press, 2001), 237–38.

10. Ricardo Llamas and Francisco Javier Vidarte, *Homografías* (Madrid: Espasa, 1999), 216.

11. Pérez reportedly remarked that "los libros de tema lésbico son más difíciles de vender y desde que salen al mercado tienen el mismo ritmo de ventas—normalmente muy bajo—, sin las alzas de ventas que se producen en los de temática gay" [lesbian-themed books are harder to sell and once they're on the market they have the same rhythm of sales—normally quite low—without the spikes in sales that gay-themed books have]. "La editorial Odisea entregó sus premios de literatura gay y lésbica," *Yahoo! Noticias* (February 7, 2003).

12. Laura Freixas, *Literatura y mujeres: Escritoras, público y crítica en la España actual* (Barcelona: Destino, 2000), p.36. Future references to this text will be noted by author's last name and page number in parenthesis.

13. The owners of both Berkana and Librería Mujeres noted that a schism developed between the stores due to the ideological split in the feminist movement itself regarding the role of lesbians.

14. Jill Robbins, "Globalization, Publishing, and the Marketing of 'Hispanic' Identities," *Iberoamericana* 3.9 (2003): 89–101.

15. The situation is particularly ironic if we consider how Latin American women residing in Spain have helped to shape literature and literary studies on the peninsula. Some of these women—Cristina Peri Rossi, Beatriz de Moura, Noni Benegas, and Iris Zavala, for example—have had a prominent role for many years in reforming the canon and the theoretical orientation of writers and scholars in post-Franco Spain through their work in publishing houses, in creating anthologies, and in Spanish universities. Thus the Uruguayan Peri Rossi has played a key role in the Editorial Lumen, the publishing house that Esther Tusquets and her brother Oscar inherited. Under their direction, Lumen ceased to publish religious texts and became the first Spanish publishing house to promote the work of gays and lesbians, and women in particular, including Spanish authors like Ana María and Terenci Moix, Jaime Gil de Biedma, Leopoldo María Panero, Gloria Fuertes, Esther Tusquets and Rosa Chacel, and such foreign writers in translation as Djuna Barnes, Monique Wittig, and Virginia Woolf. The Brazilian Beatriz de Moura, sister-in-law of Esther Tusquets and director of Tusquets Editores after splitting with Esther and Lumen in 1968, also profoundly changed the Spanish publishing business by publishing "high culture" books that questioned the hard-line positions of both the Left and the Right: that is, she wanted a business "a que no sólo irritaba profundamente al beaterío nacional-católico de la época, sino que hería la sensibilidad de cierta izquierda ortodoxa" [that not only profoundly irritated the beatific National-Catholics but that also wounded the sensibility of a certain wing of the orthodox left]. Her three goals, as she describes them, were to reassert the importance of the avant-garde, to promote debate on culture and ideas, and to publish fiction by Spanish and Latin American novelists. The Argentine Noni Benegas, an award-winning poet in her own right, published in 1997 the first

poetry anthology dedicated exclusively to the work of Spanish women—*Ellas tienen la palabra: Dos décadas de poesía española* [*The Women Have the Floor: Two Decades of Spanish Poetry*]—to which she contributed a thoughtful preliminary study of the category of "women's poetry" in contemporary Spain. Her selection and study of these young poets changed the image of contemporary poetry in Spain, which had been dominated by the almost exclusively male group of *poetas de la experiencia* [poets of experience]. She also played a key role in securing the National Prize in Poetry for a Spanish woman (Julia Uceda) for the first time since Franco's death. The Puerto Rican Iris Zavala, meanwhile, has collaborated with the University of Barcelona for many years, and her scholarly work on feminism and post-colonialism has profoundly marked younger scholars in Spain. It cannot be denied that these Latin American women have played a ground-breaking role in Spanish intellectual life, even where their influence might not be immediately visible.

16. It is ironic that Hernández criticizes the Librería Mujeres for a similar move toward merchandising feminist T-shirts, mugs, music, and so forth, and for having received subventions from the state. (Personal interview, July 2000).

In a 1998 interview published in *El País*, Begoña Aguirre interviews Alonso Ramírez, a thirty-nine-year-old Madrid lawyer and director of Servi G, the first multiservice network of "pink businesses." According to Ramírez, Servi G was established because "queremos demostrar que los gay no solo sabemos montar empresas de ocio" [we want to show that gays can create businesses that are not just for recreation]. "Es una forma de reivindicar el ser homosexual las 24 horas y no sólo a la hora del amor y el sexo" [It's a way of vindicating homosexuals 24 hours a day, and not just at the moment of love and sex]. Although the enterprise could be seen to reinforce the closet, Ramírez believes the opposite to be true: "Hay muchas personas que soportan una dualidad, por la noche son gay y en su trabajo ocultan sus preferencias. Nosotros las expresamos abiertamente y eso puede romper estigmas" [There are many people who can tolerate duality; they can be gay by night but they prefer to hide their preferences at work. We express them openly, and that can eliminate stigmas]. He goes on to insist that the network will change the image that the public at large has of the gay community: "Creemos que sirve para integrar o normalizar. Es como el barrio de Chueca, que ha sacado la imagen del homosexual del cuarto oscuro. Antes si se hablaba de un gay siempre se tenía la imagen de las saunas con zona oscura; ahora cualquiera que vaya a Chueca ve que se ha convertido en un barrio vivo y más cuidado y relaciona lo homosexual con algo positivo, no con el morbo" [We believe that it serves to integrate or normalize. It's like the Chueca neighborhood, which has taken the image of the homosexual out of the dark room. Before, the mention of gays always brought to mind the saunas of dark zone; now anyone who goes to Chueca can see that it's become a lively and well-tended neighborhood, and can relate the gay with something positive and not just with sexual curiosity]. ("Chueca ha sacado la imagen del homosexual del cuarto oscuro" [Chueca has taken the image of the homosexual out of the dark room], www.elpais.com, September 11, 1998).

17. The bookstore El Cobertizo in Valencia, for example, closed its doors in April 2004, after seven years in business.

18. This was the layout of the store as of summer 2005.

19. Shortly after I had written these lines in the summer of 2004, I met some friends for a drink at one of the terrazas in the Chueca plaza. As we chatted, a man came to our table with flyers—which he offered exclusively to the

women—advertising a new store, La Juguetería: Erotic Toys. The flyer told us that the store was not exclusively for women, but stocked: "Juguetes orgásmicos para todos los sexos. Diseños exclusivos para lesbianas + gays + transgéneros" [Orgasmic toys for all sexes. Exclusive designs for lesbians, gays, and transgendered people]. Clearly, however, the owners were targeting lesbians with their flyer marketing campaign, presumably because they thought that the gay men and transgendered people would find the store on their own. The store can be accessed online at lajugueteria@wanadoo.es.

20. Personal interview, July 1999. The book does include the following Spanish men, however: Luis Cernuda, Federico García Lorca, Salvador Dalí, Luis Antonio de Villena, Eduardo Mendicutti, Jaime Gil de Biedma, and Terenci Moix.

21. Luis Antonio de Villena, *Amores iguales: Antología de la poesía gay y lésbica* (Madrid: La Esfera de los Libros, 2002).

22. Alberto Mira, *Para entendernos: Diccionario de cultura homosexual, gay y lésbica*, 2nd ed. (Barcelona: Ediciones de la Tempestad, 2002).

23. Mabel Galán, *Donde comienza tu nombre* (Madrid: Odisea, 2004).

24. Eric O. Clarke, *Virtuous Vice: Homoeroticism and the Public Sphere* (Durham, NC: Duke University Press, 2000), 10.

25. The same held true for Lucía Etxebarría's *Beatriz y los cuerpos celestes* when it won the Nadal prize in 1998.

26. Ana Paula Ferreira, *Fantasmas e fantasias imperiais no imaginário português contemporaaneo*, ed. Margarida Calafate Ribeiro and Ana Paula Ferreira (Porto: Campo das Letras, 2003).

27. de Certeau, *Practice of Everyday Life*, 101.

REFERENCES

Aguirre, Begoña. "Chueca ha sacado la imagen del homosexual del cuarto oscuro." www.elpais.com, September 11, 1998.

Alas, Leopoldo. *Ojo de loca no se equivoca: Una irónica y lúcida reflexión sobre el ambiente*. Barcelona: Planeta, 2002.

Benegas, Noni, and Jesús Munárriz. *Ellas tienen la palabra: Dos décadas de poesía española*. Madrid: Hiperión, 1997.

Cela, Julia. *Galería de retratos: Personajes homosexuales de la cultura contemporánea*. Madrid: Egales, 1998.

Chisholm, Dianne. *Queer Constellations: Subcultural Space in the Wake of the City*. Minneapolis: University of Minnesota Press, 2005.

Clarke, Eric O. *Virtuous Vice: Homoeroticism and the Public Sphere*. Durham, NC: Duke University Press, 2000.

Cruz-Malavé, Arnaldo, and Martin F. Manalansan, IV. *Queer Globalizations: Citizenship and the Afterlife of Colonialism*. New York: New York University Press, 2002.

de Certeau, Michel. *The Practice of Everyday Life*. Translated by Steven Rendall. Berkeley: University of California Press, 1984.

Ferreira, Ana Paula. *Fantasmas e fantasias imperiais no imaginário português contemporâneo*. Edited by Margarida Calafate Ribeiro and Ana Paula Ferreira. Porto: Campo das Letras, 2003.

Freixas, Laura. *Literatura y mujeres: Escritoras, público y crítica en la España actual.* Barcelona: Destino, 2000.

Galán, Mabel. *Donde comienza tu nombre.* Madrid: Odisea, 2004.

Gallotti, Alicia. *Kama-sutra lésbico: Para vivir la sexualidad en libertad.* Madrid: Martínez Roca, 2004.

García Martín, Antonio, and Andrés López Fernández. *Imagen social de la homosexualidad en España.* Madrid: Asociación Pro Derechos Humanos, 1985.

Giorgi, Gabriel. "Madrid en tránsito: Travelers, visibility, and gay identity." *GLQ* 8.1–2 (2002): 57–79.

"La editorial Odisea entregó sus premios de literatura gay y lésbica." *Yahoo! Noticias* (February 7, 2003).

Lefebvre, Henri. *The Production of Space.* 1974. Translated by Donald Nicholson-Smith. Oxford: Blackwell, 1991.

Llamas, Ricardo, and Francisco Javier Vidarte. *Homografías.* Madrid: Espasa, 1999.

Mira, Alberto. *De Sodoma a Chueca: Una historia cultural de la homosexualidad en España en el siglo XX.* Madrid: Egales, 2004.

———. *Para entendernos: Diccionario de cultura homosexual, gay y lésbica.* 2nd ed. Barcelona: Ediciones de la Tempestad, 2002.

Moura, Beatriz de. http://www.literaturas.com/faroni/beatriz de moura.htm

Robbins, Jill. "Globalization, Publishing, and the Marketing of 'Hispanic' Identities," *Iberoamericana* 3.9 (2003): 89–101.

———. "The (In)visible Lesbian: The Contradictory Representations of Female Homoeroticism in Contemporary Spain." *Journal of Lesbian Studies* 7.3 (2003): 107–31.

"Tusquets suspende el Premio La Sonrisa Vertical." *El País.ES* Cultura (May 25, 2004).

Veksler, Bernardo. *Del Barquillo a Chueca: Transformaciones y glamour de un barrio madrileño.* Madrid: Vision Net, 2005.

Villaamil, Fernando. *La transformación de la identidad gay en España.* Madrid: Los Libros de la Catarata, 2004.

Villena, Luis Antonio de. *Amores iguales: Antología de la poesía gay y lésbica.* Madrid: La Esfera de los Libros, 2002.

———. *El mal mundo: Dos relatos sobre el amor masculino.* Barcelona: Tusquets, 1999.

Walters, Suzanna Danuta. *All the Rage: The Story of Gay Visibility in America.* Chicago: University of Chicago Press, 2001.

Part II

"Sisters Are Doing It for Themselves": Lesbian Identities in Contemporary Spanish Literature

Jacky Collins

> Considero que abordar el lesbianismo como parte de la normalidad cotidiana es la única forma de avanzar en el proceso de socialización de las homosexuales. Precisamente, la Literatura es un instrumento muy útil para avanzar en este proceso.
>
> Gemma Retamero[1]

> [I consider that dealing with the subject of lesbianism as a part of everyday life is the only way to move forward in the process of lesbian socialization. In particular, literature is a most useful tool in this process.]

IN HER STUDY ON LESBIAN IDENTITIES, OLGA VIÑUALES LAMENTS that invisibility and negation are two of the most sinister discriminations society is capable of producing, discriminations to which the majority of lesbians in Spain have been subject.[2] Likewise Fefa Vila affirms that there has been a distinct lack of cultural representations of lesbians in Spain when compared to such representations of gay men.[3] Clearly, it is to be acknowledged that the creation of an identity is rendered problematic from a position of invisibility. However, the introduction of a lesbian space within the context of literary texts allows for the construction of a lesbian subjectivity and for the development of both social and sexual lesbian identities.[4] Through reading lesbian texts lesbians are able to identify themselves and thus construct a lesbian subjectivity; likewise, through the production of lesbian writing authors are able to challenge the social, political, and cultural subordination that heteropatriarchy has until now exerted over this group.

The importance of the production of lesbian fiction with re-

gard to the formation of lesbian identities is foregrounded in
Bonnie Zimmerman's landmark text *The Safe Sea of Women:
Lesbian Fiction 1969–1989.*[5] It is therefore particularly encouraging to note that 2005 saw the formation of the Ellas Editorial
publishing company in Barcelona, a group with the stated aim of
dealing solely with works based around lesbian themes, in contrast to previously established groups such as Egales and Odisea
Editorial that deal with both gay and lesbian publications. Ellas
Editorial's first published author, Thais Morales, commented in
an article that was published in *La Vanguardia* that "[a]ún hay
diferencias dentro del mundo de la homosexualidad, entre hombres y mujeres. El gay está mejor aceptado, sobre todo si forma
parte de una nueva clase social con fuerte poder adquisitivo. Pero
la mujer sigue siendo invisible, sale poco, no frecuenta locales
de ambiente, es menos admitida" [there are still differences
within the homosexual world, between men and women. Gay
men are better accepted, especially if they form part of the new
social class with strong purchasing power. But [gay] women continue to be invisible, they go out less,and they are less ac-
cepted].[6] She goes on to state that there is a need for such a
publishing company that is devoted to disseminating works that
contain a lesbian theme that "ayudaría a la normalización'
[would assist normalization].

Initially this chapter will present a comparative study of three
texts published since 1999—*Plumas de doble filo,* Lola Van
Guardia (1999); *El lago rosa,* Illy Nes (2004); *Donde comienza tu
nombre,* Mabel Galán (2004)—in order to examine the extent to
which it is possible to determine the emergence in literature of
a lesbian identity out of the shadows of shame, rejection, and
self doubt, to inhabit a place of acceptance and self-affirmation.[7]
Such development is reflective of more broad-based changes in
Spanish society with regard to an emerging lesbian community,
as well as recent legal developments in the recognition of same-
sex marriage. Moreover it is possible to interpret the inclusion
of these aspects within the narrative as the normalization of lesbians and lesbianism in contemporary Spanish society.

However, in contrast to the aforementioned views that es-
pouse normalization as a means to ensure lesbian visibility,
Sally Munt has argued in favor of an alternative literary expression of lesbian identities, claiming that:

[h]eroes offer a metaphor of the self in movement, change and
process . . . , a lesbian success story, an icon of struggle, and both

we and "mainstream" culture need her versatility. Normalization is resisted by the public discourse of lesbianism—if our lesbianism is kept secret, then our private desires become domesticated—hence the importance of images like the heroic, which exist in the popular, public realm.[8]

Recent years have seen the development of such public discourse in Spain, alongside a significant growth in the number of lesbian texts produced by Spanish lesbian authors, to the extent that it is now possible to point to an additional literary manifestation, that of the textual configuration of a Spanish heroic lesbian body. With a view to examining this emerging trend, this chapter will go on to consider three further novels from the Spanish lesbian fiction genre of the last ten years, namely Mabel Galán's *Desde la otra orilla* (1999), Lais Arcos's *72 horas* (2004), and Paz Quintero's *Destino programado* (2005).[9]

Returning to the notion that novels published by and for lesbians in Spain towards the end of the twentieth century presented a considerably more positive portrayal of lesbian characters, relationships, and identities than had appeared earlier, Illy Nes's *El lago rosa* will be the first text to be examined. This narrative represents one woman's journey of self-discovery expressed through the metaphor of travel. Susana, a young photographer based in Barcelona, decides to fulfill one of her dreams by traveling to Senegal to undertake an interview with Amira, a retired model who now works to help and support the marginalized of her country. Conveyed as a first-person narrative, this text enables the emerging lesbian to speak for herself from the privileged position of the subject.

Before embarking on the journey, Susana has already begun to question her relationship with her male partner, Marcos, which has become restrictive and abusive. On meeting Amira for the first time in Senegal, Susana is struck by her physical beauty and refers to her as "aquella hermosa diosa de ébano" (that lovely ebony goddess), going on to liken her to "la mismísima Afrodita" [Aphrodite herself] (39), which could be read simply as one woman appreciating the beauty of another. However, she also senses that Amira is flirting with her, a first for Susana, which produces in her conflicting reactions of embarrassment and delight. After the first intimate moment between the two women, Susana questions this perplexing shift in her sexuality: "¿Desde cuándo me gustaban las mujeres? Aquella era una idea descabellada. ¡Yo no era lesbiana!" [Since when did I like women? That was a ridiculous idea. I wasn't a lesbian] (52). Later, when questioned about her sexuality by her co-worker Leo, she is adamant that "no me van los vicios raros" [I'm not into kinky stuff], again declaring "¡Yo no soy lesbiana. Nunca me gustó una chica!" [I'm not a lesbian! I never liked girls!] (55). Leo's response speaks to a fluid rather than a fixed notion of sexuality when he recommends that Susana "debería [. . .] probar con una tía" [should . . . try it with a chick] (55). As the two women become closer physically, Susana continues to struggle with her sexual identity, embarrassed and unnerved by her own actions. Yet even as she categorically states to Amira "[l]o siento [. . .] pero yo no soy lesbiana" [I'm sorry . . . but I'm not a lesbian], at the same time she is depicted as longing for the other woman to do whatever is necessary to win her (74–75).

It is only after a problematic visit from Marcos that Susana finally acknowledges her love for Amira and makes it plain that what she is feeling is more than just a passing phase (99), a common retort levied at same-sex attraction. However, Susana is unaware of Amira's fatal illness that ultimately ends her life before the two can build a lasting relationship. Nevertheless, in Amira's dying breath she acknowledges that Susana is "la mujer con la que siempre he soñado" [the woman I have always dreamed of] (119). Thus, although no depiction is presented here of an enduring lesbian relationship, Nes portrays a love that has the power to overcome many obstacles: prejudice, gender, culture, and death; further, we are shown a woman who wrestles with her own self-doubt and fears to come to accept the person she has become and who is proud to recount the love that she has experienced for another woman. Further, contrary to earlier representations of lesbian relationships in Spanish literature (Esther Tusquets and Ana María Moix), which depicted women having lesbian affairs while remaining in unhappy heterosexual marriages, here the central character makes a conscious, self-empowering choice to end her relationship with Marcos and live her life on her own terms. It is also worth mentioning that when Amira speaks of how the relationship between herself and Susana could have been if she were not dying, she refers to their union as a marriage. After they share an intimate meal together, Amira declares to Susana, "Si fueras lesbiana, te pediría que te casaras conmigo" [If you were a lesbian I would ask you to marry me] (91). Despite Amira's fatal illness, no mention is made of a marriage being legally impossible, and when her death is imminent, she still speaks of the relationship they could have enjoyed as a marriage (109).

While Nes's narrative centers on the self-realization of the individual, Galán's *Donde comienza tu nombre*, is constructed around a framework that speaks to the notion of a continuum, of a network or community of lesbian solidarity, rather than of an individual existing in isolation, as appears to be the case with earlier publications (*Si tú supiéras*, Antonio Rufo Gómez (1997), *La mancha de la mora*, Dolores Soler Espiauba (1997) and *Con la miel en los labios*, Esther Tusquets (1997).[10] With her second novel, Galán offers a postmodern text that resists literary conventions by employing techniques such as an unstable chronology and narrative voice and by creating an unconventional plot structure. Reality and fiction are interwoven as the main protagonist, Isabel, a lesbian writer from Madrid, acts as narrator for three separate strands; firstly, her own experiences; secondly, those of two thirty-something lesbians, Ana and Silvia, who also live in Madrid; and finally, the depiction of the love story between Irene and Rosalía, the principal characters in Isabel's latest novel.

Through this spectrum of women, Galán provides significant insight into the way that lesbian experience in Spain has changed over the last thirty years. Focusing on just one of these strands here, it is perhaps the story of the two friends and former lovers, Ana and Silvia, that best serves to illustrate this transformation, particularly regarding women living in major cities such as Madrid and Barcelona.

The friends are initially depicted looking to put an ad in a lesbian online magazine in order to find other lesbians to date. Their debate over the wording they should use illustrates how the language that lesbians use to self-reference and express their desires has evolved to reflect changes in attitudes around sexuality within the lesbian community. Rather than being a "lesmadura" [older lesbian] who is looking for someone "[c]ariñosa, inteligente y capaz de sincera entrega" [loving, intelligent, and capable of commitment] (37), Silvia advises Ana to instead use expressions that will attract "las pibitas jóvenes, jaraneras y atrevidas, con su rollito fresco de lesbiana libre nunca reprimida" [the daring, young lesbians who are always out partying, with her free-and-easy-lesbian-up-for-anything banter] (38), such details serving to challenge previous proscriptive stereotypes of how lesbians view and behave in sexual relationships with other women.

A subsequent account of the many alternatives that the two friends have at their disposal to find possible partners, both in real space and online, affords insight into the expansion and practices of Spain's city-dwelling lesbian communities. The reference to an authentic website, chueca.com, advertising a lesbian literature forum, which Ana and Silvia attend, also provides the novel with a measure of intertextuality, reminding the reader that although these characters are fictional, they are indeed representative of the communities of lesbians that exist in contemporary Spain. Moreover, the author's depiction of this event, where one of the presenters encourages her audience to get together to discuss issues that really concern them, can be read more broadly as an encouragement to lesbians to collaborate to combat the invisibility that continues to affect this community.

Lola van Guardia's popular text, *Plumas de doble filo*, will finally be examined in this section to consider recent legal developments in Spain around the recognition of same-sex marriage and what that has meant for the lesbian community. This novel appeared at a time when Spain's conservative party, el Partido Popular, had been working to prevent the introduction of same-sex partnership laws that would seek to secure equal citizenship rights for gays and lesbians. Van Guardia's novel presented an ironic view of this discussion and could be viewed as a rallying cry to the lesbian community to take up the political struggle to bring about "la normalización del lesbianismo en la sociedad española" [the normalization of lesbianism in Spanish society].

The mystery in *Plumas* centers on the apparent murder of Laura Mayo, a prominent left-wing politician. Crucially however, a parallel theme of the novel deals with the prospective introduction of a fictional statute (Ley de Familias Ejemplares [LEFE] [the Exemplary Family Law]) which proposes that, for a family unit to be recognized at law, it must include a male head of the household ("un varón") and a female spouse ("una hembra") (124). Under the new law families with more than three children, at least one of which is male, would be elevated to the status of FEP (Familia Ejemplar de Rango Preferente [High Ranking Exemplary Family]), entitling them to a range of privileges; families which failed to meet these criteria would be penalized, for example by exclusion from state employment, from obtaining credit and from entitlement to any social security benefits (125)—such legislation being reminiscent of the social structure developed during the Franco regime, which clearly framed the acceptable and desirable configuration of the ideal family.

By the end of the novel, through the concerted efforts of the main protagonists, who inspire the lesbian community in Barcelona to literally "come-out" in support of Laura Mayo and against the LEFE, Van Guardia reinforces the notion that a community united can indeed make a difference, and that the "what might be" is not an unattainable goal. In this way she succeeds in providing Spanish lesbian readers with not only a text in which they can discover themselves, but also a literature of hope, an inspiration for the present and the future.

It is interesting to note that in 2004, five years after *Plumas* first appeared, the new Socialist government of Spain began a campaign to legalize same-sex marriage. This legislation was finally passed by Las Cortes, the Spanish parliament, making same-sex marriage officially legal on July 3, 2005. Despite this considerable measure of progress, Spanish lesbian and (gay) married couples continue to experience difficulties with regard to issues of parenting and adoption.

This question of lesbian parenting is also broached by Van Guardia in *Plumas* through the established couple, Ana and Clara, who encounter innumerable difficulties as they struggle to adopt a child. I would suggest therefore that this work can still serve to encourage the present lesbian community to "dar la cara" [stand up and be counted] and continue to lobby for equal rights. As Pedro Zerolo observed in an article that appeared in *El País Semanal*, "La visibilidad es una arma de transformación social que se ha revelado extraordinariamente eficaz" [visibility is a weapon for social change that has proven to be extraordinarily effective].[11] Although this statement was made in reference to famous male homosexuals that had *come out,* the same advice could be said to hold true for lesbians, as Van Guardia's text clearly suggests.

In present-day Spain, against a backdrop of groundbreaking legislation and ongoing social change, it is possible to observe female subjects who are willing to explore their identity, confront their fears, break free from the past, and embrace their sexuality. In the first set of texts considered, lesbian sexuality is portrayed openly, and the lesbian subject has been positioned, not as marginalized other but rather as privileged self at the center of the text. Moreover, from the lesbian characters in these novels, and other works by Libertad Morán, Susana Guzner, Olga Martí, and Arancha Apellániz published since 2000, there appears to be a move towards a multivocal deconstructed lesbian identity, one that speaks of a growing and diverse community. This trend provides a distinct shift from the portrayal of a lone individual battling external and internal homophobia from a position of isolation, as featured in many earlier novels. It is to be hoped that this range of literary expression will continue to proliferate, as it has done in particular in the last six years.

With a view to examining the notion of the heroic lesbian body serving as resistance to the normalization of lesbian identities, this chapter will now consider three further novels from the Spanish lesbian fiction genre, these being Mabel Galán's *Desde la otra orilla* (1999), Lais Arcos' *72 horas* (2004), and Paz Quintero's *Destino programado* (2005). The discussion around these texts will argue that the lesbian body (or rather bodies) is granted a tangible corporeality or presence which works to resist the eradication constantly threatened by the dominant patriarchal order, with the positioning of lesbians as principal characters within the narrative, ensuring that these repeatedly marginalized body/ies is/are placed at the center of the text. This operation results in these bodies being transferred from a position of outsider to insider, from functioning as other to subject. Consequently, they are imbued with the power to effect change not only within their own space, but also without. It is this power, then, created through lesbian desire, that will be the focus in proposing that the bodies found within the chosen texts can indeed be said to be heroic.

Zimmerman posits the notion of the Lesbian Hero, as depicted in many of the coming out novels published in the United States and the United Kingdom between 1969 and 1989. She highlights "the quest, the picaresque and the *bildungsroman*" (60) as the main conventions employed by lesbian authors of the period. It is interesting to note that the works of Galán, Arcos, and Quintero can also be said to incorporate such literary devices, notwithstanding that they were published more than a decade after the period referred to by Zimmerman—an occurrence that is perhaps understandable given the relatively late emergence of Spanish lesbian literature. Further, the critic goes on to identify specific heroic types appearing within such fiction, these being warrior, outlaw, witch, magician, androgyne, and artist. Accordingly, Zimmerman's terminology will be taken as a starting point from which to explore the lesbian bodies located in the following texts considered here.

As an example of the lesbian heroic, *Desde la otra orilla*

points to the picaresque subgenre. Within the setting of present-day Madrid, the author offers an intriguing postmodern twist to this classic literary form by creating a character that uses the Internet to veil her true gender and sexual identity—Galán's roguish hero Andrea, who by day waits tables in a city café and by night tends bar in one of the numerous mixed gay and straight venues in Chueca, a popular gay and lesbian neighborhood in Madrid city center. For nearly a year Andrea has been secretly observing Alicia, one of her regular customers at the café, and she is willing to try every means at her disposal to win over the object of her desire.

Although structured as a linear narrative, Galán's first novel is presented from a retrospective viewpoint, using both first- and third-person narrative voices, thus offering a multivocal subject. Tellingly, the opening page presents the reader with a sensual description of an oil painting of a woman's naked body which, although presented as an image on canvas, is depicted in terms which incite the observer to reach out and stroke her. From the outset then, it is evident that the textual focal point of desire will be the female body itself. However, since this reaction of desire is evoked in another woman, the corporeal elements described—"los ojos grises, la piel morena, el vello púbico, la inexplorada geografía y el tesoro allí escondida" [the gray eyes, dark skin, pubic hair, unexplored territory, and the treasure hidden within] and "la delgadez extrema de aquellos dedos, sus labios de una suavidad acogedora, prometían oscuras caricias, impensables para la mayoría de los humanos" [the extreme slenderness of those fingers, her soft welcoming lips, promised dark caresses, unthinkable for most people] (11)—refer therefore to the focus of lesbian desire, rather than to the female being objectified by the male gaze, or simply to an anodyne appreciation of the female form.

In this initial chapter—which contemplates, one year on, a fulfilling lesbian relationship whose origins are explored in the rest of the novel—the centrality of lesbian desire and the lesbian body to the text is further evident in the note that the object of desire (Alicia) writes and leaves for the lover (Andrea) who, as the unfolding narrative reveals, has succeeded in winning her heart. This communication evinces the desire that exists between these two bodies and the impact that this connection has had on the writer. Alicia also speaks of "la necesidad de amar a tu cuerpo y retenerte a mi lado" [the need to love your body and keep you by my side] (13); and her final comment in the note bears witness to the transforming power that Munt refers to as "the sheer reproductivity of lesbian desire" (165), which in this instance has led to one woman's discovery of who she is—for Alicia admits, *"poco a poco me fui encontrando a mi misma, lentamente, entre tus manos . . ."* [little by little, in your hands, I slowly began to find myself] (14).

As mentioned, Galán's text develops so as to portray the instability of the paradigms of gender, sexuality, and identity. The resultant fluidity of bodies is demonstrated in Alicia's dilemma regarding whom she should love—from an assortment of two males, a nongendered virtual suitor, and a female: Juan, her long-term, though often absent, partner; Arturo, a lover who is charming in every way, but who fails to really capture Alicia's heart; her "ciber-caballero andante" [cyber knight-errant], whose true identity (Andrea) is unknown to her; and Andrea herself, to whom she finds herself inexplicably attracted, but whom loving would challenge all her preexisting notions of society's expectations of the female body.

As indicated in Zimmerman's taxonomy of heroic types "the magician . . . has become a lesbian archetype because the lesbian transforms what are traditionally identified as the laws of nature" (67). In *Desde la otra orilla* Andrea appears to embody the magician in seeking to attract Alicia by means of illusion. She begins by leaving her anonymous letters and goes on to establish contact with Alicia via cyberspace. It is this virtual suitor that Alicia refers to as "su ciber caballero" [her cyber knight], unaware of the true identity of the person who is sending her these amorous e-mails. Andrea's actions thus serve to remove the physical body from the exchanges, and Alicia, with her heteronormative preconceived ideas of gender and sexuality, in no way suspects that such attention could come from another woman. As Lisa Haskell points out, the Internet provides a "site for the connection of virtual bodies, offer[ing] us the possibility of divesting ourselves of identities defined by our bodies"; she goes on to suggest that in "the ephemeral nation of cyberspace . . . I have no body."[12]

This device of the temporary suspension of fixed, gendered bodies is reinforced by the reaction of Eloisa, Alicia's tarot-reading Cuban neighbor when, during one of her readings, she explains that "las cosas no son lo que parecen" [things aren't what they seem] (119), and again when, in response to Alicia's question whether the friend she is predicted to lose will be male or female, Eloisa tells her "con las cartas nunca se sabe" [with the cards, you can never tell) (140). Further, these tarot sessions, which point to Alicia's undergoing some form of transformation, underscore a reading of Andrea as magician, with Eloisa advising that the configuration of "[e]l Mago, sobre la Torre y al lado de la lámina XIII" [the Magician, over the Tower and next to Card XIII (Death)] suggests that Alicia will be "otra persona" [someone else], and that she will have "otra vida diferente y un nuevo amor" [a different life and a new love] (17). The transforming power of Andrea's desire for Alicia is echoed in the note that Alicia leaves for her, in which she declares "la primera vez que tus manos me acariciaron en silencio, yo me rompí en mil pedazos, y mi voluntad dejó de pertenecerme, para comenzar ese largo viaje del que no he retornado jamás" [the first time that your hands caressed me in silence, I shattered into a thousand pieces, my will no longer my own, to start that long journey with you from which I have never returned] (13). Thus Alicia, herself wooed by anonymous written communications, in turn uses the written word to express and acknowledge the intensity of her feelings for Andrea.

In the following text, the heroic lesbian body as outlaw will be considered, a device described by Zimmerman as "the woman who journeys through patriarchy and exits it for Lesbian Nation [thus] plac[ing] herself outside the laws and customs of the old world" (61). Paz Quintero's first novel, *Destino programado*, which was awarded II Premio Terenci Moix de Narrativa Gay y Lésbica Fundación Arena [II Terenci Moix Gay and Lesbian Literature Award], recounts the archetypal "love conquers all" story, again with urban settings—in this case the cities of Barcelona, Madrid, and Seville—serving as location for the lesbian body.[13] The key protagonists, Elisa and Marta, are repeatedly referenced by their contrasting physical attributes—"la rubia"/"la morena" [the blonde/the brunette], "cabello dorado"/"pelo azabache" [golden hair/jet-black hair]—a pairing which may be seen to imply the ideal binary of heterosexual male fantasy, but which could also be said to represent "a perfectly sealed world of female desire" from which the masculine body is denied access.[14]

The narrative, spanning twenty-three years from 1979 to 2002, and developed in postmodern nonlinear style, is based loosely around the traditional bildungsroman in that it traces the emotional development of two teenage girls into adulthood. Rather than conforming to the heteronormative tendency of a single hero, *Destino* offers a multivalent heroic body in the char-

acters of Marta and Elisa, both of whom are positioned initially
as outlaw. Their 'heroic quest' for the childhood sweet-
hearts—to be reunited—begins when they are discovered together by one of the nuns at the boarding school they attend,
leading to their expulsion from school and ensuing separation.
The author describes the physical union between the two in contrasting terms; as the girls sleep peacefully together after their
first night of lovemaking, the scene is described idyllically thus:

> La luz del exterior se colaba furtivamente por las rendijas de la per-
> siana, tatuando en los cuerpos de ambas amantes un sinfín de dora-
> das líneas. La muchacha del pelo oscuro yacía tranquilamente
> acurrucada sobre el pecho de su compañera. Marta, en cambio, per-
> manecía en una posición recta, que parecía inmóvil. Sus manos esta-
> ban unidas, y sus mejillas estaban muy próximas. La fina sábana que
> las envolvía sólo las cubría de cintura para abajo" (86–87).

> [Sunlight stole secretly through the slats of the blind, infusing the
> lovers' bodies with a myriad of golden lines. The dark-haired girl lay
> peacefully curled up on the bosom of her companion, while Marta
> remained stretched out, perfectly still. Their hands were clasped and
> their cheeks pressed together. The thin sheet they were wrapped in
> covered them from the waist down.]

In contrast, once they are discovered by Sor Inés [Sister Inés],
who had been alerted to the situation by a jealous classmate,
Marta and Elisa are referred to as "desgraciadas" [wretched] and
their intimate body parts, earlier described in such aesthetic
terms, are now "las partes pecaminosas" [sinful members] (88).
All too briefly these bodies seem to occupy a temporal space of
belonging, only to be abruptly cast out into a space of rejection
and condemnation; rather than being desired bodies, they are
portrayed as unwanted outlaws.

Quintero's lesbian bodies suffer further injustice at the hands
of an unmerciful, heterosexual, patriarchal society, in the form
firstly of Elisa's father, who arranges for his daughter to enter
into an unwanted heterosexual marriage, and subsequently of
her abusive husband, Carlos, who, on discovering that it is
Marta she really loves, physically and mentally torments his
wife, as well as hiring hit men to harass and assault Marta and
her gay friend and business partner. Nevertheless, despite this
"journey through patriarchy" (as described by Zimmerman,
1990), which is fraught with danger, these lesbian bodies, located at first as outlaw, are both ultimately transformed from

the position of victim and outsider to one of agency and belonging; through Elisa's father's later acknowledgement and acceptance of his daughter's sexuality, and Marta and Elisa's successful collaboration with the police authorities to bring Carlos to justice, the lesbian body can be perceived to have progressed from the margins to the center.

Further, the exile or escape theme typical of the bildungsroman is clearly evident in the separation endured by Marta and Elisa, with the heroic outlaw lesbian body subsequently transmuting into the warrior, as Marta works undauntedly to rescue Elisa from the misery of her abusive relationship with Carlos and bring her back to the safety of a loving relationship so that "las dos amantes, que durante tanto tiempo estuvieron separadas, se unieron en un enternecedor abrazo" [the lovers, who for so long had been separated, came together in an emotional embrace] (118). Thus here, as with *Desde la otra orilla*, lesbian desire is shown to give rise to a body with the power to produce change.

Having considered the lesbian body as magician and outlaw, the subject's positioning as warrior will be examined more closely in Lais Arcos's first novel *72 Horas*. Here the author presents a lesbian body that is skillfully replaced as Other in the narrative and delivers what Munt refers to as "an heroic aesthetic, one that provokes a 'pride' response in order to rebut the shame produced by homophobia" (6). The lesbian bodies here are truly multiple since they account not only for two of the main protagonists, Laia and Marion, but also for an array of minor characters. Arcos situates these bodies again in present-day urban settings—Paris, Barcelona, and Lyon—and very much at the center of established society, with Laia and Marion working within the diplomatic corps and national press respectively. Moreover, the two characters are depicted as financially independent and able to sample the finer things in life—autonomous bodies, therefore, who appear to enjoy a privileged position in society despite their lesbian sexuality.

As the title suggests, the plot develops over the course of three days and, in keeping with postmodern tradition, is related from the point of view of a number of characters that are at once central and marginal to the narrative. It soon becomes evident that the heroic lesbian body—in this instance Laia—finds herself on dangerous ground when, as she attempts to find out who has been tampering with her computer, she unwittingly makes connection with the leaders of a terrorist plot. From that point she is targeted by terrorist cell member Karim, who is involved in orchestrating an imminent terrorist attack. This desire to eliminate Laia, as voiced by Karim, evokes the manner in which the lesbian body has traditionally been disappeared from countless cultural, literary, social and legislative sites; he asserts that "tenía que acabar con la pequeña sanguijuela" [he had to put an end to that little bloodsucker] (75), and that homosexuals are "una degeneración de la naturaleza" [a degenerate manifestation of nature] (82).

However, despite considerable efforts, Karim is unable to eradicate Laia and, in keeping with literary conventions, this lesbian warrior must then embark on a quest to thwart the villains, portrayed here as Algerian Muslim separatists who plot not (as the authorities suspect) to attack the G7-P8 summit being held in Paris, but to detonate a bus full of Parisian soccer fans into an international laboratory in Lyon where research into deadly viruses is carried out. In her readiness to take whatever action is needed to prevent the attack, the lesbian body here epitomizes perhaps the fundamental characteristic of the hero— the willingness to make the ultimate sacrifice for the greater good: she places herself in the way of the oncoming bus and shoots the suicide bomber who is at the wheel.

It is interesting to note again that, as Laia and Marion join forces with Manu (a Spanish police officer working at the Spanish Embassy in Paris) and Philippe and Thierry (French secret police agents), the otherwise frequently peripheral lesbian entity works in tandem with the establishment to effect positive societal change. Indeed in Arcos's text, the lesbian body is displaced from the margins by a body which is seen to represent a greater threat to the fabric and stability of society—the terrorist body. Consequently the transgressive lesbian body is transformed from performing as the (moral) lawbreaker into one who acts to protect society, operating against those who would seek to inflict harm and suffering. It may be noted that in 1970s U.S. lesbian fiction the warrior figure was especially evident, a result perhaps of the prevalence at that time of wars of national liberation, for instance in Vietnam and Algeria, as well as the Black liberation struggle of that era (Zimmerman, 64). Thirty years on, the textual embodiment of a heroic lesbian body in Spanish literature comes at a time of perceived threat to Spain's national security, both from within and from outside its borders, and when the perceived menace to society—previously trangressive sexualities—is now global terrorism.

The lesbian entities represented in the second set of texts are portrayed as nonalienated bodies, able to cross virtual and geographical borders. They are located centrally to the text and, by means of the power generated from the merging of such bodies in acts of lesbian desire, are transformed into agents of action. Indeed as Elizabeth Grosz, in her contemplation of Deleuze and Guatarri's work on affectivity, argues, "a body is what a body does."[15] She goes on to point out that lesbian lifestyles produce lesbian bodies, which derive from sexual practices that fashion the body itself, as illustrated in the novels examined here.

Further, as Zimmerman explains, lesbian writers, "in adapting conventional literary figures to the particular realities of lesbian life, create powerful and evocative codes for the lesbian self" (60). The texts considered here can indeed be said to create such codes through their portrayals of the heroic lesbian body, the authors in question offering up a corporeality with the capacity to transcend essentialist notions of self to present the reader with a multiple hero and a multivalent lesbian self. The importance of such representations should not be underestimated for, as Munt asserts, "[h]eroic narratives . . . are particularly relevant to a culture required to present a self as active and visible. Twentieth-century lesbian culture . . . grappled constantly with this need" (10). I would contend the same holds true for lesbian cultures in twenty-first-century Spain.

To conclude, Wilfredo Hernández has pointed out that "[t]he late appearance of the lesbian subject in Spain is a direct consequence of the political and religious repression exercised during the Francoist regime" (29).[16] However, with the transformation that Spanish society has undergone since the Transition, and more recently, with the advent of the new millennium, Spanish lesbian authors have been developing a space from which a range of lesbian subjects are being presented and being brought to the fore. As witnessed by the characters that inhabit the novels examined in this chapter, lesbian writers and protagonists are undoubtedly speaking for themselves, and in their own words. This is confirmed by Angie Simonis who comments thus on the way contemporary Spanish lesbian literature is changing:

> Las temáticas se abren y el espíritu libre se avanza. La escritura se despliega en un vuelo de libertad, de querer demostrar que la imagen y el discurso equivocado pueden transformarse, de que hay más cosas que decir que nunca y de que hay que decirlas con nuestra propia voz, con nuestra propia gramática y con nuestras propias imágenes.[17]

[Different subject matter is appearing and a free spirit is pushing back the boundaries. Writing is taking off in search of freedom, wanting to show that mistaken images and discourse can be changed, that there are more things than ever to be said and that they must be said with our own voices, our own language, and our own images.]

Therefore, despite what may appear initially to be opposing perspectives (to work toward or to eschew normalization) regarding the manner in which lesbian literary identities should be presented and elaborated, it is perhaps prudent to encourage proliferation in order to allow for a multiplicity of voices, stemming from a wide range of lesbian writers and characters, the volume of which would demand society's attention and recognition.

NOTES

1. Gemma Retamero, "Prólogo," in *Efecto retrovisor*, by Thais Morales (Barcelona: Ellas Editorial, 2005), 11.

2. Olga Viñuales, *Identidades lésbicas* (Barcelona: Ediciones Bellaterra, 2000), 177–81.

3. Fefa Vila, "Voces y ecos de la comunidad gay en España," in *Identidad y diferencia: sobre la cultura gay en España*, eds. Juan Vicente Aliaga and José Miguel G. Cortés (Barcelona: Egales, 1997), 199–237.

4. Tamsin Wilton, *Lesbian Studies: Setting an Agenda* (London: Routledge, 1995), 135.

5. Bonnie Zimmerman, *The Safe Sea of Women: Lesbian Fiction 1969–1989* (London: Onlywomen Press, 1990).

6. Thais Morales, "Nace una editorial especializada en obras de temática lesbiana," *La Vanguardia*, Sección Cultura (March 24, 2005): 31.

7. Lola Van Guardia, *Plumas de doble filo* (Barcelona: Egales, 1999); Illy Nes, *El lago rosa* (Barcelona: Ediciones Bellaterra, 2004); Mabél Galán, *Donde comienza tu nombre* (Madrid: Odisea, 2004).

8. Sally Munt, *Heroic Desire: Lesbian Identity and Cultural Space* (New York: New York University Press, 1998), 2.

9. Mabel Galán. *Desde la otra orilla* (Madrid: Odisea, 1999); Lais Arcos, *72 horas* (Barcelona: La Tempestad, 2004); Paz Quintero, *Destino programado* (Barcelona: La Tempestad, 2005).

10. Antonio Rufo Gómez, *Si tú supiéras* (Barcelona: Ediciones B, 1997); Dolores Soler Espiauba, *La mancha de la mora* (Barcelona: Ediciones B, 1997); Esther Tusquets. *Con la miel en los labios* (Barcelona: Anagrama, 1997).

11. Pedro Zerolo in "Lesbiana sin complejos," Luz Sánchez Mellado, *El País Semanal* (June 29, 2003): 46.

12. Lisa Haskell, "Cyberdykes: Tales from the Internet," in *Assaults on Convention: Essays on Lesbian Trangressors*, eds. Nicola Godwin, Belinda Hollows, and Sheridan Nye, 50–61 (London: Cassell, 1996).

13. This literary prize was established in 2005, in memory of the author Ter-

enci Moix in collaboration with the Arena Foundation which supports the gay and lesbian community in Cataluña.

14. Barbara Creed, "Lesbian Bodies: Tribades, Tomboys and Tarts," in *Sexy Bodies: The Strange Carnalities of Feminism*, eds. Elizabeth Grosz and Elspeth Probyn (London: Routledge, 1995), 101.

15. Elizabeth Grosz, *Space, Time and Perversion: Essays on the Politics of Bodies* (London: Routledge, 1995), 214.

16. Wilfredo Hernández, "From the Margins to the Mainstream: Lesbian Characters in Spanish Fiction (1964–1979)," in *Tortilleras: Hispanic and U.S. Latina Lesbian Expression*, eds. Lourdes Torres and Inmaculada Pertusa (Philadelphia: Temple Press, 2003), 29.

17. Angie Simonis, *Cultura, homosexualidad y homofobia. Vol. 2, Amazonia: Retos de visibilidad lesbiana* (Barcelona: Laertes, 2007), 137.

References

Arcos, Lais. *72 horas*. Barcelona: La Tempestad, 2004.

Creed, Barbara. "Lesbian Bodies: Tribades, Tomboys and Tarts." In *Sexy Bodies: The Strange Carnalities of Feminism*, edited by Elizabeth Grosz and Elspeth Probyn, 86–103. London: Routledge, 1995.

Galán, Mabel. *Desde la otra orilla*. Madrid: Odisea, 1999.

———. *Donde comienza tu nombre*. Madrid: Odisea, 2004.

Grosz, Elizabeth. *Space, Time and Perversion: Essays on the Politics of Bodies*. London: Routledge, 1995.

Haskell, Lisa. "Cyberdykes: Tales from the Internet." In *Assaults on Convention: Essays on Lesbian Trangressors*, edited by Nicola Godwin, Belinda Hollows, and Sheridan Nye, 50–61. London: Cassell, 1996.

Hernández, Wilfredo. "From the Margins to the Mainstream: Lesbian Characters in Spanish Fiction (1964–1979)." In *Tortilleras: Hispanic and U.S. Latina Lesbian Expression*, edited by Lourdes Torres and Inmaculada Pertusa, 19–34. Philadelphia: Temple Press, 2003.

Morales, Thais. "Nace una editorial especializada en obras de temática lesbiana." *La Vanguardia*, Sección Cultura (March 24, 2005).

Munt, Sally. *Heroic Desire: Lesbian Identity and Cultural Space*. New York: New York University Press, 1998.

Nes, Illy. *El lago rosa*. Barcelona: Ediciones Bellaterra, 2004.

Quintero, Paz. *Destino programado*. Barcelona: La Tempestad, 2005.

Retamero, Gemma. "Prólogo." In *Efecto retrovisor*, by Thais Morales, 11–13. Barcelona: Ellas Editorial, 2005.

Rufo Gómez, Antonio. *Si tú supiéras*. Barcelona: Ediciones B, 1997.

Simonis, Angie. *Cultura, homosexualidad y homofobia. Vol. 2, Amazonia: Retos de visibilidad lesbiana*. Barcelona: Laertes, 2007.

Soler Espiauba, Dolores. *La mancha de la mora*. Barcelona: Ediciones B, 1997.

Tusquets, Esther. *Con la miel en los labios*. Barcelona: Anagrama, 1997.

Van Guardia, Lola. *Plumas de doble filo*. Barcelona: Egales, 1999.

Vila, Fefa. "Voces y ecos de la comunidad gay en España." In *Identidad y difer-*

encia: sobre la cultura gay en España, edited by Juan Vicente Aliaga and José Miguel G. Cortes, 199–237. Barcelona: Egales, 1997.

Viñuales, Olga. *Identidades lésbicas.* Barcelona: Ediciones Bellaterra, 2000.

Wilton, Tamsin. *Lesbian Studies: Setting an Agenda.* London: Routledge, 1995.

Zerolo, Pedro in "Lesbiana sin complejos," Luz Sánchez Mellado. *El País Semanal* (June 29, 2003): 36–47.

Zimmerman, Bonnie. *The Safe Sea of Women: Lesbian Fiction 1969–1989.* London: Onlywomen Press, 1990.

"All L Breaks Loose":
Lola Van Guardia's Lesbian Trilogy

Nancy Vosburg

THE OPENING IN 1993 OF THE FIRST GAY AND LESBIAN BOOKSTORE IN Spain—Berkana, in the Madrid neighborhood of Chueca—marked a new period in the development of what can be considered a literature for and by lesbians.[1] In 1995, Berkana's owner, Mili Hernández, along with Connie Dagas and Helle Bruun (co-owners of Cómplices, a gay and lesbian bookstore which had just opened in Barcelona) founded Egales, the first independent gay and lesbian publishing company in Spain. Two years later, Oscar Pérez founded the publishing company Odisea and opened a second gay and lesbian bookstore in Madrid, A Different Life. Both publishing companies had as their objective to fill their shelves with Spanish LGBT literature and to educate their clients about their own history in a country that was still overcoming the oppressive influence of the thirty-six years of the Franco dictatorship.

While many of the early offerings of Egales and Odisea were didactic or "light" literature offering seductive homoerotic scenarios, a new plateau was reached with the 1997 publication by Egales of *Con pedigree* (With Pedigree), the first volume of what would subsequently be a trilogy penned by a mysterious Lola Van Guardia, the pseudonym employed by the emerging humorous writer Isabel Franc.[2] The other titles in the trilogy, launched by Egales in their "Salir del armario" [Coming Out of the Closet] series, are *Plumas de doble filo* (1999) [Double-Edged Feathers/Pens] and *La mansión de las tríbadas* (2002) [The Mansion of the Tribades]. Initiated at the time that the ruling Partido Popular, under the leadership of José María Aznar, was lacerating the gay and lesbian community with an ever increasingly conservative legislative and educational agenda based on so-called "family values," the novels lambaste the lamentable political climate while lovingly lampooning the identity politics of the diverse lesbian community in Spain, particularly in Barcelona.

193

In this chapter, I propose to provide an overview of Lola Van Guardia's trilogy from the perspective of its innovative approach in presenting and critiquing not only its target audience, the lesbian community in Spain, but the larger sociopolitical community that surrounds it. Van Guardia's trilogy performs what Philip Fisher has identified as "the valuable 'work' of transforming the exotic or the revolutionary into the ordinary," in the sense that the community depicted, which heterosexuals might consider "exotic," is shown to share the anxieties and ambitions of society at large.[3] While there are major differences between the literary trilogy and Showtime's television series *The L Word* that emanate primarily from the necessities and conventions of the two distinct media forms, I will occasionally invoke the latter because of certain similarities that I wish to draw out. Above all, both Van Guardia's trilogy and *The L Word* respond to a desire by their creators to make visible the diverse lives and lifestyles of a community of lesbians. To achieve this, they use an ensemble cast whose divergent story lines are intertwined in a narrative structure which harkens back to Dickens. By dramatizing more than one lesbian plot at a time, both these cultural phenomena strive to bring about a qualitative difference in the audience response to social reality. As Eve Kosofsky Sedgwick has said about *The L Word*, and which holds true for Van Guardia's trilogy, "The sense of the lesbian individual, isolated or coupled, scandalous, scrutinized, staggering under her representational burden, gives way to the vastly livelier potential of a lesbian ecology."[4] Furthermore, both series, constituting as they do two forms of popular fiction, have the capacity to mediate social conflict. As Scott McCracken has asserted, popular fiction "acts as a medium between reader [or viewer] and world through which the social contradictions of modernity can be played out."[5] By making visible the lesbian within the matrices of social and sexual identities, Van Guardia's trilogy underscores the "normality" of lesbian lives in diverse social and professional roles.

Among the ensemble cast of Van Guardia's trilogy, some of the star players are Adelaida Duarte, "la gran diva de las letras lésbicas" [the great diva of lesbian literature]; Dorotea (or Tea) de los Santos, the self-proclaimed "hetero y muy hetero" [hetero and very hetero] journalist, literary critic, and television talk show hostess; radio personality Matilde Miranda, who becomes the passionate lover of the "hetero" Tea; Clara and Ana, who are trying to adopt a baby; "cyberhippies" Candi, Gabi, and Nati, always on the prowl; Channel 4 technician Marga Sureda and her esoteric lover Inés Villamontes; wannabe film director Remei G., who finds herself picking up odd jobs (catsitter, house-cleaner, cook) while waiting for her big break; and Karina, Ce-cilia, and Gina, owners of the lesbian locale Gay Night. The supporting cast includes militants from the GLUP (Grupo de Lesbianas Unidas y Pioneras [Group of United and Pioneer Les-bians]), ALI (Alegría Lesbiana Independiente [Independent Les-bian Happiness]), LA (Lesbianas Autosuficientes [Self-Sufficient Lesbians]), Paca the hairdresser, Emi the taxi driver, Azucena from the gym, Rita Padilla and her lover "desde tiempos inmem-oriales" [from time immemorial], Neus Deus, and *las organiza-das, las independientes, las radicales, las históricas, las nuevas, las desconocidas, las locas,* and *las separatistas.*[6]

While oblique references are made in the novels to males and to heterosexuals—the RadiGays and Tea's one-night stands, it is women, and more specifically, lesbian women, who occupy cen-ter stage. As Elina Norandi has affirmed, "estas mujeres no viven al margen de la cultura oficial, todo lo contrario, participan acti-vamente de ella, incidiendo y transformando su devenir. Más bien diría que lo que la autora consigue es construir una sociedad que no está determinada por la heterorrealidad" [these women do not live on the margins of the official culture, on the contrary, they participate actively in it, inciting and transforming its proc-esses. I would go so far as to say that what the author achieves is constructing a society that is not determined by heteroreality].[7]

All of the active characters, from the *fontaneras* [plumbers] to the *Mosses d'Escuadra* [Catalan police force] to the *ministras* [ministers], are female. This all-female ensemble dominates both public and private space, and every woman is viewed as being or having the potential of being a lesbian.[8] But despite this homogenizing potential, the diversity of the lesbian community, characterized by competing identity politics and personal and public rivalries, contests what patriarchal forces and institu-tions have configured as a homogenous and stereotyped "other." The "pedigree" in the title of the first novel, for instance, is a term that some Spanish lesbians use to refer to women who have been conscious of their lesbianism from a young age and thus have never had sexual relations with men.[9] The tension between the so-called "authentic" lesbians (those with "pedigree") and lesbians who have had sexual relations with men is just one of the numerous "ideological" positions that Van Guardia lam-poons in the series.

Van Guardia makes visible and gives voice to a variety of lesbian identities, lifestyles, and looks. Like the characters on *The L Word*, and in every good soap opera, these characters live, love, lust, get hurt, and struggle with family, relationships, and their work.[11] The group endogamy that binds the characters together, far from a homogenizing force, reflects the importance of friendship networks as a basic element in maintaining and supporting sexual identity, as social anthropologist Olga Viñuales has noted in her important study of real Spanish lesbian lives (127). While Van Guardia's depiction of the gossip and confidence-sharing of her characters may seem exaggerated, Viñuales observes that:

> Además de mantener a las ex amantes o ex pareja como amigas, entre heterosexuales y lesbianas existen tres diferencias más: para las lesbianas que encubren su identidad sexual y que carecen de filiación, las amistades son la única fuente de soporte emocional cuando surgen problemas. Horas y horas de teléfono, de conversaciones, de compañía, de consuelo compartido con otras amigas, hacen de la red de amistades el único soporte emocional cuando se rompe una relación de pareja. Una segunda diferencia es que las amistades cumplen un importante papel moldeador de la identidad sexual. Con las amigas o amiga se acude al ambiente, se conocen nuevos locales, en ellos se hacen bromas, se cotillea y se seduce. *Estas son las cosas que no se pueden compartir con las amigas heterosexuales.* Y, por último, [. . .] la red de amistades lésbicas fortalece la autoestima e identidad de sus miembros. (126–27).

> [Besides maintaining ex-lovers or ex-partners as friends, there are three more differences between heterosexuals and lesbians: for lesbians who hide their sexual orientation and who lack group affiliation, friendships are the only source of emotional support when problems arise. Hours and hours of telephone [calls], of conversations, of company, of mutual consolation, make the friendship network the only emotional support when an intimate relationship fails. A second difference is that friendships fulfill an important role in shaping sexual identity. With friends or with a friend one can frequent gay spots, get acquainted with new locales, where lesbians joke, gossip, and seduce. *These are the things that a lesbian cannot share with heterosexual friends.* And, finally, . . . lesbian friendship networks strengthen the self-esteem and identity of their members.]

In Van Guardia's novels, the diverse characters move within their own friendship networks, yet these networks intersect and converge in the various locales of the lesbian *ambiente* (i.e., gay-lesbian encounter spaces). The *ambiente* offers the characters the possibility of transcending the relative isolation of their particular clique or network and creates intrigue as member identity is challenged and/or reaffirmed in the group interactions.

Structured as a series of soap-opera installments ("entregas"), the first novel of the trilogy (*Con pedigree*) is a light-hearted lampoon of the lesbian community in and around Barcelona.[11] What intrigue there is develops from the attempt by Karina, Cecilia, and Gina to successfully launch a new lesbian locale, Gay Night, and the seductions, couplings, frustrations, and uncouplings of the various ensemble characters. Gay Night's possibilities and potential clientele come under the scrutiny of the different lesbian factions, who all want to shape it into their own particular vision of what a lesbian bar should be and who should be admitted. When Karina, Cecilia, and Gina finally succeed in inaugurating the bar, the locale offers the diverse characters a type of "hipermercado de ocio" [leisure supermarket] in which to live out their respective *amores y desamores* [love relationships and break-ups]. Always-on-the-prowl Nati Pescador, for instance, finally manages, after several failed seduction attempts at Gay Night, to "reel in" a partner, and the novel closes with their wedding ceremony at the bar, for which the entire lesbian community turns out.

While humorously "pegging" the petty squabbling and divisive gossip of Barcelona's diverse lesbian cliques, Van Guardia introduces in the first novel what will be the underlying theme of the trilogy: the necessity for lesbians, particularly those in prominent positions, to own their sexual identity and come out in the public sphere. In the process, she explores the various impediments to "coming out." This may seem odd given that Van Guardia's own identity as author was a mystery to most of her reading public until 2003. Nevertheless, Franc was simply ceding to the wishes of her publisher, who saw the use of a pseudonym as a way of creating more intrigue around the novels.[12]

Given her inability to acknowledge publicly, even to her closest friends, her lesbian orientation, the character Tea de Santos constitutes one of the central focal points of not only the first novel but the entire trilogy, as she delights in "outing" others while keeping covert her own lusty relationship with Mati Miranda. As Franc (Van Guardia's real-life alter-ego) has eloquently stated in an opinion piece in the lesbian journal *Sales* on the necessity to be more open, "No se trata de explicar nuestra vida privada ni de revelar con quién nos acostamos. Es mucho más que eso. Es afrontar una opción de vida con valentía y dejarnos de rodeos, edulcoraciones y otras falacias" [It's not about explaining our private lives or revealing with whom we're sleeping. It's much more than that. It's confronting a life option with courage, without evasions, sugarcoating or lies].[13]

In the second novel, *Plumas de doble filo*, the series takes on the characteristics of the lesbian thriller.[14] While the lesbian thriller has been a constant in Anglo-American literature since the beginning of the 1980s, it has just barely begun to appear in Spanish literature. Barbara Sjoholm (the former BarbaraWilson), one of the initiators of the genre, has spoken of the possibilities that the lesbian thriller, such as her Pam Nilsson mysteries, offers in terms of contesting the ideologies that have forced lesbians to play the role of the silent victims of crimes against women.[15] For Sjoholm, the fact that a lesbian becomes the investigator, instead of the victim, offers opportunities to bring about a justice many times denied to lesbians. In *Plumas*, "all L breaks loose" when the parliamentary representative from the Arco Iris [Rainbow] Coalition, Laura Mayo, is supposedly found liquidated in her Madrid garden, face down on her barbecue grill with her hands and face "marcada[s] a fuego como un solomillo" [grilled like a sirloin steak] (38).[16]

While the characters find themselves, either through their relationship to Mayo or through coincidence, involved in solving the crime, Van Guardia introduces yet another character who turns the thriller into a parody of the *novela negra*, which by the late 1990s was enjoying its heyday on the Spanish bestseller list.[17] Police inspector Emma García, who in part tries to model herself after special agent Dana Scully of *The X Files* and in part after the tough loners of the hard-boiled novel, is dispatched from Madrid to Barcelona to unravel the various threads of the investigation. The methodical yet bumbling García is constantly challenged by a series of impediments, from her uniform skirt to her lack of knowledge of Catalan to her tendency to fall in love with the prime suspects in the investigation. Like Tea de Santos, the García character becomes an important comic character in both this and the third novel as she attempts to "perform" her detective role in line with her chosen media/literary models.

In keeping with her critique of the conservative politics of the time, Van Guardia has her cast speculating that the crime was motivated by Mayo's opposition to the new legislation—the homophobic Ley de Familias Ejemplares [Law of Exemplary Families]—that the Minister of Family Affairs, Beatriz Panceta, is about to present in parliament. Panceta's objective is to "limpiar el país de la proliferación de parejas de hecho, que contaminaba de forma amoral y anárquica el principio básico de una sociedad como dios manda: la familia nuclear" [cleanse the country of the proliferation of domestic partners that were contaminating in an amoral and anarchic manner the basic principle of a god-ordered society: the nuclear family] (*Plumas*, 88).[18] The suspense mounts as not only García but the ensemble cast working in their separate ways close in on the truth of the matter and collectively manage to solve the crime.

Just as the lesbian community rallies around the new lesbian locale, Gay Night, in the first novel, so they come, or are brought, together by the nefarious crime in Madrid, a crime motivated by the perceived need to "cover up" nonnormative sexual identity at the highest levels of the government. When the alleged victim of the crime, Laura Mayo, is publicly "outed" and vituperated in the sensationalist press, Tea, Ade, and Mati speak out from their public positions of prominence to denounce the homophobic campaign. But when their "pen," or public voice, proves to be insufficient, they decide to employ the other *pluma* at their disposal (see note 3) and "out" themselves in public. So begins an initiative that the entire lesbian community, even the "very hetero" Tea and others who have been reluctant to publicly acknowledge their sexual identity, quickly adheres to, and soon the phrase, "I'm gay too" is resounding throughout the country.[19] In Van Guardia's utopian universe, the visibility of the lesbian community and the solidarity it inspires are enough to turn the tide. This, incidentally, is a vision shared by Juan Vicente Aliaga y Jose Miguel G. Cortés in their *Identidad y diferencia: Sobre la cultura gay en España* [Identity and Difference: About Spanish Gay Culture], in which they state: "Estamos convencidos que hacernos visibles, salir del armario, crea un importante cambio en las actitudes y reacciones sociales" [We're convinced that making ourselves visible, coming out of the closet, creates an important change in social attitudes and reactions] (121). Minister Panceta's involvement in the crime and her machinations to impose her projected law without parliamentary debate come under scrutiny as politicians respond to the lesbian campaign. After all, as the author concludes tongue-in cheek, "¿[q]ué gobierno democrático habría rechazado discutir sabiendo que la respaldaba una ingente mayoría de votantes?" [what democratic government would have refused to discuss [these issues] knowing that a huge majority of voters supported the debate?] (256).

In the third novel, *La mansión de las tríbadas*, Cecilia and Gina, in disagreement with Karina about how to run Gay Night, have decided to sell their interest in it, buy a *masía* [farmhouse] in the countryside and convert it into a *casa de turismo rural* [rural bed-and-breakfast] for women only. Even though the renovations haven't been completed yet, reservations for Easter week come pouring in from the major players in the ensemble cast, who all have their particular reasons for getting out of the city. Tea and Matilde, for example, convince Ade, who has just published her latest best seller, *Más allá de tu frondoso pubis* [Beyond Your Luxuriant Pubis], and is experiencing her normal post-literary-partum depression, that a week in the country will improve her spirits. Clara and Ana's new baby, engendered in the previous novel by a revolutionary new technique that does not involve sperm, is suffering allergies in the city. Even Police Inspector García, whose preoccupation with a lump in her breast is interfering with her duties in Chueca, has seen the ads for the *casa rural* and decides to spend a few days there, since her superiors have sidelined her anyhow. Good thing she's there, too, as nefarious events soon begin to occur: arson, a presumed kidnapping/perhaps murder, and an attempt by the autonomous government, in cahoots with developers of a theme park, to expropriate the *masía* and its surrounding property. As in the previous novel, the ensemble cast, this time augmented by a group of Basque lesbians who have traveled to the *masía* for the holidays, becomes involved in solving the mysteries and bringing the novel to its resolution, while García bumbles along in her inimitable fashion.

While the humorous parodies of lesbian identity politics, soap operas, and the *novela negra* form the connective tissues which give shape to the divergent stories, the real comic tour de force of the novels lies primarily in Van Guardia's sophisticated wordplay, linguistic farces, and intertextual references to both high and low cultural forms, particularly the music, films, and television programs that have become either national or international lesbian cultural icons (i.e., Luz Casal, Melissa Etheridge, k.d. lang, Ani DiFranco, Patricia Cornwell's Kay Scarpetta, Dana Scully of *The X Files*, the movie *A mi madre le gustan las mujeres*). Isabel Franc, in talking about her "split personality" as a writer, remarked that

Lola Van Guardia es sobre todo muy gamberra escribiendo, a mí me resulta fácil escribir como Lola Van Guardia porque con ella el gag más insólito es el que más funciona. Isabel Franc intenta trabajar de una forma literaria un poco más seria.[20]

[Lola Van Guardia is above all outrageous when she writes; it's easy for me to write as her because with her the most unusual gag is the one that works best. Isabel Franc tries to produce literature that's a little more serious.]

Van Guardia seems to have the most fun with Tea (or Dorotea) de Santos, the egotistical literary critic and television hostess who makes a habit of self-promotion in the titles she devises for her programs: TE ADORO TEA, AbreTE A la noche, TE Acuerdas de TEA, TE Acuestas con TEA, and AtréveTE A, with its accompanying slogan, "AtréveTE A verlo, AtréveTE A participar."[21] Her insistence on her heterosexuality, even after she becomes involved in a lusty relationship with Mati Miranda, makes of her not only the buffoon of the novels but the centerpiece of the theme of the visibility of lesbians in the public sphere.

Another comic character is Gina, the American partner of Cecilia, who is a type teachers will recognize in their beginning Spanish classes, the person still struggling to get her mind around subject/verb agreement, *ser* and *estar, por* and *para*, and of course, gender agreement. When her partner Cecilia advises her to go for the feminine ending when in doubt, the results, of course, are disastrous. While Gina's linguistic mishaps correspond to a comic stereotype a la Sender's Nancy,[22] her "gender troubles" serve to lay bare an essential problem in the linguistic construction of a feminine, nonpatriarchal universe—the sexist nature of the Spanish language. Women's inability to escape phallologocentric language is never resolved adequately in the otherwise all-female world of the novels, but Gina's utterances underscore the challenges that women, particularly lesbians, face in trying to forge an alternative reality not circumscribed by the gender binary and heteronormativity.

Inspector Garcia's ignorance of Catalan pronunciation likewise provides hilarious scenes when she speaks to women in the upper echelons of the Catalan government and the *Mosses d'Escuadra* (in this case, the all-female Catalan police force) with whom she's working. Cognizant that a Castilian but non-Catalan reading public would miss the comic results produced, the author has her narrator direct a mini-lesson in Catalan pronunciation to her reader, one of many interventions by the narrator directed at a presumed female reader. Since García represents both the political power of the central state and the linguistic domination of Castilian over the other languages spoken in Spain (Catalan, Euskerra or Basque, and Galician), Van Guardia underscores an additional challenge that the majority of her main characters face in constructing a nonnormative, nonperipheral identity in what she calls the new *estado pluriautonómico* [multiautonomous region state], while poking fun at the presumed superiority of the dominant Castilian culture every time García makes a linguistic faux pas (e.g., Campmany = Camain).

The author's penchant for erotic literature also finds expression in the trilogy of *culebrones*. As a finalist for the Sonrisa Vertical prize for erotic literature with her first novel, *Entre todas las mujeres* [Among All Women] (1992), and having been expelled from school on one occasion for writing pornographic stories, Franc/Van Guardia engages her poetic and linguistic imagination in her descriptions of the intimate relationships of her characters. In this regard, the author disposes of the water/marine images that have been consecrated in Spanish lesbian writing by such well-known Spanish authors as Esther Tusquets and Carme Riera.[23] In *Con pedigree*, Gabi, who perceives that her national pride is at stake when she picks up a German tourist at Gay Night,

> empezó por explayarse en sus artes acariciatorias hasta ponerle los pezones como puntas de Everest. *"Hem fet el cim,"* le dijo antes de lanzarse a lamerlos con fruición y, al mismo tiempo, hacer uso de una dactilología a noventa revoluciones que hizo levitar a la alemana a una altura similar a la de la puerta de Brandemburgo. Pero la aria no quiso ser menos y como si se tratara de un partido entre Steffi Graff y Arantxa Sánchez Vicario, devolvió el peloteo llevando su vigorosa lengua hasta el clítoris de la Gabia que creyó estar volando en un *jet* (129).

> [began by extending her caressing arts until [the German's] nipples were like the peaks of Mt. Everest. "We've reached the summit," she said before she began licking them with pleasure and, at the same time, making use of a digital dexterity at ninety revolutions that made the German levitate to a height similar to that of the Brandenburg Gate. But the Aryan, not to be outdone, as if it were a match between Steffi Graff and Arantxa Sánchez Vicario, returned the volley, taking her vigorous tongue toward Gabi's clitoris. Gabi felt like she was flying on a jet].

In *Plumas,* the description of a *casteller* [human tower] competition in Ade's housing development is interwoven with the actions taking place in a nearby bedroom.[24] The description begins:

> Laura y Eva se erguían desnudas en el lecho y entrelazaban sus muslos y sus brazos del mismo modo que los brazos y los muslos de las *castelleras* se trenzaban entre sí y las que subían zigzagueaban cual lagartijas por los cuerpos de las que ya estaban situadas y sus vientres rozaban las espaldas y las nalgas de las otras hasta situarse encima y apostar las plantas de los pies en sus hombros. Y las manos de las *castelleras* se asían con fuerza las unas a las otras en un entramado de pieles y sensaciones. El vientre de Eva contra el vientre de Laura. Subieron las *quartes* frotando su pectoral contra el dorso de aquellas a las que escalaban. Vientre contra vientre en el lecho y en la torre pecho contra nalga (192–93).

> [Laura and Eva were sitting up naked on the bed and intertwining their thighs and arms in the same way that the arms and thighs of the *castelleras* were woven together. The ones that were climbing zigzagged like lizards around the ones that were already in place, and their bellies brushed the backs and the buttocks of the others, until they reached the top and planted their feet on the shoulders of the ones immediately below. And the *castelleras* held each other's hands tightly in a framework of skins and sensations. Eva's belly against Laura's belly. The *quartes* climbed up, rubbing their pecs against the backs of those they climbed over. Belly against belly in the bed, and in the tower, breast against buttock.]

The description continues in an even more explicit vein as the various steps in the raising of the *casteller* are related, intertwined with the caresses of Laura and Eva as they too reach a climax. A symphony and the formation of a hurricane provide similar poetic inspirations for the humorous eroticism of *La mansión.*

In these lusty love scenes, Van Guardia's sense of humor, rather than the erotic, is at the forefront, so that even the sex scenes become parodies of serious erotic literature. Lola's alter ego, Isabel Franc, admits that Lola needed some prodding from the Egales publishers:

> Yo les estaba dando el libro por entregas y un día me dijeron: "está bien y nos gusta mucho, es muy divertida pero—como son muy diplomáticas—quizá le falta un poco de acción." ¿Acción? Pregunté yo. "Sí, un poco de ya sabes, ¿no? Un poco más de acción porque . . ."

Total, querían decir escenas de cama, yo me quedé a rombos. "Sí, ya sabes que a las chicas les gusta un poco de sexo explícito." Total que de ahí salieron la escena del vibrador japonés, las castelleras, porque tal y como les dije: es sexo a mi estilo (Colomer and Roca, 4:27).

[I was giving them the book in installments and one day they said to me: "It's going well and we like it a lot, it's very funny but"—since they're very diplomatic—"perhaps it lacks a little action." "Action?" I asked. "Yes, a little of you-know-what, no? A little more action because . . ." To sum up, they were trying to say bedroom scenes, which threw me for a loop. "Yeah, you know the girls like a little bit of explicit sex." So out came the scene of the Japanese vibrator, the scene of the *castelleras*, because, as I told them: it's sex, my style.]

As with other offerings from the "Salir del armario" series, and despite their character of postmodern parody, Van Guardia's novels are affirmative depictions of lesbian lifestyles and eroticism which aim to "normalize" lesbian desire. But in so doing, do they challenge in any way heteronormativity? Jill Robbins, in her exploration of the "contradictory" representations of lesbians in Spain, asserts that the majority of novels in the "Salir del armario" series "in fact represent lesbian women as 'normal citizens,' often with children and eventually 'married' to other lesbians, thus reaffirming the norms of the heterosexist public sphere."[25] Certainly characters such as Clara and Ana, whose melodrama centers on their desire for a child, are examples of this contradiction in lesbian representation. Yet Van Guardia does give the couple the ability to achieve their dream through a revolutionary new technology that bypasses the need for sperm. And while Nati celebrates a wedding at the end of the first novel, the marriage does not last. At the least, as Jacky Collins has argued, Van Guardia's novels present a "destabilized world, where the inversion of social and cultural norms is taken to an extreme," particularly in the second and third novels, where male characters, who receive oblique reference in the first novel, "have been disappeared from the narrative altogether" (79–80). Yet her claim that "Van Guardia has created a world that is freed from patriarchal, though not necessarily institutional, oppression" (89) is somewhat undercut by Van Guardia's own attention to the linguistic challenges of creating a utopian model of lesbian separatism.

Perhaps the trilogy's greatest strengths reside in the fact that the novels can be read at different levels, depending on the sophistication of the reader. In their cultural intertextuality, their engagement with the contemporary political climate, and their exploration of the linguistic challenges to achieving true freedom from the dominant gender and political realities, the novels represent, albeit as a postmodern parody, a more sophisticated approach to lesbian identity than the often pedagogical and somewhat "dumbed-down" coming-out stories from which the "Salir del armario" series takes its name. Van Guardia effectively breaks with the "heteroreality" of the public sphere, "naturalizing" lesbianism as the "normal" way for women to relate to one another (Collins, 88). In the process, she makes an urgent call to lesbians, particularly those in prominent positions, to own their identities in public, as a first step in challenging lesbian invisibility.

Van Guardia's recourse to humor as a means not only to deliver a sociopolitical critique of contemporary Spain but also as a way of representing the lesbian community is fresh and refreshing. Reflecting on Van Guardia's use of humor, Franc has stated that

> Lola Van Guardia hace culebrones con estructura de culebrón, y además con culebrones paródicos o humorísticos, como quieras llamarles, con lo cual hay poco espacio para la seriedad. La reflexión, en todo caso, está detrás. El humor es algo muy serio. Yo creo que la mejor manera para hacer llegar las cosas es desde el humor, sobre todo la autocrítica y a las mujeres y a las lesbianas en particular nos ha faltado muchísima autocrítica. Parece que los personajes de Lola Van Guardia no reflexionan, pero están dando pie a que la lectora pueda reflexionar sobre nuestra propia historia, nuestros propios dramas, nuestras tragedias (Colomer and Roca, 24).

> [Lola Van Guardia writes soap operas with the structure of soap operas, and what's more, parodic or humorous soap operas, whatever you want to call them, so there's not much room for seriousness. [Serious] reflection, however, is behind it. Humor is very serious. I believe that the best way to deliver things, particularly self-criticism, is through humor, and women in general, but lesbians in particular, have lacked self-criticism. It seems there's not much self-reflection on the part of Van Guardia's characters, but they open the door for the [female] reader to reflect on our own history, our own dramas, our own tragedies.]

Gone are the stereotypes of classic lesbian fiction (i.e., the "strange" girl, butches and femmes, the repressed *soltera* [unmarried woman]), as well as the tragic vein of humiliation, marginalization, and persecution that is all too present in realist lesbian fiction, in which the characters must challenge societal, as well as internalized, homophobia. Since lesbianism is the "norm" in Van Guardia's novels, with all the characters surrounded by a large and diverse lesbian community, the notion of the "Other" is inverted. Even Van Guardia's characters who are reluctant to "come out" and proclaim their homosexuality in public have a self-confidence and certitude in their sexual relations that reinforces Franc's contention that lesbians must overcome their own cowardice or hesitation in confronting the world.

Finally, one has to recognize as well the popularity of the novels in Spain—the first is now in its fourth edition, the second and third in their second—and the extent to which the fictitious author Lola Van Guardia has herself become an important lesbian cultural icon, just like the real and fictitious media/literary icons in her novels. Two comic books, entitled *The Lola's World* (Ediciones de la Tempestad, 2005) and written by a couple of lesbians whose "literary" pseudonym is ELENApuntoG, feature a thirty-something lesbian in rebellion against the status quo and the reactionaries who still seem to manage the world.[26] It is no coincidence that the very first frame depicts lesbians floating on air after getting Lola Van Guardia's autograph at a book signing. Another recently published book, *SEXutopías* (2006), by Sofía Ruíz, includes a rather long short story, "Buscando a Lola desesperadamente" [Desperately Seeking Lola], which itself is a parody of Lola Van Guardia's parodies. In the short story, the narrator takes on the persona of Police Inspector Emma García as she attempts to track down the elusive fictitious author, who is one of the subjects of her as-yet-to-be-completed doctoral dissertation.

With *Con pedigree* now translated to French and Italian (quite a feat for a Spanish lesbian novel) and her fans clamoring for more, Isabel Franc has not dismissed the possibility of taking Lola Van Guardia "out of the closet" again.[27] In fact, Franc told this writer in conversations during the summer of 2006 that Van Guardia has already come up with a theme for what will undoubtedly be another humorous lesbian best seller.

NOTES

My title is borrowed from an episode of Showtime's *The L Word*, a Sapphic soap whose sexy ensemble cast includes Mia Kirshner, Jennifer Beals, and Laurel Holloman. The show debuted in January 2004 and has now completed its sixth and final season. The series creator/executive producer is Ilene Chaiken, a former executive at Spelling Television and Quincy Jones Entertainment. The first season of *The L Word*, dubbed into Spanish, was not televised in Spain until the winter of 2005–6 on the Spanish pay-per-view channel, Canal +. I do not wish to suggest by using this title that the Lola Van Guardia series was influenced by this American phenomenon, as that would have been impossible, but rather that Van Guardia's trilogy "broke loose" the existing norms in Spanish lesbian literature through humor and parody. Both the Spanish literary trilogy and the American television series do, however, share the common theme of the lives and loves of a tight-knit group of friends within a lesbian community.

1. For a more detailed overview of the development of Spanish lesbian literature, see Inma Pertusa and Nancy Vosburg, *Un deseo propio* (Barcelona: Bruguera, 2009), 7–44.

2. The first edition of Van Guardia's trilogy was titled *Con pedigree: Culebrón lésbico por entregas*. "*Culebrón*" is a word used in Spain to designate a television soap opera. The subtitle was pulled in subsequent editions because bookstores seemed unwilling to display a novel that was blatantly lesbian.

3. Philip Fisher, *Hard Facts: Setting and Form in the American Novel* (New York: Oxford University Press, 1987), 19–20.

4. Eve Kosofsky Sedgwick, "Forward: The Letter 'L,'" in *Reading The L Word: Outing Contemporary Television*, eds. Kim Akass and Janet McCabe (London: I.B. Tauris, 2006), xxi.

5. Scott McCracken, *Pulp: Reading Popular Fiction* (Manchester: Manchester University Press, 1998), 6.

6. English translations of the various lesbian groups would be: the organized, the independents, the historicals, the new ones, the unknown, the crazies, and the separatists. Van Guardia's parodic universe reflects the diverse and divisive ideological positions that have created animosities in the Barcelona lesbian community (political divisions that characterize the Madrid lesbian activists as well), as is documented by scholars such as Olga Viñuales in her *Identidades lésbicas: discursos y practicas*, (Barcelona: Ediciones Bellaterra, 1999).

7. Elina Norandi, "La trilogía de Lola Van Guardia: Un fenómeno de fans entre las jóvenes lesbianas," in *Mujeres jóvenes ¿Nuevos Feminismos?*, coord. Alicia Gil Gómez (Castellón: Universitat Jaume I de Castellón. 2006), 260.

8. Jacky Collins, "'A World Beyond': The Lola Van Guardia Trilogy," in *Hispanic and Luso-Brazilian Detective Fiction: Essays on the Genero Negro Tradition*, eds. Renee W. Craig-Odders, Jacky Collins, and Glen S. Close (Jefferson, NC: McFarland, 2006), 80.

9. In her discussion of bisexuality in Spain, Viñuales has pointed out that some Spanish women who have had sexual relations with men do recognize—in private—their bisexuality (86). But within the lesbian community, they are subject to

[u]na incomprensión que proviene de las que piensan el lesbianismo en términos excluyentes y que se evidencia en expresiones como "lesbianas de pedigrí," dando a entender que existen lesbianas *auténticas*, desde siempre, de pura raza, que no han pasado por una fase heterosexual (my emphasis) (Viñuales 86).

[a lack of understanding that emerges from those who think about lesbianism in exclusive terms, which can be seen in the use of expressions such as "lesbians of pedigree," suggesting that there exist *authentic* lesbians, those who have always identified themselves as such, of pure race, who have never gone through a heterosexual phase].

The lesbian "with pedigree" is equivalent to the "gold-card lesbian" in the United States, a phrase used in a fourth-season episode of *The L Word*.

10. In fact, the lyrics of the theme song by the band Betty, introduced in season two of *The L Word*, apply just as handily to Van Guardia's novels: "Talking, laughing, loving, breathing, fighting, fucking, crying, drinking, writing, winning, losing, cheating, kissing, thinking, dreaming . . . It's the way that we live and love."

11. Although initially the work was to be published one or two chapters at a time, not only to provoke a certain anticipation, but also to bring the lesbian reading community by the Cómplices bookstore in Barcelona on a regular basis, technical problems prevented this from happening. Instead, it was published in its entirety (Isabel Franc, "From Tragedy to Parody: Lesbian Fiction in the Spanish State," keynote speech delivered at the XVIII Southeast Foreign Languages and Literatures Conference, Stetson University, February 22, 2008).

12. Franc divulged this anecdote about the mystery pseudonym to the author in a conversation in July 2006.

13. Isabel Franc, "Sobrevivir al final trágico con orgullo y elegancia," *Sales* 4 (June 2006): 10.

14. The word "plumas" is itself a double entendre: on the one hand, it translates as "pens," which the character Adelaida Duarte takes up to denounce governmental homophobia. But "pluma" or "tener pluma" [to have a feather] is also used to refer to ambiguous visual mannerisms that indicate the real or hypothetical homosexuality of a person.

15. Paulina Palmer, "The Lesbian Thriller: Transgressive Investigations," in *Criminal Proceedings: The Contemporary American Crime Novel*, ed. Peter Messent, (London: Pluto Press, 1997), 88.

16. "All L Breaks Loose" is the title of one of the episodes from the third season of *The L Word*.

17. "Novela negra" is the Spanish designation for hard-boiled detective fiction.

18. In Spain, domestic partner laws that recognized and gave legal benefits to two cohabiting adults began to be legislated in practically all the autonomous regions after Catalonia was the first to approve its own "ley sobre parejas de hecho" en 1998. The autonomous laws were important precursors to the 2004 national law recognizing same-sex marriages.

19. Franc remarked to the author in a conversation in 2007 that the "I'm gay too" campaign was a spoof on the "I've aborted too" campaign during the legislative abortion debates of the early post–Franco Transition period.

20. Alba Colomer and Jorgeleta Roca, "El humor es mi forma de supervivencia: Entrevista con Isabel Franc," *Sales* 4 (June 2006): 24.

21. While English translations could be rendered for these titles, it is enough to observe how Tea manages to insert her name into each one she dreams up.

22. In Ramón Sender's humorous 1962 novel, *La tesis de Nancy*, the eponymous protagonist is an American college student spending a year of study abroad in Seville. The novel centers on her mishaps with Andalusian colloquial language, as well as her failure to recognize false cognates.

23. For a discussion of the archetypal aquatic images of lesbian sexuality in Spanish fiction, see Inma Pertusa's *La salida del armario: Lecturas desde la otra acera* (Gijón, Spain: Llibros del Pexe, 2005).

24. A "casteller" is a tower formed with human bodies. Competitions are held throughout Catalonia throughout the year, and while men have traditionally been the only participants, Van Guardia, in keeping with her all-female aesthetic, has women performing these difficult structures.

25. Jill Robbins, "The (In)visible Lesbian: The Contradictory Representations of Female Homoeroticism in Contemporary Spain," *Journal of Lesbian Studies* 7.7 (2003): 113.

26. The creators of *The Lola's World* are Elena Guardia (graphics) and Maria Angels Cabrè (text).

27. In 2004, Franc, "in collaboration with" Lola Van Guardia, published *No me llames cariño* [Don't Call Me Honey], which included some of the characters from her trilogy, including Police Inspector Emma García. While there are several humorous episodes in the novel, including García's continuing efforts to learn Catalan, the novel is markedly different from the trilogy in both theme and tone.

REFERENCES

Akass, Kim, and Janet McCabe, eds. *Reading the L Word: Outing Contemporary Television*. London: I.B. Taurus, 2006.

Aliaga, Juan Vicente, and José Miguel G. Cortés. *Identidad y diferencia: Sobre la cultura gay en España*. Barcelona: Editorial Gay y Lesbiana, 1997.

Collins, Jacky. "'A World Beyond': The Lola Van Guardia Trilogy." In *Hispanic and Luso-Brazilian Detective Fiction: Essays on the Genero Negro Tradition*, edited by Renee W. Craig-Odders, Jacky Collins, and Glen S. Close, 79–90. Jefferon, NC: McFarland, 2006.

Colomer, Alba, and Jorgeleta Roca. "El humor es mi forma de supervivencia: Entrevista con Isabel Franc." In *Sales* 4 (June 2006): 24–27.

ELENApuntoG. *The Lola's World: Historias de Lola*. Barcelona: Ediciones de la Tempestad, 2005.

Franc, Isabel. "From Tragedy to Parody: Lesbian Fiction in The Spanish State." Keynote Speech delivered at the XVIII Southeast Foreign Languages and Literatures Conference, Stetson University, February 22, 2008.

Fisher, Philip. *Hard Facts: Setting and Form in the American Novel*. New York: Oxford University Press, 1987.

McCracken, Scott. *Pulp: Reading Popular Fiction*. Manchester: Manchester University Press, 1998.

Norandi, Elina. "La trilogía de Lola Van Guardia: Un fenómeno de fans entre las jóvenes lesbianas." In *Mujeres jóvenes, ¿Nuevos feminismos?* Alicia Gil Gómez, coord. 257–62. Castellón: Universitat Jaume I de Castellón, 2006.

Palmer, Paulina. "The Lesbian Thriller: Transgressive Investigations." In *Criminal Proceedings: The Contemporary American Crime Novel*, edited by Peter Messent, 87–110. London: Pluto Press, 1997.

Pertusa, Inma and Nancy Vosburg. *Un deseo propio*. Barcelona: Bruguera, 2009.

Robbins, Jill. "The (In)visible Lesbian: The Contradictory Representations of Female Homoeroticism in Contemporary Spain." *Journal of Lesbian Studies* 7.7 (2003): 107–31.

Ruíz, Sofía. *SEXutopías*. Barcelona: Egales, 2006.

Van Guardia, Lola. *Con pedigree*. Barcelona: Egales, 1997.

———. *La mansión de las tríbadas*. Barcelona: Egales, 2002.

———. *Plumas de doble filo*. Barcelona: Egales, 1999.

———. "Sobrevivir al final trágico con orgullo y elegancia." *Sales* 4 (June 2006): 10.

Viñuales, Olga. *Identidades lésbicas: discursos y prácticas*. Barcelona: Ediciones Bellaterra, 1999.

The Aesthetics of Murder in Carme Riera's "Gloria": Writing Sexually Subversive Violence

Maria DiFrancesco

—Gloria, me da la impresión de que te estás
enamorando . . .
Y Gloria sonreía con aquella sonrisa suya, lejana, enigmática,
un poco triste. Sonreía más con los ojos que con los labios.
                    —¿Y, si fuera verdad, te molestaría?[1]

"Gloria, it seems to me that you're falling in love . . ."
And Gloria smiled with that smile of hers, distant, enigmatic, a little sad. She smiled more with her eyes than with
her lips. "And, if that were true, would it bother you?"]

CARME RIERA (PALMA DE MALLORCA, 1948) HAS WON CRITICAL AC-
claim as a provocative writer who began pushing the envelope
regarding feminine identity and cultural agency in Spain following Franco's dictatorship in 1975. Two of the writer's most examined tales, "Te dejo, amor, en prenda el mar" ["I Leave You,
My Love, the Sea as a Token"] (1975) and "Y pongo por testigo a
las gaviotas" ["I Call on the Seagulls as Witness"] (1977), intimately dialogue with each other as each uniquely describes the
erotic love relationship between an adolescent girl and her
teacher, María, an older woman.[2] Curiously, "Gloria," another
tale published around the same time that also deals with subversive sexuality, including lesbian and bisexual identities, has received little, if any, critical consideration.[3] Perhaps this
inattention is partially due to the tale's emphasis on constantly
shifting erotic boundaries and the anxiety surrounding gender
identity. Indeed, until fairly recently, few academic publications
existed that were dedicated to the study of homosexual and lesbian identities in Spanish-language literature, much less the exclusive study of lesbianism in Iberian literature.[4]

211

According to Ana Morey Planas, the first-person narrator of
Riera's story, her writing serves as legal testimony to Gloria's
mysterious disappearance, murder, and bodily preservation
through taxidermy. As her account of events unravels, the reader
comes to see Gloria Canals Santandreu as part of a love triangle,
the object of desire of two rivals, one the female narrator, the
other a male adversary, Hans Norbert Eizemberg, who threatens
to take Gloria away from Ana when he asks her to marry him. It
appears that, since neither the narrator nor Hans can ever
wholly possess their object of desire, the two conspire to murder
and keep Gloria's embalmed body. Taxidermy, defined as "the
act of preparing and preserving the skins of animals, and stuffing
and mounting them so as to present the appearance, attitude,
etc. of the living animal," thus becomes a fundamental metaphor used to convey the erosion of limits placed on gendered desire.[5] I argue that through the aesthetics of this gothic murder,
Riera blurs the boundaries separating the acceptable from the
unacceptable, the private from the public, and shows that gender
can be a monstrous masquerade of many configurations. Relying
on theoretical materials by critics such as Thomas De Quincey,
Joel Black, and Judith Butler, I conclude that the ruptures between inside and outside exploited in the acts of murder and
taxidermy are tropes employed to represent sexual identities as
no longer fixed within binaries of masculine and feminine.

Perhaps it would be most helpful to begin this analysis of
"Gloria" by discussing what I mean when I refer to the "aesthetics" of murder. Following Black, an object, concept, action, or
event can obtain artistic status by virtue of being invented by
one who calls himself an artist. In this case, any effective, individual engagement in creation automatically renders such an
object, idea or event "artistic."[6] Nevertheless, Black likewise
notes that a thing, notion, performance, or occurrence can be
equally considered art if the viewer beholding any one of these
perceives it as such.[7] Anything once contemplated as aesthetically pleasing gains the status of art object.

But how is it that one might come to look on the ghastly offense of murder—criminal homicide involving both intent and
premeditation—as "aesthetic"? Although at first glance unusual, the notion that murder may be considered "beautiful," an
artistic event worthy of being observed and evaluated through
an aesthetic lens, is not at all unique to this study of Riera's
"Gloria." Most notably, in his series of essays entitled "On Murder Considered as One of the Fine Arts," nineteenth-century

British author Thomas De Quincey acknowledged that the act of killing, together with the crime scene fashioned by the murderer, could be considered productive as well as creative by onlookers. Murder once distanced from the scope of moral judgment and classification becomes sublime, expanding the human imagination. If Kant defined the sublime as that which does "violence to our imagination," De Quincey saw murder as uniquely capable of inspiring onlookers to observe killing from an "aesthetic-critical" rather than a "moral-rational" point of view.[8] The movement away from moral judgment and rationalization permitted witnesses to perceive killing as culturally subversive in a way that it had not been before. Transgressing Judeo-Christian and humanist limits of morality by proposing that murder be viewed from a purely aesthetic perspective, De Quincey challenged the cultural fabric, creating a potential space for a release from existing social values and taboos.

What's more, and perhaps most provocative, De Quincey suggested that those who write about violent crime come to share the same sphere of influence as the murderer who throws the social moral balance into disequilibrium. Drawing a parallel between the two, De Quincey asserted that pleasure and power motivate both the writer and the murderer to succeed in their respective arts.[9] The writer of crime literature, like the murderer, becomes an agent of cultural transgression. Authorship as well as the ownership of language used to describe criminal activity become inherently dangerous. For De Quincey, the writer and murderer equally seek "freedom by outstripping or subverting the social institutions they feel thwart or confine them."[10] Nonetheless, the writer who successfully presents murder as art must portray a normally terrible deed as nothing less than somehow agreeable. The artist-criminal must present murder "according to the institutionalized conventions of the art world—as a stable, interesting event to be regarded from different perspectives and debated from different points of view by critics and connoisseurs."[11] In this respect, it may be that the writer creates a narrator who makes the murderer appear to be an artist, thereby heightening "his own artistry by projecting it upon his awe-inspiring subject."[12] Thus, although news of a murder generally evokes horror, revulsion, and the requisite need for a community to follow up with some formal declaration of pious morality regarding the scene and any victims, viewed aesthetically—in relation to good taste—the vile act becomes something entirely distinct. The writer transforms the abject into something so seductively palatable that readers come to voraciously consume it.

So it is in "Gloria." The art of narrative seduction, in this case through murder, is nothing new to Riera, who has boldly attested to the seductive quality of literature, especially the short story form, in several interviews.[13] Readers familiar with Riera's oeuvre will further notice a striking similarity between "Gloria" and many of the author's early tales that employ the confessional mode, an enticing literary device used to captivate readers and incite them to continue reading. Yet unlike the narrators of tales such as "Te dejo, amor, en prenda el mar," "Y pongo por testigo a las gaviotas" or her latest novel, *La mitad del alma* [*Half of the Soul*], Ana Morey does not employ the epistolary form to intimately address her audience but makes use of a legal report. If the phrase "testimonial literature" has been most recently used to refer to first-person accounts of social oppression, violence, and war, the narrator of "Gloria" returns the literature of testimony to its fundamental origins. Writing an official statement about the sordid events leading up to and including the murder of her illegitimate cousin and best friend, she writes and submits a document to the scrutiny of the law, implicitly making a solemn claim that what she has written is a declaration of fact. This testimony begins with the words:

> Dudo mucho de que mis declaraciones puedan resultarles útiles. Ya se lo he repetido durante estos días, mientras ustedes, con una insistencia propia de profesionales, me han pedido que les contara todo lo que supiese. Ahora, cuando intento ordenar en mi pobre cerebro todos los sucesos que conozco, con el fin de exponerlos con la máxima objetividad y precisión, siento, con inusitada intensidad, escalofríos recorriéndome el cuerpo.[14]

> [I highly doubt that my testimony will be useful to you. I've already repeated it to you over these last days, while you all, with the insistence of true professionals, have asked me to tell you all that I might know. Now, when I try to organize in my own mind all the events with which I'm familiar, with the intention of exposing them to maximum objectivity and precision, I feel, with rare intensity, goosebumps running up and down my body.]

Although fully aware that her testimony will be read by legal officials and used in a court of law, the testimony Ana renders to her audience is far from objective, far from fact-driven. Writing these words, the narrator confesses that she feels mental confusion, physical disorder, and emotional upset. Later, this language becomes reflective of Ana's inability to acknowledge and accept her own sexual identity as a lesbian woman as well as indicative of her duplicitous criminal role within the narrative. As she alludes to her personal experiences and feelings toward Gloria, Ana's story begins to "fix" Gloria's body in literature in much the same way as Hans "fixes" Gloria's preserved body as an objet d'art through taxidermy. The narrative produces an increasingly complex image of Hans and Ana, both of whom participate in committing a heinous murder in order to settle their own sexual anxieties through art.

"Gloria's" classic gothic elements, including the confessional mode, immediately entrench the story's narrator and characters within an aesthetically rich style that shapes and informs the reader's understanding of the text. Beyond the narrative style and gory murder, which itself takes place in a dark, isolated cabin in the woods, the narrator makes numerous references to Gloria's intrinsically marginal status within conservative Spanish culture. Namely, Ana presents Gloria as the fruit of an uncle's illicit affair. Ana's aunt, either unwilling or incapable of accepting the reality of her partner's romantic interlude with another woman, effectively coerces her husband to send Gloria to a remote convent school managed by strict nuns while forcing him to send his lover, Gloria's mother, to Argentina where she would be unable to contact him or ask him for monetary support in the future. According to Ana, Gloria grew up believing she had well earned her marginal status within conservative Spanish society as a child of sin.[15] Although happily welcomed back into the extended family by Ana's mother to be raised with Ana as her adoptive sister, the narrator suggests that Gloria spent years performing sacrificial acts before finally appearing to accept her position within the family, "Gloria se sometía a penitencias y sacrificios inusuales en una jovencita de veintiún años."[16] [Gloria submitted herself to acts of penitence and sacrifices unusual in a young woman of twenty-one years.]

That this tale of murder should contain such classic gothic elements is not at all surprising given that gothicism has always presented writers and readers with the opportunity to encounter thrilling nonconventional sexual relationships in literature.[17] Eve Kosovsky Sedgwick suggests a likely link between nontraditional sexual relationships and a preoccupation with limits in her quintessential book *The Coherence of Gothic Conventions*, stating that gothic literature often involves an experience with otherness, the violation of limits (especially those of the body), and the anxiety that comes from such experiences of otherness and transgression of boundaries.[18] Within this larger literary context, Riera not only implicitly frames Gloria's early marginal sexual status within the gothic, but she explodes the limits of this status, making it possible for readers to explore the concept of gender in murder as art.

Perhaps nowhere else is Riera's preoccupation with the limits and boundaries of the gothic more evident than in Ana's discussion of taxidermy. For all intents and purposes, the goal of the taxidermist is to transform a once-living organism, typically some prey that has been hunted, into an object to be publicly exhibited and admired by observers. The taxidermist generally takes great pains to conserve the natural look and appeal of the organism, often mounting the animal within a larger naturalistic setting to maintain a sense of the creature's authenticity and realism. Within this context, we may begin to analyze Ana's testimony regarding Hans as well as his unusual hobby: "Soy testigo de que tocaba el violín con virtuosismo supremo, con la misma meticulosidad con la que se dedicaba a disecar pájaros. He guardado en el desván los ejemplares, una abubilla, una lechuza, un vencejo, un buitre [. . .], que como si se tratara de ramos de flores, le mandaba a Gloria."[19] [I can testify that he played the violin with supreme virtuosity, with the same meticulousness with which he dedicated himself to preserving birds. I have saved examples of his work in the attic, a hoopoe, a barn owl, a swift, a vulture . . ., like some send flower bouquets, he sent these to Gloria.] Ana's description is important for several reasons. On the one hand, her characterization distances Hans from the traditional, heterosexual male hunter who collects big game in order to mount his prize and gain the recognition of others who might observe and admire his skill. For such a hunter, prey might be said to symbolically function as a substitute for the phallus. The larger and more terrifying the game, the more virile and powerful the hunter who acquires authority over his victim. On the other hand, Hans's status as a virtuoso violinist, together with later revelations that he works for a Swiss bank, speaks several languages fluently, and enjoys classical music, categorically places him within the upper class. His affluent status within a privileged social group may initially account for his interest in avian taxidermy. Rather than cultivate an interest in large game that would necessitate his participation in savage expeditions, he cultivates an interest in diminutive creatures. These delicate and attractive animals more appropriately appeal to his character and rank within society. They hold an aesthetic charm that other, fiercer creatures might not.

On another level, Hans's preoccupation with avian taxidermy is curiously fascinating since it is closely tied to the subversion of gender categories and conventions within the tale. Ana most emphatically draws attention to the relationship between ambiguous gender limits and taxidermy through references to Gloria's dead body at the end of her testimony. Discussing the way in which the police found Hans kneeling down before her stuffed corpse, Ana states, "[Hans] [t]enía el cuerpo cubierto de flores. Había sido embalsamada como si se tratara de un pájaro más."[20] [[Hans] had covered the corpse with flowers. She had been embalmed as if she were one more bird.] For Hans, taxidermy becomes the art form through which he not only attempts to gain artistic control of his object of desire, Gloria, but also through which he artfully attempts to gain control of his own sexual anxieties. If the ordinary hunter who practices taxidermy learns about the anatomy, skeletal structure, movement, and natural habitat of a living thing—in this case, birds—in order to gain authority over them, Hans learns all this to regulate how his object of desire will be perceived. To the degree to which he succeeds at this, he will succeed at regulating how he himself will be perceived by others. He uses the creative artistry of taxidermy to reinforce and legitimate a set of power relations. Through this hobby, he legitimates and maintains his status as artist-murder while inscribing male aggression on Gloria, a feminized object to be victimized and mutilated for his own profit.

The narrator draws several parallels between Hans's birds and Gloria, making the link between the two obvious. Ana tells how she initially reacted to Hans's prefered pastime saying, "A mí, aquellos animalitos, inmóviles, cadáveres disfrazados, me producían una impresión desagradabilísima, ya que se les obligaba a representar su papel, ostentoso e inútil, de vivos, sin tener cuenta para nada de su propia voluntad de muertos que reclaman sepultura."[21] [To me, those little animals, immobile, disguised cadavers, made a very disagreeable impression on me, since they were forced to play their parts, ostentatious and useless, when living, without considering their own wills as dead beings that demand burial.] She declares that the birds, located and displayed in a glass case for all to see, cause her a great deal of psychological upset. Their listless bodies constantly remind her of death, a foreshadowing of Gloria's untimely demise. According to Ana, the birds seem to ask for a permanent reprieve from this world.

In much the same way that Ana portrays Hans's birds as passive creatures exhibited for pleasure, she, too, begins to describe Gloria in bird-like terms, a tell-tale sign of the appeal she might hold for Hans:

> Gloria era una niña alta, pálida, triste de ojos, desorientados y grandes, del color de miel. Apenas hablaba cuando alguien le preguntaba alguna cosa, contestaba tan escuetamente como podía, con voz dulce y en un tono suavísimo, fruto de su larga estancia con las monjas, en el mejor—eso sí—colegio de Palma. Su padre, un tipo insensato que presumía de calavera, quiso pagarle siempre lo más costoso económicamente hablando, ya que le negaba cualquier afecto. Así que, desde pequeña, Gloria llevaba vestidos caros. Eso y el esmero que ponía en no mancharse, en no arrugarse, hacía que siempre pareciera que acababa de salir de un estuche de lo limpia y planchada que iba.[22]

> [Gloria was a tall, pallid girl with sad, disoriented, big eyes the color of honey. She hardly spoke when anyone asked her anything, she'd answer as concisely as possible with a sweet voice and in a suave tone, the fruit of her long stay with the nuns, in the best—that's a fact—high school in Palma. Her father, a foolish type that fancied himself a playboy, always wanted to provide her with the most expensive things, economically speaking, since he denied her all affection. So, since childhood, Gloria always wore expensive dresses. That and the care that she took to not get dirty, to not get her clothes wrinkled, made it so that she always appeared to have just come out of a display case, because of how clean and pressed she went.]

Ana represents her illegitimate cousin and best friend as naturally submissive, describing Gloria as having pale skin and honey-colored, disoriented eyes, traits that convey physical weakness as well as a lack of agency and movement. By depicting Gloria as having confused eyes, eyes that clearly cannot focus on objects, Ana implies that, rather than see, Gloria is seen. She, like the stuffed birds kept in the glass case, appears to be visually restricted, unable to gaze back at the lecherous, menacing gaze of those who would look upon her, particularly Hans. Ana also methodically draws attention to the bird-like quality of Gloria's voice and accent by foregrounding its sweet, perhaps songlike, softness.[23] If Hans's preserved birds must be kept and controlled in glass cabinets, the language that Ana uses to describe Gloria equally defines her as a kept bird, a product of strict Catholic schooling and an absent father who would have her always look physically attractive. Like the stuffed birds that must be skillfully prepared for public exhibition, Gloria epitomizes molded perfection. Wearing the expensive clothes chosen and given to her by her father, and taking immaculate care of her outward appearance, she embodies the artifice of a dictated, static femininity, one in which she appears to take no active role in having created.

I emphasize this imagery not only because it underscores Gloria's passive objectification by the narrator, but also because it sharply contrasts with later, dissonant images that represent a far different picture of Gloria as a protagonist. At first glance, one might explain these engaged, active images of Gloria by asserting that they result from her growing trust in the relationship she shares with Hans:

> La veía más alegre, con ganas de salir, de charlar. Me fijé, incluso, en un detalle que me pareció *sintomático:* todas las mañanas, antes de salir a la calle para acudir a su trabajo en la Diputación, pasaba por el salón de los espejos y se miraba detenidamente de pies a cabeza, desde todos los ángulos [. . .] Gloria, que no había tenido adolescencia, se estaba convirtiendo en una adolescente.[24]

> [I saw that she was happier, she had a desire to go out, to chat. I even noticed a detail that seemed *symptomatic:* each morning, before going out to her job at the County Council, she'd pass by a salon of mirrors and she'd carefully look at herself from head to toe from every angle. . . . Gloria, who had never had adolescence, had become an adolescent.]

The narrator would have her readers believe that, as the relationship between Hans and Gloria naturally developed, so too did Gloria's need to fly away from the safety of the proverbial nest in which she had been living, Ana's home. Gloria's increased agency and interest in the world around her appears to result from being in love.

Although this description links heterosexual feminine satisfaction with giving and getting heterosexual male pleasure and approval, it concurrently destabilizes the notion of femininity as aligned with meek compliance. If Ana artfully describes Gloria as having disoriented eyes in a previous passage, she now depicts Gloria as looking at herself from head to toe and from every angle in shop windows. She is not only seen by those around her as an object of desire, but comes to appreciate herself as such an object. While she may well be providing satisfaction to a male partner, her relationship with Hans may be viewed as ultimately resulting in a coming of age that permits her to both see and seek her own sexual pleasure. What's more, and perhaps most striking, the narrator's use of the word "sintomático" implies that this coming of age, like an illness, is accompanied by symptoms. Taken a step further, we shall see that taxidermy becomes a method by which both Hans and Ana attempt to cure their own symptomatic anxieties around gender roles and sexual identity. By killing Gloria, they attempt to manage Gloria's increasingly indefinable sexuality with all its infirm implications.

But how do images of Gloria hint at anxieties around gender conventions and sexual identity? And how does taxidermy serve as a metaphor for the destabilization of the sexual positions played by Hans and Ana? Mark Seltzer suggests a possible answer to these questions, saying that "murder is where bodies and history cross."[25] For Seltzer, the killer, and in this case the taxidermist as well as his accomplice, resolve the instability and uncertainty of bodies through the act of murder.[26] As we shall see, Ana's testimony, her "historia" of the events as they occurred, depicts a female victim whose sexuality is described in increasingly ambiguous terms. Gloria comes to embody a sexuality that jeopardizes both heterosexual male and lesbian identity. Specifically, as Hans becomes more cognizant of the closeness of the erotic relationship shared by Ana and Gloria, he comes to feel his own sense of male sexual security as overtly threatened. In much the same way, as Ana becomes cognizant of the very real possibility of losing Gloria to Hans, she reacts by becoming Hans's accomplice. As his partner in crime, Ana sacrifices Gloria, eternally keeping her love from his clutches.

As previously suggested, Hans occupies a dangerous position as a man in love with a woman whose sexuality constantly transgresses gender conventions. The inherent peril of this position becomes evident in a telling passage wherein Ana tells of her last meeting with Hans before Gloria's demise:

> La noche en que Gloria salió para no volver nunca más, su prometido subió a buscarla. Mientras esperaba impaciente que Gloria acabara de arreglarse, se sentó a mi lado en el cuarto de estar y comenzó a explicarme—en un mallorquín correctísimo, que *me admiraba*—cómo quería a aquella mujer excepcional y el enorme cambio que se produjo en su vida desde el momento en que la conoció. Había vehemencia en sus palabras, emoción, incluso. Estaba algo nervioso, entrecruzaba las manos una y otra vez con un gesto que no me gus-

taba demasiado, no sabría decir por qué. No tuvimos mucho tiempo que hablar; Gloria apareció, sin hacer ruido, por detrás del cortinaje que cubría la puerta. *Nos sorprendió y nos levantamos.*[27]

[The night Gloria went out never to return, her fiancé came up to get her. While he impatiently waited for Gloria to get ready, he sat down at my side in the living room and he began to explain—in a very correct Majorcan dialect, that I admired—how he loved that exceptional woman and the enormous change that had taken place in his life since the moment he met her. There was vehemence in his words, emotion even. He was somewhat nervous, crossing and uncrossing his arms once and again with a gesture that I didn't like too much, I wouldn't know how to explain why. We didn't have much time to speak; Gloria appeared, without making any noise, from behind a curtain that covered the door. She surprised us and we got up.]

While his actions might be characteristic of any anxious lover awaiting the imminent arrival of a love, Hans's body language calls to mind the fretful concern of a would-be assassin at work on a scheme to commit murder. From the way he vehemently expresses himself, to the way in which he restlessly fidgets, crossing and uncrossing his hands, Hans's gestures emphatically reinforce the notion that nervous energy coincides with the contemplation and decision to carry out a heinous transgression.

Just as the passage underscores Hans's murderous scheming, so too it foregrounds emerging concerns regarding the sexualities of both Hans and Ana. As Tania Modleski points out, female bisexuality poses a danger to the conventions of traditional male-female structured relationships.[28] If, as I will suggest, it is the case that Gloria is attracted to both males and females, then this attraction blurs the limits of heterosexual love under patriarchy. This aberrant love that cannot be named endangers Hans's otherwise proper identity within patriarchy as a well-to-do Swiss banker and businessman with fine taste in classical music, good food, and fine wines. Details within the paragraph make this threat clear. Most notably, the narrator reveals her admiration for Hans. While it is true that she specifically articulates high regard for his ability to speak Majorcan, a language not his own, in my estimation, Ana's admiration also draws attention to her own growing interest in Gloria's love object. Her appreciation suggests that she recognizes Hans as a rival. He is an "other" who vies for—and successfully receives—Gloria's attention. The fact that Ana later mentions that neither Hans nor she heard Gloria arrive to meet the two that evening—that they were in fact surprised by her arrival—further promotes this interpretation of the passage. That is, the narrator gives the reader the impression that the two competitors, Hans and Ana, had been engaged in a level of discussion about Gloria so intense as not to have heard the protagonist draw near.

Discussing Alfred Hitchcock's *Psycho*, a film sharing more than one parallel with Riera's "Gloria," Modleski argues that instability of male subjectivity leads to violence against women.[29] In much the same way as Modleski describes in her book, Hans uses taxidermy to rid himself of any reminders of Gloria's bisexuality.[30] By killing her, yet preserving her very feminine body, he artfully constructs her to be whatever he would have her be. If she had, while alive, threatened his sexuality under patriarchy, her stuffed body cannot continue to threaten him. Hans uses his skills as a taxidermist to eradicate any ambiguous sexual subjectivity once embodied by Gloria and to restore her to a proper place within patriarchy.

Ana, for her part, denies having had a lesbian affair with Gloria while time and again implicitly coming out of the proverbial closet only to implicate herself as an accomplice in the crime. From the beginning of the testimony, Ana refutes rumors that she had had any romantic relationship with Gloria, declaring that theirs was nothing more than a platonic friendship based in adoptive sisterhood, "Sé que ustedes creen que nos unía un sentimiento mucho más fuerte que la pura amistad, y que mi última afirmación confirma sus sospechas."[31] [I know that you believe that a much stronger feeling than friendship united us, and that my last statement confirms your suspicions.] Yet at the same time that Ana candidly rejects the allegation that she shared a sexual relationship with Gloria, she affirms and acknowledges the existence of social values that would have denied her the ability to freely publicize this kind of intimate connection with another woman. In one telling passage, she directly addresses her audience, the police and detectives involved in the murder case, in an attempt to defend herself from those who would accuse her of having had a lesbian relationship: "Tal vez, ustedes crean que los criados han sido sobornados y mienten o que nosotras, Gloria y yo, reservábamos nuestras intimidades sólo para aquellos momentos en los que permanecíamos solas en la habitación, al amparo de la noche. Pero yo les aseguro, por la sagrada memoria de Gloria, que entre nosotras todo fue de una limpieza absoluta."[32] [Perhaps you believe that the servants have been bribed and that they're lying or that we, Gloria and I, reserved our private interactions to those moments when we were alone, in the bedroom, in the refuge of the night. But I assure you, on Gloria's sacred memory, that between us there was absolute purity.] Later, she vehemently reiterates, "No les negaré que Gloria fue la persona más importante de mi vida y la que más me interesó de todas cuantas he conocido. Pero les aseguro que en nuestras relaciones siempre prevaleció la más absoluta moralidad, así que no tuvieron nada de prohibidas."[33] [I won't deny to you that Gloria was the most important person in my life and the one who most interested me of all the people I've known. But I assure you that the most absolute morality always prevailed in our relations, so there was nothing forbidden between us.] These statements unambiguously communicate recognition of cultural mores placing any sexual desire beyond orthodox heterosexuality as out of bounds. She discounts any possibility that she might identify as a lesbian, and in doing so, she acquiesces to the limits placed on her by patriarchy. Rather than confront or effectively contend with patriarchal powers, she appears to surrender to them, admitting the total censorship placed on such aberrant love under Franco.

Indeed, Ana's refutation of having had an intimate relationship with Gloria and of identifying as a lesbian can be interpreted as perfectly in line with the values of Spanish culture during the 1970s. From the beginning of the Franco regime in the 1930s until its end in 1975, the vast majority of women followed a politics of state-mandated conservatism. Imposed from without by the church and state, women internalized "a repressive and hypocritical code of morals wherein male promiscuity was unofficially acceptable whereas female sexual expression was confined to procreation and the fulfillment of the husband's conjugal rights."[34] One could hardly discuss one's sexual desires as a heterosexual woman, much less hope to ever candidly acknowledge or talk about lesbian desires and activities. To do so would not only be to tread into forbidden and immoral territories that violated the rules of church law, but to risk legal and political retribution at the hands of state representatives. In Spanish literature, this too was the case. Writing about sexual relationships and desires was considered at the very least aesthetically questionable, and at the very most ethically reprehensible.[35]

Details in Ana's testimony that indicate that the narrator *did* share a romantic relationship with Gloria fit within this cultural framework of secrecy. If, on the one hand, Ana follows the rules of Spanish patriarchy by persistently disputing that she identified as a lesbian, her narrative concurrently subverts these rules by consistently depicting an intimate portrait of denied Sapphic love. Ana effectively reveals her true sexual preferences, as well as those of Gloria, when she inquires as to Gloria's relationship with Hans:

> —Gloria, me da la impresión de que te estás enamorando [. . .]
> Y Gloria sonreía con aquella sonrisa suya, lejana, enigmática, un poco triste. Sonreía más con los ojos que con los labios.
> —¿Y, si fuera verdad, *te molestaría?*[36]

> "Gloria, it seems to me that you're falling in love . . ."
> And Gloria smiled with that smile of hers, distant, enigmatic, a little sad. She smiled more with her eyes than with her lips.
> "And if that were true, would it bother you?"

Gloria's enigmatic smile and expressive eyes together with her verbal response show a degree of playful seduction. She knowingly performs to tease and entice Ana, making the narrator jealous of the relationship she shares with Hans by directly asking her whether the nature of that relationship troubles her. To be sure, it is possible that the relationship bothers Ana because she realizes that the friendship the women share will soon be torn apart by impending marriage. Nonetheless, since Ana later conveys a sense of rage at Hans, it is necessary to argue that the love the two women share is not that of platonic, heterosexual women, but rather an erotic, passionate love at the brink of ruin. Nowhere is Ana's rancor towards Hans more evident than when she declares, "El día en que [Gloria] me pidió prestado el aderezo hacía tres meses justo que había conocido al hombre que *nos tenía que resultar tan pernicioso.* Siete años más joven que Gloria, se dedicaba a negocios de banca; nos dijo que estaba en Mallorca, como delegado de una agencia sueca, para gestionar la compra de unos terrenos en los que proyectaban instalar un hotel de lujo."[37] [The day [Gloria] asked to borrow my jewelry it had been just three months that she'd met that man who was going to be *so exceedingly harmful to us.* Seven years younger than Gloria, he was dedicated to banking; he told us he was in Mallorca, as a delegate of a Swiss agency, to negotiate the buying of some land on which they planned to build a luxury hotel.] Ana's use of the possessive pronoun "nos" is particularly significant because of its inclusive nature. Simply put, the pronoun signifies a sense of mutual victimization. Ana insinuates feeling just as threatened and enraged by Gloria, a lover who Ana perceives as imminently abandoning her for a man, as by Hans, who has successfully vied for Gloria's attention and won her in their rivalry.

Ana's feelings of fear and abandonment by Gloria escalate and come to a head when she finds out that Hans has asked Gloria to marry him:

> Temía que la llevara a vivir en su país, a otro lugar lejos de Mallorca, o, simplemente, a otra casa, y el egoísmo me hizo ser espléndida hasta el extremo de ofrecerle a Gloria el caserón en que vivíamos las dos. Yo me conformaría con instalarme en la parte de abajo, en el estudio, que, con un poco de obra, quedaría espacioso y agradable. De ese modo, estaría preservada su intimidad y yo no me quedaría sin su compañía. Gozaba pensando que, puesto que la boda parecía inminente, al cabo de un año, habría otro huésped en el piso de arriba. Gloria era joven todavía y me había manifestado, a menudo, que le gustaría mucho tener media docena de niños. El deseo de convertirme en tía, casi casi en madre, aunque los sobrinos no llevasen mi sangre, aunque los hijos fuesen de otro, me llenaba de satisfacción. Por todo eso y, sobre todo, porque veía lo feliz que era Gloria, consentí en su matrimonio con aquel hombre, extranjero y más joven que ella.[38]

> [I feared that he would take her to live in another country, another place far from Mallorca, or simply, to another house, and my ego made me be generous to the extreme so that I offered Gloria the big house in which we both lived. I'd make due by moving in downstairs, in the studio, which, with a little work, would turn out spacious and agreeable. That way, they'd have their privacy and I would still have her company. I enjoyed thinking that, since the wedding would be imminent, within a year, there would be another guest upstairs. Gloria was still young and she'd told me, often, that she would like to have half a dozen children. The desire to become an aunt, almost a mother, though the children wouldn't have my blood, though they'd be another's children, filled me with satisfaction. Because of all this and, above all, because I saw how happy Gloria was, I consented to her marrying that man, a foreigner who was much younger than she.]

Again, Ana's words might be interpreted as indicative of a normal fear over the possibility of losing any close friend. In addition, given the nature of families in Spain, that Ana would offer Gloria the opportunity to continue living with her in the house that they had shared even after marrying is not uniquely indicative of a lesbian romantic interest or desire. Extended families, including grandparents, aunts, uncles, and children, have habitually cohabited as this has been a custom of Spanish people for centuries. What is unsettling and particularly illuminating, however, is the import Ana places on Gloria to have children. Rather than see Hans as father and Gloria as mother of any potential offspring, Ana articulates her own active involvement in this undertaking. She states that she would accept Gloria's children as her own and that, while they would not share her blood, Gloria's children would fill Ana with satisfaction. What's more, in dreaming about the life they would live and fantasizing about being like a mother to Gloria's children, Ana reveals an erotic connection to Gloria. Through her fantasy, she not only displaces her male rival, Hans, but also symbolically eradicates the power of patriarchy in conventional family structures. Her consenting to the marriage, in itself an interesting detail that demonstrates Ana's power within the triangulated relationship, seems to hinge on the fact that the two—Hans and Gloria—would both agree to live with Ana under one roof. The foreigner and rival, Hans, would thus be surrendering his privileged place of authority within the patriarchal family to Ana.

For her part, Gloria relentlessly defies traditional feminine gender roles as she appears to uphold them. I have already shown that the narrator paints the figure of a woman who espouses traits long associated with heterosexual feminine desire. Beyond playing the role of the passive bird—a character that, no doubt, Hans finds attractive—she accepts Hans's petition of matrimony and otherwise behaves to make herself look the part of an exemplary partner in a typical male-female heterosexual relationship. Drawing attention to this model behavior, Ana describes how Gloria meticulously readies for her last date with Hans, "Entré en su habitación mientras se estaba arreglando. La encontré sentada ante el espejo del tocador, maquillándose ligeramente las pestañas con un sombreador liláceo, después se pintó los labios con un tono pálido. Llevaba puesto un traje largo negro que estrenaba aquella noche."[39] [I walked into her bedroom while she was getting ready. I found her sitting in front of the dressing-table mirror, lightly applying a lilac eye shadow to her eyelashes, then she painted her lips a pale tone. She wore a long black dress that she was putting on for the first time that night.] Yet the way Gloria prepares herself for the outing—elegantly dressing and perfectly applying makeup—again duplicitously foregrounds this femininity not as passive, but as an active process that involves artful consideration and creative production on the part of an engaged agent. Taken to its logical limit, Ana's characterization demonstrates the way in which Gloria skillfully, perhaps even theatrically, manipulates her appearance to conform to the regulations of a male-female binary that stipulates that the female sex should display certain and specific sexual attributes. As Judith Butler explains, "Even if the sexes appear to be unproblematically binary in their morphology and constitution (which will become a question), there is no reason to assume that genders ought also to remain as two."[40] According to Butler, the presupposition of a binary gender scheme unreservedly maintains the belief in a mimetic relation of gender to sex wherein gender reflects physical sex or is in some other way controlled by it. If we perceive gender as detached from biological, physical sex, then gender itself can be observed as "free floating artifice, with the consequences that man and masculine might just as easily signify a female body as a male one, and woman and feminine a male body as easily as a female one."[41] The "gender trouble" at work in the narrative is that Gloria, while often appearing to perform in very feminine ways to attract Hans, also sexually performs to attract Ana. She masterfully shows gender to be a masquerade played to attract all interested parties.

Finally, if there remains an ultimate, unspoken complicity between Hans and Ana to murder Gloria, it stems from the fact that each realizes the impossibility of "fixing" Gloria's ability to perform sexually in life. Gloria, while alive, escapes gender conventions by aesthetically appealing to and unsettling both male and female counterparts. Once she is killed, however, Hans and Ana can both negotiate their sexual anxieties around her fixed, now unalterable body. Scenes that depict Gloria's dead body not only represent this fixing, but also represent the renegotiation and ultimate liberation of gender conventions that occur upon her death. Describing the way in which naive hikers find Hans and Gloria, Ana recounts:

La descubrieron por casualidad unos excursionistas. Un temporal les obligó a hacer noche en la montaña, porque la niebla no les dejaba avanzar. Entonces fue cuando encontraron la caseta de aperos, aparentemente abandonada, y forzaron la puerta de entrada. Al abrirla vieron a un hombre arrodillado junto a una mujer que parecía dormida. A la luz de la linterna brillaban las joyas, que adornaban una blancura enfermiza. El hombre ni les miró y se limitó a decir en tono autoritario: "Márchense, aquí no caben." Anduvieron toda la noche

bajo el aguacero, el miedo hizo que desistieran de quedarse en aquel
refugio. Al amanecer divisaron las luces de un pueblo; cuando llegaron ya era casi de día. Agotados, lívidos, mojados como sopas, ater-
rorizados hasta la punta de los pelos, dieron parte a la guardia civil
de lo que habían visto. Hacia las tres de la tarde, llegaron ustedes,
acompañado por un grupo de gente que conocía el paraje. Creían que
ya no encontrarían a nadie. Pero, no. Él continuaba allí al lado de
Gloria, que yacía en un catre, en un ángulo del pequeño cuartucho,
su rostro, palidísimo, sonreía enigmáticamente. Tenía el cuerpo cubierto de flores.[42]

[Some hikers found her by coincidence. A storm forced them to pass
the night in the mountains, because the fog wouldn't let them ad-
vance. So they entered the cabin, which had been apparently abandoned, and they forced their way in. Upon entering, they saw a man
kneeling before a woman who seemed asleep. By the light of the lan-
tern, her jewels sparkled, adorning a sick white complexion. The
man didn't even look at them, and he limited himself to saying in
an authoritative tone, "Leave, you don't belong here." They walked
the entire night in the rainstorm, the fear made them desist from
looking for refuge there. At dawn, they discerned the lights of a
town; when they arrived it was already almost daylight. Tired, livid,
soaking wet, petrified to the point of having goosebumps, they reported what they had seen to the Civil Guard. Around three o'clock
in the afternoon, you arrived, accompanied by a group of people who
knew the spot. They thought that they wouldn't find anyone there.
But, no. He was still at Gloria's side, who lay in a cot, in a corner of
the small room; her face, very pallid, she smiled enigmatically. Her
body was covered with flowers.]

The narrator's testimony again interweaves gothic elements
connecting nonconventional sexual relationships to a preoccupation with physical and psychological limits. Ana not only
calls attention to geographical limits (the boundaries defined by
the placement of the cabin in the woods), but also calls attention
to the limits of the physical bodies of the characters involved.
By locating the killing and preservation of Gloria's body in a remote, sparsely decorated cabin, the narrator situates her readers
outside culture and civilization. It is a solitary world wherein
unspeakable atrocities occur. The innocent hikers who unwittingly venture into the crime scene to avoid the rainstorm, and
later the Civil Guard, represent intrusive elements impinging on
the transgressions that take place in this secret world.
    Regarding the physical limits of the body and the violent act
of taxidermy itself within this framework, at no time does the

narrator give us any indication of how, exactly, Hans kills or preserves Gloria's body. Ana includes no reference regarding the actual dissection of the cadaver, the tools used to perform the process, the removing of bodily fluids, or the stuffing and sewing together of the skin. Thus, though taxidermy has been said to represent "the most literal expression of male violence," it dually represents the unspoken, invisible volatility at the heart of patriarchy.[43] Hans brutally violates the limits of the physical body by murdering Gloria. Rendering her inactive, he quashes any question regarding his own male power and authority. What's more, by dissecting her only to fill her up with whatever elements he deems fit, he validates his own subjectivity and sexual identity within patriarchal culture without appearing to consider or recognize the ramifications of these acts on other such subjects. Indeed, not only does Hans stay at Gloria's side when the hikers enter his cabin, but he remains there until the police arrive to collect him as her murderer. In Gloria's lack of being, her hollow passivity, he reifies and projects his own manliness and desires. Once dead and preserved, she cannot react to him or reject him. She is artfully composed and framed within a "proper" position. As an object of art, she will be eternally gazed upon but will never again be able to see for herself. She will never be able to object to his needs. Likewise, he no longer needs to react to what others might say regarding the murder because he has already reconfirmed and fixed his own identity within the social structure. If his sexuality had been, at any time, in question, the act of killing proves his manly position.

Ana's complicity in Gloria's killing also becomes evident, in part because she incriminates herself in the offense. Pointing out that several gaps remain to be filled regarding the murder, Ana wonders where Hans obtained the roses and gladiola to cover and adorn Gloria's corpse, "El monte bajo de Andratx es absolutamente yermo. Y en enero, sólo en los invernaderos se cultivan rosas y gladiolos. ¿De dónde los sacaba Hans? ¿Quién se los mandaba? Apunto la posibilidad de que tenga un cómplice, un encubridor. Ustedes tienen la obligación de encontrarlo. Pero, en mi delirio, era yo misma quien llevaba flores a Gloria."[44] [The Andratx scrubland is absolutely barren. And in January, only in greenhouses are roses and gladiolas cultivated. Where did Hans get them? Who sent them to him? I'd like to point out that he might possibly have an accomplice, a collaborator. You have the obligation to find him. But, in my delirium, it was I who brought flowers to Gloria.] Though Ana insists her confession results from delirium, a symptom of the trauma she undergoes upon hearing of the demise of Gloria, the innumerable subtleties to which I have alluded establish the real possibility that Ana wanted Gloria killed as much as did Hans. Indeed, if Hans kills with his taxidermy tools, then Ana kills with her pen in writing this sordid testimony of love and murder.

But can the aesthetics of this killing be read in some more positive, if still sexually subversive, way?

To answer this question, I must first state that Carme Riera ultimately tells a story not only of gender oppression, but also of self-determination and independence. While some might suggest that Riera does a disservice to feminist politics, and perhaps most to lesbian readers, because she implies a complicity between Hans and Ana in this murder, I do not believe that this complicity communicates full adherence to patriarchal structures that would construct Gloria as a typical feminized object and victim who suffers at the hands of male cultural authority and violence. Instead of viewing Gloria as having provoked her own oppression by "playing on both teams," attracting both male and female lovers, I believe that the aesthetics of her killing fits into a much more significant literary framework that ironically liberates gender conventions as it seductively fixes them. Gilbert and Gubar discuss this phenomenon in their readings of gothic literature, saying that "women must kill the aesthetic ideal through which they themselves have been killed into art."[45] Rather than accept being "fixed" into art, Gilbert and Gubar declare that female authors and their critics "really must dissect in order to murder."[46] By closely examining and scrutinizing often binary representations of women—so-called angels and monsters—created by women authors, Gilbert and Gubar attempt to better understand what these depictions tell us about the female imagination.[47] Thus, it may be that what appears to be female complicity in women's victimization by men occurs so that authors might free women from their previously "fixed" positions in art. If this is the case, then perhaps Riera's tale of taxidermy attempts to do the same. By first "dissecting" and then stuffing the protagonist, Riera not only frees Gloria from having to inhabit a male-defined position as a female victim, but also liberates the limits of heterosexual and lesbian desire through her pen.

The position of Gloria's corpse at the end of the text is emblematic of this rebellious movement. When the police arrive at the rustic cabin where Hans has kept the preserved body, they find him kneeling beside Gloria. If at first Gloria practiced acts of martyrdom to symbolically purge herself of the sinful history that engendered her, we find that Hans paradoxically elevates her body from a position of base abjection to a position of sacred veneration. Prostrate at her bedside, he now performs in a way that shows he will continue to gaze upon her, worshipping her as a goddess. As her name suggests, he glorifies her in this process. Having implicated herself in the murder by suggesting that it is she who supplied the roses and gladiola that adorn Gloria's corpse, Ana likewise appears to elevate Gloria to the status of the divine. Roses, often representative of erotic love, passion and unity, are profoundly symbolic. Especially useful in Riera's text is the rose as a sign of silence or secrecy, hence the Latin term *sub rosa* (literally meaning "under the rose") used to refer to something confidential.[48] The gladiolus, while perhaps less commonly referred to in literary circles, is equally significant since the flower symbolizes remembrance. Beyond this, the term *gladiolus* derives from the Latin "galdius" meaning "sword."[49] By confessing that she supplied the roses and gladiola with which Hans covered Gloria's body, Ana communicates not only the piercing love the two women shared but also beautifully conveys the sense of secrecy under which their lesbian relationship lay hidden for so long.

Thus, while Hans and Ana work together to "fix" Gloria's sexual identity, allaying their own sexual anxieties and fears, they simultaneously raise their object of desire to the status of the divine. The sexually ambiguous Gloria thereby comes to embody a volatile sexuality that cannot be defined within the status quo of patriarchy. Consequently, Riera not only aligns the violence of this crime within a tradition of aesthetic murder but within a larger literary context that appreciates the act of writing itself as directly aligned with the violation of sociocultural limits. If Hans commits a heinous, unspeakable act in performing taxidermy on Gloria, Ana commits an equally unspeakable transgression by acting together with him. What's more, Ana threatens the normative heteropatriarchal order by continually masking and unmasking her sexual subversions in what is a public, legal document. Although not particularly dangerous by today's standards, where popular literature and horror films alike often include references to violence as well as homosexual and lesbian desire, the Spain of the 1970s was not open to such unambiguously ambiguous sexual deviancy. By creating these characters, especially the figures of Ana and Gloria, Riera takes up a politically charged position outside the text to champion the rights of those who would otherwise be silenced. While neither of these female characters openly affirms her participation in a lesbian affair, innumerable coded references used to refer to their relationship repeatedly challenge the social and political climate of the time. Perhaps most provocative, through these characters, Riera addresses the existence of Sapphic and bisexual desire without treating lesbians or bisexuals as homogeneous. If anything, "Gloria" paints a picture of human sexual desire—heterosexual, bisexual, lesbian, gay—as truly spanning a continuum that paradoxically has no extremes and cannot be fixed.

NOTES

1. Carme Riera, "Gloria," *Te dejo el mar* (Barcelona: Austral, 1991), 89. All subsequent references to "Gloria" are from this Spanish translation. "Gloria" was originally published in Catalan as part of the collection *Te deix, amor, la mar com a penyora* (1975).

2. Both "Te dejo, amor, en prenda el mar" and "Y pongo por testigo a las gaviotas," translated to Spanish by Luisa Cotoner in the collection *Te dejo el mar* (Barcelona: Austral, 1991), were originally published as "Te deix, amor, la mar com a penyora" (1975) and "Je pos per testimoni les gavines" (1977), respectively. Several articles have been written about the intertextual nature of these tales as well as the way in which each individually treats lesbianism. Of special interest are Brad Epps's "Virtual Sexuality: Lesbianism, Loss, and Deliverance in Carme Riera's *"Te deix, amor, la mar com a penyora,"* in *¿Entiendes?: Queer Readings, Hispanic Writings*, eds. Emilie L. Bergmann and Paul Julian Smith (Durham, N.C.: Duke University Press, 1995), 317–45; Inmaculada Pertusa's "Carme Riera: (Un)covering the Lesbian Subject or Simulation of Coming Out?," in *Tortilleras: Hispanic and U.S. Latina Lesbian Expression*, eds. Lourdes Torres and Inmaculada Pertusa, (Philadelphia: Temple University Press, 2003), 35–46; as well as Kathleen Glenn's "Voice, Marginality, and Seduction in the Short Fiction of Carme Riera," in *Recovering Spain's Feminist Tradition*, ed. Lisa Vollendorf (New York: Modern Languages Association, 2001), 374–89; and Maria DiFrancesco's "Absence and Presence: Traces of Sapphic Love in Carme Riera's 'Te dejo, amor, en prenda el mar,'" in *Convergencias Hispánicas: Selected Proceedings and Other Essays on Spanish and Latin American Literature, Film, and Linguistics*, eds. and introd. Elizabeth Scarlett and Howard Wescott (Newark, DE: Cuesta, 2001), 69–78. Both tales invoke the same principle characters. Nonetheless, while the narrator of "Te dejo, amor, en prenda el mar" is named "María," the unnamed teacher/lover who narrates "Y pongo por testigo a las gaviotas" insists that her lover was not named "María" but rather "Marina."

3. To my knowledge, only passing references are made to "Gloria" in the available body of critical literature. For example, Luisa Cotoner mentions Hans as a "personaje claramente decadentista" in her introduction to *Te dejo amor* ("Introducción," 25). Riera, for her part, briefly alludes to "Gloria" in an interview with Geraldine Cleary Nichols found in *Escribir, espacio propio: La-*

foret, Matute, Moix, Tusquets, Riera y Roig por sí mismas (Minneapolis, MN: Institute for the Study of Ideologies and Literature, 1989), 224.

4. See Emilie L. Bergmann and Paul Julian Smith, eds., *¿Entiendes?: Queer Readings, Hispanic Writings* (Durham, N.C.: Duke University Press, 1995); Lourdes Torres and Inmaculada Pertusa, eds., *Tortilleras: Hispanic and U.S. Latina Lesbian Expression* (Philadelphia: Temple University Press, 2003); David William Foster and Roberto Reis, eds., *Bodies and Biases: Sexualities in Hispanic Cultures and Literatures* (Minneapolis: University of Minnesota Press, 1996); David William Foster, ed., *Spanish Writers on Gay and Lesbian Themes* (Westport, CT: Greenwood Press, 1999); Sylvia Molloy and Robert Mckee Irwin, eds., *Hispanisms and Homosexualities* (Durham, N.C.: Duke University Press, 1998); and Josiah Blackmore and Gregory S. Hutcheson, eds., *Queer Iberia: Crossing Cultures, Crossing Sexualities* (Durham, N.C.: Duke University Press, 1999).

5. "Taxidermy," *Oxford English Dictionary*, ed. J.A. Simpson and E.S.C. Weiner. 2nd ed. Oxford: Clarendon Press, 1989. OED Online Oxford University Press. <http://ezproxy.ithaca.edu:2073/cgi/entry/50247808?single=1&query_type=word&queryword=taxidermy&first=1&max_to_show=10>

6. Joel Black, *The Aesthetics of Murder: A Study in Romantic Literature and Contemporary Culture* (Baltimore: Johns Hopkins University Press, 1991), 12.

7. Ibid., 12.

8. Thomas De Quincey, "On Murder Considered as One of the Fine Arts," in *On Murder*, ed., intro. and notes Robert Morrison. New York: Oxford University Press, 2006), 11.

9. Thomas De Quincey, "On the Knocking at the Gate in Macbeth," in *On Murder*, 4–5.

10. Robert Morrison, "Introduction," in *On Murder*, xi.

11. Joel Black, *Aesthetics*, 112.

12. Ibid., 39.

13. In an interview with Kathleen Glenn, Riera definitively states, "I believe that a writer's first mission is to seduce, because the world is full of books, and if you don't seduce the reader in the first few lines, your book will surely not be read and, in that case, why publish it? Therefore, seduction is an absolute necessity" ("Conversation with Carme Riera" in *Moveable Margins: The Narrative Art of Carme Riera*, eds. Mary S. Vasquez, Mirella Servodidio, and Kathleen M. Glenn, 39–57 (Lewisburg: Bucknell University Press, 1999), 40).

14. Riera, "Gloria," 85.

15. Ibid., 90.

16. Ibid.

17. Claude J. Summers, ed. *The Gay and Lesbian Literary Heritage: A Reader's Companion to the Writers and Their Works, From Antiquity to the Present* (New York: Routledge, 2002), 312.

18. Eve Kosovsky Sedgwick, *The Coherence of Gothic Conventions* (New York: Arno, 1980), 38–39.

19. Riera, "Gloria," 88–89.

20. Ibid., 100.

21. Ibid., 89.

22. Ibid., 86–87.

23. I cannot but wonder whether the author intentionally wished to make a play on words by implying that Gloria had acquired the accent of the Canary islands.

24. Riera, "Gloria," 89 (my italics).

25. Mark Seltzer, *Serial Killers: Death and Life in America's Wound Culture* (New York: Routledge, 1998), 6.

26. Ibid., 3.

27. Riera, "Gloria," 92 (my italics).

28. Tania Modleski, *The Women Who Knew Too Much: Hitchcock and Feminist Theory* (New York: Routledge, 1989), 5.

29. Several parallels exist between Alfred Hitchcock's classic horror thriller *Psycho* and Riera's "Gloria." First, both Hitchcock's Norman Bates and Riera's Hans share the unusual hobby of avian taxidermy, and both make references to the bird-like characteristics of the women. What's more, both the movie and the short story include sexually ambiguous male characters who brutally kill their respective objects of desire and then preserve these women through taxidermy. Finally, although Norman Bates works at the family business of running a hotel, Hans is in Mallorca on behalf of a Swiss bank interested in building hotels in the region. In a personal interview with Riera concerning the subject, I asked the author if she had been influenced in her writing by Hitchcock's *Psycho*. She refuted any coincidence as just that: coincidence.

30. Tania Modleski, *Women Who Knew Too Much*, 8.

31. Riera, "Gloria," 85.

32. Ibid., 86.

33. Ibid., 85–86.

34. Alision Maginn. "Female Erotica in Post-Franco Spain: The Will-to-Disturb," *Ciberletras* 8 (2002), http://www.lehman.cuny.edu/ciberletras/v08/maginn.html.

35. Lesbian voices and depictions of lesbian identities remained largely invisible during the Franco years. Ana María Moix proved a noteworthy exception to this rule, publishing the novels *Julia* (Barcelona: Seix Barral, 1970) as well as *Walter ¿por qué te fuiste?* (Barcelona: Barral Editores, 1973) during this period. Not surprisingly, considering it contained a myriad of sexual taboos, including sodomy and masturbation, as well as lesbian and bisexual characters, censors edited the latter no fewer than forty-five times before finally allowing the book to go to press.

36. Riera, "Gloria," 89 (my italics).

37. Ibid., 88 (my italics).

38. Ibid., 91.

39. Ibid., 88.

40. Judith Butler, *Gender Trouble: Feminism and Subversion of Identity* (New York: Routledge, 1990), 6.

41. Ibid., 6.

42. Riera, "Gloria," 99–100.

43. Jeffrey Niesel, "The Horror of Everyday Life: Taxidermy, Aesthetics, and Consumption in Horror Films," *Journal of Criminal Justice and Popular Culture*, 4(2), (1994), http://www.albany.edu/scj/jcjpc/vol2is4/horror.html.

44. Riera, "Gloria," 100–1.

45. Sandra Gilbert and Susan Gubar, *The Madwoman in the Attic: The Woman Writer and the Nineteenth-Century Literary Imagination* (New Haven: Yale University Press, 1979), 17.

46. Ibid., 17.

47. Ibid.

48. "Sub-rosa," *Oxford English Dictionary*. http://ezproxy.ithaca.edu:2073/

cgi/entry/50240429/50240429se12?single = 1&query_type = word&queryword
= sub + rosa&first = 1&max_to_show = 10&hilite = 50240429se12.
    49. "Gladiolus," *Oxford English Dictionary.* http://ezproxy.ithaca.edu:
2073/cgi/entry/50095086?.

REFERENCES

Black, Joel. *The Aesthetics of Murder: A Study in Romantic Literature and Contemporary Culture.* Baltimore: Johns Hopkins University Press, 1991.

Butler, Judith. *Gender Trouble: Feminism and Subversion of Identity.* New York: Routledge, 1990.

Cotoner, Luisa. "Introducción." In *Te dejo el mar*, by Carme Riera, 11–34. Barcelona: Austral, 1991.

DeQuincey, Thomas. "On the Knocking at the Gate in Macbeth." In *On Murder*, edited, introduction, and notes by Robert Morrison, 3–7. New York: Oxford University Press, 2006.

———. "On Murder Considered as One of the Fine Arts." In *On Murder*, edited, introduction, and notes by Robert Morrison, 83–84. New York: Oxford University Press, 2006.

Gilbert, Sandra, and Susan Gubar. *The Madwoman in the Attic: The Woman Writer and the Nineteenth-Century Literary Imagination.* New Haven: Yale University Press, 1979.

Hitchcock, Alfred. *Psycho.* 1960. Collector's Edition. Universal City, CA: Universal, 1999.

Maginn, Alison. "Female Erotica in Post-Franco Spain: The Will-to-Disturb." *Ciberletras* 8 (2002). http://www.lehman.cuny.edu/ciberletras/v08/maginn .html.

Modleski, Tania. *The Women Who Knew Too Much: Hitchcock and Feminist Theory.* New York: Routledge, 1989.

Morrison, Robert. "Introduction." In *On Murder*, by Thomas De Quincey, vii–xxvii. New York: Oxford University Press, 2006.

Niesel, Jeffrey. "The Horror of Everyday Life: Taxidermy, Aesthetics, and Consumption in Horror Films." *Journal of Criminal Justice and Popular Culture* 4(2), (1994). http://www.albany.edu/scj/jcjpc/vol2is4/horror.html.

Riera, Carme. *La mitad del alma.* Translated by Carme Riera. Madrid: Alfaguara, 2004.

———. "Gloria." In *Te dejo el mar*, translated by Luisa Cotoner, 85–101. Barcelona: Austral, 1991.

———. "Te dejo, amor, en prenda el mar." In *Te dejo el mar*, translated by Luisa Cotoner, 53–68. Barcelona: Austral, 1991.

———. "Y pongo por testigo a las gaviotas." In *Te dejo el mar*, translated by Luisa Cotoner, 129–39. Barcelona: Austral, 1991.

Sedgwick, Eve. *The Coherence of Gothic Conventions.* New York: Arno, 1980.

Seltzer, Mark. *Serial Killers: Death and Life in America's Wound Culture.* New York: Routledge, 1998.

Summers, Claude J., ed. *The Gay and Lesbian Literary Heritage: A Reader's Companion to the Writers and Their Works, From Antiquity to the Present.* New York: Routledge, 2002.

Flavia Company: From Lesbian Passion to Gender Trouble

Inmaculada Pertusa-Seva

> it is important not only to understand how the terms of gender are instituted, naturalized, and established as presuppositional but to trace the moments where the binary system of gender is disputed and challenged, where the coherence of the categories are put into question, and where the very social life of gender turns out to be malleable and transformable.
>
> —Judith Butler

Flavia company's prolific literary career began in 1987 when, at the age of 23, this young Argentinean-Spanish writer published her first novel, *Querida Nélida*,[1] almost by chance.[2] Combining journalism and translation with literary writing, in the last nineteen years Flavia Company has published ten novels, several collections of stories and a significant number of articles in the *ABC*, the *Vanguardia, Diario 16, El periódico de Cataluña, Avui, Revista de libros de Madrid*, and *Quimera*, among others. Looking at the themes that have appeared in her fictional world, we can see how Company includes many different aspects of the human condition, perhaps insisting more on those connected to interpersonal relationships: love and lack of affection, passion and lust, and the limits between friendship and desire. Along with these almost universal commonplaces in her fiction, we find several stories of love between women that, far from classifying Company as a lesbian writer, facilitate an experimental and innovative frame to her writing. Among the large number of novels written by Company, we see *Querida Nélida* (1987), *Dame placer* (1999)[3] and *Melalcor* (2000)[4] as novels where this "[autora] inquieta y de múltiples registros" [anxious author of multiple levels] according to Eva Gutiérrez Pardina, and "de obra autorreflexiva que . . . se plantea y resuelve desafíos formales en diálogo íntimo con la tradición literaria que la precede y la acompaña de modos diversos" [of autorreflexive work that . . . considers and solves formal challenges in intimate dialogue with the literary tradition that precedes her and accompanies her in different ways] in the opinion of Meri Torras,[5] moves from an inescapably precocious and intimate narrative to an obsessive and self-referential monologue, to culminate in her most ambitious narrative experiment, where the limits between time and space, identity and gender, are questioned in order to introduce a defamiliarizing vision of the heterosexual system that affirms the possibility of sexual expressions that exceed the predominant gender norm.

Even though Company's literary production is characterized by the structural and formal diversity of almost each one of her works, it is important to recognize that this creative originality parts nonetheless from a common aesthetic and ideological conception that is difficult to ignore when connecting her work. In Company's creative universe we find *Querida Nélida*, written as an epistolary narrative between the two protagonists; *Dame placer*, that reproduces the uninterrupted monologue of the narrator with a psychoanalyst; and *Melalcor*, where the narrative voice displayed in brief sections unexpectedly changes from first to third person as the sexual attributes of the main characters also change.[6] It is necessary not so much to recognize the differences that make the works so original, but rather the similarities that connect them and, more concretely, the subversive elements of each text that model the destabilization of the power strategies of the dominant heterosexual discourse in which they are inscribed.

Initially, the bonds necessary to connect the literary production of Company in general, and the three novels that we discuss here in particular, are revealed by the author herself not only through her fictional work, but also by means of playful incursions in literary reviews and newspaper columns, and in the few interviews with the author that have been published. In a 2001 interview for the magazine *Barcelona Review*, Company gave the following response to Ana Alciana's question about whether a writer always writes the same book:

Fins a cert punt, aquesta idea que sempre s'escriu el mateix llibre és un tòpic. Només fins a cert punt, insisteixo. El que passa és que una és sempre—més o menys—la mateixa persona i, encara que pugui evolucionar, **l'obra és el reflex més directe de l'aprenentatge, de la**

maduració, de la percepció sobre la vida i el món. I de la relació amb el que t'envolta i amb els altres. En aquest sentit es podria parlar, sí, d'una sèrie d'inquietuds o de temes recurrents. En el meu cas podrien ser, potser, la frontera entre ficció i realitat—entre bogeria i enteniment—, les relacions humanes, la incertesa sobre l'existència d'alguna veritat, la llibertat.] (Alciana 2001) (emphasis added).[7]

[To a point, the idea that one always writes the same book is a cliché. What happens is that one is, more or less, the same person, and while one can evolve, **the work is the most direct reflection of learning, maturation, the perception of life and the world.** And of your relation with what surrounds you and with others. In this sense it would be possible to speak of a recurrent series of personal interests and repeated themes. In my case they could be the border between fiction and reality—between madness and understanding—human relations, the uncertainty about the existence of some truth, freedom.] (emphasis added).

Although each of the three novels that we analyze here is an independent work,[8] the relation that we propose between the three takes into consideration Company's conception of the creative development of her writing. In the three novels we can see how the protagonists personify the same learning process characterized by the maturation of their "perception on life and the world," although with different results in each case. In our reading of the three novels, life and the world are metaphors for the ability of the lesbian subject (the lesbian life) to exist in the heteronorm that denies her existence (the heterosexual world). In this way, each protagonist expresses her uncertainty about the meaning of her identity, looking for answers through intense physical and emotional connections with another woman and trying to create a space in which to express the lesbian identity denied by the heteronorm. We also see in the three novels a progression of the representation of lesbian sexuality that goes from the exposition of an intimate relationship between two women in *Querida Nélida,* to the confirmation of an absolute passion in *Dame placer,* concluding with the proposal of a fluid lesbian sexuality in *Melalcor* that introduces gender trouble, offering an alternative gender performance in dispute with heterosexual norms.

QUERIDA NÉLIDA: THE JOURNEY BEGINS

Although Company wrote her first novel when she was only seventeen years old, in this novel we can find the aesthetic and conceptual germ of the two later novels discussed here. Characterized by a subtle lyricism, *Querida Nélida* recreates an elaborate process of self-awareness in the two main characters through the attempt of Nélida, the narrator-protagonist, to persuade her new friend, Celia, to embark with her on an incredible trip that she has been preparing for several years:

> En un lejano tiempo, donde nada se reviente contra las paredes, manchándolas de tinta, emprenderé un largo viaje, de modo que no regrese al punto de partida en dos años, igual que mi acompañante; que sean puntos imprescindibles en mi itinerario un mínimo de diecisiete países (19).

> [In a distant time, where nothing will burst against the walls, staining them with ink, I will undertake a long trip that will not take me back to the point of departure in two years, the same for my companion; essential points in my itinerary will be a minimum of seventeen countries.]

The journey is a trip conceived carefully by the protagonist and written down rigorously in six notebooks, organized with the same disturbing meticulousness with which she started her initial investigation to prepare her future adventure. Each notebook is dedicated to a particular aspect of the journey, including the profile of the person who would share the trip with her. Her accidental encounter with Celia during some archaeology lectures at the Universidad Autónoma de Barcelona, and the subsequent friendship between them makes Nélida decide that Celia would be her ideal companion, as she possesses the characteristics drawn up by Nélida:

> Penetrante.
> Abierta en círculos por el lirismo más profundo.
> Cubierta por los frutos divinos de la tierra.
> Inmortal casi. Inmortal apenas (25).

> [Penetrating.
> Opened in circles by the deepest lyricism.
> Covered by the divine fruits of the Earth.
> Inmortal almost. Inmortal hardly.]

While Celia initially rejects Nélida's offer to complete this unexpected trip with her ("No es normal para nadie que alguien desconocido le proponga un largo viaje redactado y acordado en un contrato que se firmará ante notario dos días antes de comenzar la aventura" [It is not normal for anybody that a stranger proposes a long trip written up and accepted under a contract that will have to be signed in the presence of a notary two days before beginning the adventure] (17), the two women continue developing their friendship through necessary epistolary exchanges due to the continuous and planned trips of Nélida and through physical encounters where the two women enjoy themselves inventing incredible and somewhat dangerous games, such as the proposed trip. Nélida comments: "Ella era muy hábil para los juegos. A mí me fascinaba crear aquellas competiciones minuciosas, meticulosamente preparadas, arduas, difíciles. Nuestros juegos duraban días, a veces un mes [. . .] Incluso más" [She was very good at the games. It was fascinating for me to develop those detailed competitions, meticulously prepared, arduous, difficult. Our games lasted days, sometimes a month . . . Even more] (60).

While the obsession for the trip begins to attract Celia to Nélida, the relationship between the two women becomes more personal, more intimate, to the point that both feel the need to have constant contact with each other. Although it is Nélida who is the first to express her attraction for Celia ("Celia me gustaba cada día más. Me sorprendía a todas horas con su buen humor" [I liked Celia more every day. She surprised me at all hours with her good humor] (29)), Celia also ends up formulating her attraction to Nélida, to the point of confessing to her: "No es el misterio lo que de ti me interesa, sino todo aquello que no lo es, todo lo que dejas entrever, con esa forma tan tuya de mostrarte a los sentidos de quien te mira y observa" [It is not your mysteriousness that interests me, but everything that is not mysterious, everything that you let me see, with that way you have of showing yourself to the senses of the one who watches and observes you] (48), adding later: "Ayúdame. Ahora más que nunca necesito ayuda, tu ayuda. Sé que estás ahí, al otro lado de las cartas, sé que estas palabras son ahora tuyas [. . .] No, no retires la vista, sigue conmigo un instante más. Te lo ruego, ven" [Help me. Now more than ever I need help, your help. I know that you are there, on the other side of the letters, I know that these words are now yours . . . No, don't look away, stay with me a bit longer. I beg you, come] (52). The early representation of this mutual attraction will culminate with the process of identification of each woman with the image of the other so common in the expression of the lesbian sexuality,[9] to the extent of referring to each other as part of oneself, like something they themselves created by means of word games:

> Querida Celia: Acabo de descubrir por qué te intereso yo y por qué te interesa mi vida y mis planes: porque nada es verdad en mí, porque absolutamente nada parece verdad. Y lo que no parece, no es. ¿No tienes miedo de estar escribiendo a nadie? ¿De estarte inventando a alguien y creyéndotelo? ¿Y si no existo? Y si sólo parezco? A lo mejor nada es como tú crees" (51).

> [Dear Celia: I have just discovered why I interest you and why you are interested in my life and my plans: because nothing is true in me, because absolutely nothing seems true. And what it does not seem to be, it is not. Aren't you scared of writing to nobody? Scared of inventing somebody and believing it? What if I do not exist? What if I only seem to exist? Perhaps nothing is as you believe it is.]

This first approach to the recognition of oneself through the desire of the other, in our opinion, will compel Company, two years after her first literary incursion, to return to the ideas presented in her first novel in this search for desire through the identification between lovers. Likewise, in Company's review of Andalusian poet Concha García's collection, *Lo de ella,* her reflections on the poems agree with the conclusion of *Querida Nélida,* where the two protagonists literally end up transformed into one another, forcing the reader to ask herself if Celia really existed, or if perhaps Nélida and Celia are the same character. Company wrote in 2005:

> Es también *Lo de ella* un libro sobre la identidad, como no puede dejar de serlo un libro que verse sobre el amor, sobre la distinción entre el yo y el otro—o la otra—, **sobre la fusión de dos, sobre la pluralidad del uno.** La identidad queda reflejada en una ruptura gramatical absoluta, que da cuenta de la fragmentariedad del ser, su multiplicidad irreconciliable y la paz, a veces, de encontrarse con el otro—o la otra—y de encontrar en ella el reconocimiento, la calma que otorga ser vista, ser creída, ser amada (emphasis added).[10]

> [*Lo de ella* is also about self-identity, as any book that talks about love, about the distinction between the self and the other—or the female other—, **about the fusion of two, about the plurality of one** must be. Self-identity is reflected in an absolute grammatical rupture that accounts for the fragmentation of being, its irreconcilable multiplicity, and about the feeling of peace that sometimes comes from finding oneself with the other—or the female other—and from

finding in her the recognition, the calm that comes with being seen, being believed, being loved.] (emphasis added).

Although there is a lack of explicit description in the text of the sexual contacts between the two women, as we have seen, the complicity that arises between Celia and Nélida in their encounters, their epistles, and their games demonstrates the existence of a physical relationship between the two women marginal to the heterosexual norm in which Celia is placed by living with a man who seems to be her current partner. The development of the relationship between Celia and Nélida from a simple friendship to a more intense connection, demonstrated by the mutual understanding that develops between the two women, leads us, at the end of the narration, to the (con)fusion of the identity of both women, who become a single one. Celia writes: "Te recuerdo, sencillamente toda. No podría olvidar nada. Es como sentirte en mí como a mí misma [. . .] ¿Has dicho esto ya? ¿Lo has dicho tú antes?" [I remember you, purely completely. I couldn't forget anything. I feel you in me as I feel myself . . . Have you said this already? Have you said this before?] This (con)fusion of identities is reiterated at the end of the novel by the text itself when any mention of the addressee and the sender is omitted. The last letters between both women are presented without signatures, creating *the fusion of two* and *the plurality of one* by denying the existence of each one independently and anticipating, without being clear yet, the concepts that Company will take up again years later in *Dame placer:*

Y en los momentos de lucidez, ¿no estás asustada? ¿Por las noches no te corroe un miedo extraño? ¿No sientes como un abandono de todo? ¿Y dónde tus ojos sino en los míos? ¿Y la memoria? ¿Vas más allá con los recuerdos de la época en que te encontraste en unas conferencias . . . ? Tal vez creíste que me habías encontrado a mí. ¿Y has creído que existo fuera de ti? ¿Por qué? Y los ojos en los ojos, y las manos en las manos. Y esas palabras . . .

Tuya

Querida mía:
Te he olvidado. Podemos empezar. Me he olvidado.

Sinceramente tuya (67).

[And in the moments of lucidity, aren't you scared? At night, doesn't a strange fear eat away at you? Don't you feel abandoned by everything? And where are your eyes if not reflected in mine? And your memory? Do you go beyond the memories of the time when you found yourself at a conference . . . ? Perhaps you thought that you had found me. You have believed that I exist outside of you? Why? And eyes reflected in eyes, and hands clasped in hands. And those words . . .

Yours

My love: I have forgotten you. We can begin. I have forgotten myself.
Sincerely yours.]

DAME PLACER AND YOU WILL GIVE ME LIFE

In the same way that the connections between the literary review of García's poems and Company's first novel help us recognize the possibility of a lesbian relationship able to attribute identity to its subjects, the connection between another review written by the author and her novel *Dame placer* leads us to consider the use of the confession and the search for/revelation of the truth as weapons that destabilize the heterosystem in the text.

In one of the articles that Company wrote for the Sunday cultural supplement of the Spanish newspaper *ABC* in 2003,[11] the author meditated upon a phrase by Grace Paley that says, "When truth finds its level, it floats." Company considers in this short article the relation between truth, or as she puts it the "ilusión o el anhelo de la verdad" [the illusion or the yearning of truth], and reality, concluding that fundamentally humans have replaced truth with reality, in spite of their being two completely different things. The writer, starting off from Paley's maxim, asks herself what the level of truth is, concluding later:

Naturalmente, el del conocimiento necesario para identificarla. A menor conocimiento, menor nivel y, por lo tanto, menos posibilidades de que la verdad suelte el lastre que supone la ignorancia y suba hasta la superficie para hacerse visible flotando ante ojos capaces de reconocerla y, lo que es más importante aún, decirla (*Diario ABC*).

[Naturally, the knowledge necessary to identify it. Lesser knowledge, a lower level and, therefore, fewer possibilities that truth will lose the ballast of ignorance and will rise to the surface to become visible, floating before eyes capable of recognizing it and, what is even more important, of saying it.]

Following the lead drawn up in *Querida Nélida,* in *Dame placer* (2005) Company anticipates the possibility of finding "el reconocimiento, la calma que otorga ser vista, ser creída, ser amada" [the recognition, the calm that comes with being seen, being believed, being loved] by another woman. In this novel, published almost six years before her reflections on the work of García and Paley, the narrator-protagonist reveals little by little by means of a lengthy monologue before an anonymous listener, the details of an almost involuntary passion "proveniente de un reconocimiento sucedido más allá de [sus] voluntades, de [sus] ojos, de [sus] manos" [originating from the recognition beyond their will, their eyes, and their hands] (80), to apparently acknowledge the truth of her situation, to make it float to the surface and thus to be able to say it. In a process similar to a session with a psychoanalyst, the narrator accepts the game that her imposed female interlocutor offers her in order to "say" as a confession everything that she has lived ("Vivir, he vivido, y por eso hoy puedo confesarlo" [To live, I have lived, and for that reason today I can confess it] (96)). In doing so she openly discovers the details of her lesbian relationship, recognizing herself as such in the process. The story confessed by the protagonist and lived between her lover and herself, resembles a passionate experience taken to its limits: the narrator accidentally sees her future lover in a department store and, hypnotized by her eyes, she decides to follow her. They arrive at the hotel where the woman is staying, and after the anticipated mutual seduction, amplified by the circumstance of anonymity, the two women begin a passionate sexual relationship that will lead the protagonist to feel a deep obsession for the other woman, with the relationship between them bordering on sadomasochism, ending in the final abandonment of the narrator by her lover after a love triangle between them and another woman.

In his *History of Sexuality,* the philosopher Michel Foucault established that the confession, a coercive weapon used by the dominant system to control its subjects, is

> a ritual of discourse in which the speaking subject is also the subject of the statement; it is also a ritual that unfolds within a power relationship, for one does not confess without the presence (or virtual presence) of a partner who is not simply the interlocutor but the authority who requires the confession, prescribes and appreciates it, and intervenes in order to judge, punish, forgive, console, and reconcile; a ritual in which the truth is corroborated in order to be formulated; and finally, a ritual in which the expression alone,

independently of its external consequences, produces intrinsic modifications in the person who articulates it: it exonerates, redeems, and purifies him; it unburdens him of his wrongs, liberates him, and promises him salvation.[12]

In a confession we have a subject who is aware of past events, and because of that she has the knowledge of the truth she sets out to reveal initially. Thanks to this privileged knowledge, the subject confessing will speak of her experience from her own point of view, selecting the information and arranging it in the form she wants, thus being able to control the outcomes of such a confession. But when approaching an utterance identified as confessional, it is important to consider that behind the act of "saying" a truth there also hides a mechanism of control that has to be unmasked to arrive at the extent of its effects and intentions. Therefore, when considering *Dame placer* as a confession, we must look beyond what is presented as reality, as the truth, in order to destabilize the normative system by forcing all that is repressed (the lesbian sexuality) to float to the surface and become visible for eyes unwilling to recognize it in the first place.

Located inside a heterosexual system that fights to maintain its hegemonic power over disruptive sexual behaviors, the act of confessing has to be considered as a method of control used to impose gender heteronorms, in other words, the bionomic division of the feminine/masculine, male/female that requires a heterosexual behavior fit for the social norm. Taking as a point of departure the ideas developed by Foucault about the relation between power and truth, Judith Butler states that "[t]o veer from the gender norm is to produce the aberrant example that regulatory powers (medical, psychiatric, and legal, to name a few) may quickly exploit to shore up the rationale for their own continuing regulatory zeal."[13] The confession's ritual, in the initial proposal of Foucault, is validated from beginning to end in *Dame placer* by means of the exclusive use of a narrative voice in the first person, introduced in an incessant monologue that fails to find rest even in the absent limits of the chapters; the narrative voice opens and closes its own discourse without allowing any other voice to participate in the narration and in so doing controls and monopolizes the production of meaning in the text. Openly rejecting any possible intervention from her interlocutor, and denying also the possibility that her interventions could have some effect on her, the protagonist says: "No espero contestación, no se inquiete. Sé muy bien que no la tiene, que no puede tenerla, o que a mí no me convencería, que es lo mismo" [I don't expect an answer, don't worry. I know very well that you don't have one, that you cannot have one, or that it would not convince me, which is the same] (95). The narrator later silences her listener by responding to her own questions or interpreting the received gestures: "¿Por qué actúo así? ¿Qué me pasa?" [Why do I act like this? What is happening to me?], she asks her listener rhetorically on one occasion, soon to instruct her: "No, prefiero que no me haga preguntas. Deje que le cuente. Escúcheme. Seré breve" [No, I prefer that you do not ask me questions. Allow me to tell you. Listen to me. I will be quick] (13). The silence that the narrator imposes on her interlocutor amplifies the control that the narrator has on the exposed discourse and on the result of her confession, on the authenticity of the revealed truth, and therefore on the effect that she hopes to produce with her declaration.

Initially, and taking advantage of the possibilities of her personal circumstances, the narrator admits her submission to the social heteronorm that required the confession as the most logical option to confront her situation, entering voluntarily into the power dynamics that she will disturb through her enunciation. She explains:

A ver, resulta que me había encerrado en los sesenta metros cuadrados del piso que tengo alquilado en el ensanche barcelonés a olvidarme de todo aunque sabía que era imposible, hasta que en el contestador ha sonado la voz del administrador de la finca. Que me busque un abogado, que me van a echar por falta de pago. Que ya me han echado, en realidad. Por eso estoy aquí con usted, en parte, ¿no? Y normal. Yo lo entiendo. (14)

[Let's see, I had locked myself up in the sixty square meters of the flat I have rented in Barcelona's *Ensanche* to forget everything, although I knew that it was impossible, until the voice of the landlord sounded on the answering machine. He said that I need to look for a lawyer, that they are going to evict me for skipping my rent payments. They have already thrown me out, as a matter of fact. That is why I am here, partly, isn't it? Of course. I understand.]

The protagonist, harassed as she is by the "regulatory powers" (medical, psychiatric, and legal), introduces the possibility that there is another reason for her to be speaking with her interlocutor, while she unveils the details that followed the first encounter with her lover, accepting the situation where she is now. "Por eso estoy aquí con usted, en parte, ¿no?" [That is why I am here, partly, isn't it?] (14), she says, suggesting that, in addition to the mere revelation of the facts, there is another reason for her confession before the officials that require it. This is perhaps the first indication of the game the protagonist is going to develop by means of the revelation of her secret before the medical power that more than anything "ritualiza institucionalmente la mirada del otro en tanto que interpreta sus palabras según formas organizadas de existencia; es decir, entiende el sentimiento amoroso según unos códigos de comportamiento legislados y aceptados" [institutionally ritualizes the glance of the other, while interpreting her words according to organized forms of existence; that is to say, it understands love according to legislated and accepted codes of behavior] (Torras, 631). From the beginning the narrator casually informs her listener that her true desire would be to be able to speak directly with her lover and not with her ("Lo que pasa es que lo que a mí me gustaría, en realidad, es decirle todo esto a ella, no a usted" [What's going on is that what I would really like to do is to say all this to her, not to you.] (13), to finally admit that what she wanted to do was to write a letter to her lover, a letter "que le diga lo que le estoy diciendo a usted, sin más" [that will allow me to tell her what I am telling you, simply] with the intention of convincing her to return to her. The effect of this double revelation is not perceived until the end of her storytelling process: neither her interlocutor nor the implicit reader (perhaps her lover finally reading the letter that the narrator creates from her confession through the text that we are reading) can appreciate the reach of that first complaint—her desire to speak with her lover and not with her interlocutor—until it is too late, that is, at the end of her confession, when the seduction caused by the promise to reveal the truth, to make it float to the surface, becomes the strategy used by the narrator, by the text, to take control of the power and the effect of her confession when reliving with it the lesbian passion denied by the heterosexual system in which she resides as a speaking subject. "La verdad, cuando encuentra su nivel, flota [. . .] para hacerse visible [. . .] ante ojos capaces de reconocerla y, lo que es más importante aún, decirla" [When truth finds its level, it floats . . . to become visible . . . for eyes capable of recognizing it and, what is even more important, of saying it].

In *Dame placer* the act of confessing (to speak of what stays hidden) the lesbian relationship (a sexual relationship against the heterosexual norm where it is socially inscribed) provides the protagonist the opportunity to express the passion already lived, not only to relive it and enjoy it again by the act of orally experiencing it once more, but also as a strategy to make it real (visible) in the social system that represses it (ignores it). As Butler points out, "Confession does not simply bring an already existing desire of an already accomplished deed before the analyst, but alters the desire and the deed so that neither was what they become once they are stated for the analyst" (Butler, *Undoing Gender*, 165), or as we see it, the confessed desires were not recognized as such for some (the heteronorma), or freely expressed by others (the repressed lesbian subjects). If we agree with Butler that sexual confessions are a way to reproduce the body (Butler, *Undoing Gender*, 172), we can see *Dame placer* as a process of creating the lesbian body by means of the creative function of speech in the ability that language has to represent, to recreate the body. Foucault's idea that the repression of sex is no more than a control strategy to regulate individuals develops from the emphasis that power puts on reproducing confessions that disclose repressed sexual acts. The confession in this frame becomes the result of the necessity of recognition of our sexual repressions. The subject of the speech—the producer of the confession—must be interpreted through what she says she has done or thought, and the receptor of the confession—the coercive power—encourages the production of the confession to be able to impose on the speaking subject the normalization that defines it (Butler, *Undoing Gender*, 163).

In this confessional speech unfolded by the narrator, the sexual relationship between the two women is displayed within the safety of the confession and without apparent concealments or moralistic reproaches. This characteristic of the text is increased by the detailed descriptions of the sexual act between the two women that emphasize the feeling of redemption experienced by the narrator by being able to openly admit encounters that in other circumstances were characterized by the privacy of the closed space, forced as the two women were to maintain heterosexual behavior in public places:

> Salíamos a la calle, por supuesto, porque nos gustaba que nos viera y ver el mundo; a comprar, a pasear, a tomar una copa, pero entonces, de repente, teníamos que refugiarnos en cualquier rincón para que nuestras bocas pudieran besarse, o nos metíamos en el lavabo de un bar cualquiera, o en los vestuarios de unos grandes almacenes. (82).

[We went out, of course, because we liked to be seen and to see the world; to go shopping, to take a walk, to have a drink, but then, suddenly, we had to hide in some corner so that our mouths could kiss, or we went into a bar's restroom, or to the fitting rooms in a department store.]

Anticipating the enjoyment of sexual pleasure, "la más poderosa de las drogas" [the most powerful of any drugs] (18), the encounters between the two women are meticulously described by the narrator, always focused on the dogma "dame placer y te daré la vida" [give me pleasure and I will give you life] that guided the passion experienced between the two women and that now constantly accompany the memories of the narrator. Thus, we read descriptions like:

sus pechos duros, amplios, generosos, como manzanas verdes, crujientes, brillantes y dulces a la vez. Hambrienta de mi boca hambrienta. Sonoras, jugosas, perfectas (38).

[her firm, ample, generous breasts, like green, crispy, shining, sweet apples all at once. Hungry for my hungry mouth. Melodic, juicy, perfect].

Se inquietó. Empecé a morderla. Empezó a gemir. Los suyos no eran gemidos normales, como los de las demás mujeres que yo había conocido (56).

[She got impatient. I began to bite her. She began to moan. Hers were not normal moanings, not like those of the other women whom I had known].

No tardamos mucho ya en estar las dos desnudas, bajo la sábana, y ya no en el sofá, sino en el suelo tibio y crujiente de madera. Me cogió con la mano abierta por las nalgas y me tumbó boca arriba, apoyó mi cintura en su muslo tenso . . . [. . .] Llevó su mano libre hasta mis pezones y, primero uno, después el otro, los pellizcó con suavidad, como si estuviera quitándole sal de los dedos. Yo acerqué la boca hasta sus pechos y empecé a comérmelos con delicadeza, sin apresurarme, como si de verdad no hubiera deseado tenerla toda sin más dilación. Entonces fue cuando sentí que me desmayaba: la noté dentro de pronto. Se había clavado en mí toda entera. Había desaparecido de mi lado y buceaba ambiciosa por mi interior. Se movía inquieta, me golpeaba, me arañaba, me amaba ahí, desde mí misma (63–64).

[We did not take long to undress, under the sheet, and no longer on the sofa, but on the warm and creaking wood floor. She grabbed my

buttocks with her open hand and laying me face up, she placed my
waist on her tense thigh . . . She took her free hand to my nipples
and, first one, then the other, pinched tenderly as if she was cleaning
salt from her fingers. I put my mouth to her breasts and began to
nibble them gently, without hurrying, as if I didn't really want to
have her without further delay. Then I felt like I was fainting: I felt
her inside of me suddenly. She had entered me completely. She had
disappeared from my side and she was diving ambitiously through
me. She was constantly moving, striking me, scratching me, loving
me there, from within myself.]

Mi garganta añora el sabor de su placer, el ardor de su sexo y sus lati-
dos, sus contracciones, su fuerza. El vocabulario de su lengua y el
lenguaje de sus dedos. Mis manos precisan penetrarla y hacérsele dentro, convertirla en laguna, en río, en alud; que ella sea miel y yo
abeja, y luego ella miel (106).

[My throat longs for the taste of her pleasure, the ardor of her sex and
its beats, its contractions, its force. The vocabulary of her tongue
and the language of her fingers. My hands need to penetrate her and
take her from within, to turn her into a lagoon, a river, an avalanche;
and then she becomes honey and I a bee, and later she becomes
honey again.]

The description of these very intimate moments between the
two women is justified by the narrator, by the need to explain to
her listener the origin and effect of her feelings towards her
lover, and also of those of her lover towards her. "Por eso, aunque no tuviera sentido contar la historia de principio a fin, tal
cual fue, algunos datos resultaban imprescindibles, por ejemplo
para entender que nuestro primer encuentro fuera algo tan sensual y brutal al mismo tiempo" [For that reason, although it did
not make sense to tell the story from start to finish, as it happened, some details are essential to understand why, for instance, our first encounter was something so sensual and brutal
at the same time] (147). The narrator insists on explaining that
both of them were fully aware that their relationship was something that took them beyond their own limits, beyond not only
their senses but themselves. It was, as the narrator says, "una
pasión que provenía de un reconocimiento sucedido más allá de
nuestras voluntades, de nuestros ojos, de nuestras manos" [a passion that came from a recognition that happened beyond our
control, our eyes, our hands] (79), a passion that little by little is
going to produce the same identification between the two
women that we saw arise between Celia and Nélida in *Querida*

Nélida. As the sexual relationship reaches an almost unbearable climax, the narrator begins to lose her identity, to be only a part of the one without whom she is not going to be able to live. "Siempre he sabido que perderla a ella sería extraviarme a mí misma" [I have always known that to lose her would be like losing myself] (47). "Ser la tierra, ser de tierra, ser de ella, ser sí misma en cada embate, ser nada en el momento de sentirlo todo. Olvidarse de los nombres y conservar el único posible. Ser yo las dos. Ser yo siendo ella. Ellas" [To be earth, to be made of earth, to be of her, to be her in each attack, to be nothing at the moment of feeling everything. To forget the names and to keep the only possible one. I being both of us. To be I being she. They] (35).

The revelation of her lesbianism, and the recognition of the loss of her identity and self-control due to the passion felt for the other woman, places her inside the limits imposed by the hegemonic power on the social subject (her mother had even said to her: "Yo sé muy bien que tú no eres así" [I know very well that you are not like that] (62)), apparently justifying the necessity to be judged, to be punished, pardoned, consoled, and reconciled by the power that demands the confession. She tells her interlocutor: "Tiene que creerme, ¿puede? La verdadera dimensión de lo ocurrido sólo encontrará razón de ser al entrar en contacto con usted" [You must believe me, can you? The true dimension of what happened will only find its reason for being when put in contact with you] (131). Nevertheless, the sexual details exposed, the revelations are not so much the needed truths to release her and to save her from her "faults," but rather are used by the narrator to manipulate the effect of the confession that remains incomplete because it lacks sufficient elements of credibility.

Throughout her confession the narrator controls the moment at which she is going to recall the details that produced the break in the relationship. In spite of having disclosed intimate scenes to her interlocutor, giving the impression of exposing all the truth of the situation, the protagonist prolongs the moment when she will explain the reason why her lover abandoned her. After confirming the need for the description of the indispensable details, granting herself the power to tell the truth, the narrator doubts her capacity to remember everything from an objective point of view ("Es curioso, pero a medida que hago memoria de mis propios recuerdos me da por acordarme de los suyos también, de los que nunca compartimos" [It is peculiar, but as I recall my own memories I tend to remember hers as well, memories we never shared before] (113)), introducing ambiguity and doubt into her speech. She announces to her interlocutor: "Me duele la cabeza. Sabe de sobra lo que eso supone. No me gusta. Pierdo los códigos y no entiendo nada. Igual que una rebelión." [My head hurts. You know very well what that means. I do not like it. I lose the codes and I do not understand anything. Just like a rebellion] (131). From this moment on, the story of the narrator begins to lose the touch with reality that it had maintained previously; the narrator soon confesses to having walked down the streets looking for her lover, to having gotten lost in the streets in which she had become lost with her, and to have refused to leave her house, and not gone to work, determined to take the last step. The descriptions of her feelings become almost dreamlike ("¿Y ahora qué? ¿Me hago una gargantilla que me apriete el cuello o se lo rebano a los topos y me hago una transfusión que cambie mi sangre por leche desnatada?" [And now what? Should I make myself a necklace that tightens around my neck, or should I slice it up giving it to the moles, and I give myself a transfusion that changes my blood for skimmed milk?] (152)), to end up denying the existence of the truth that she tried to reveal: "Digo que me duele darme cuenta de que todo lo que fue verdad era mentira, pero eso mismo es lo que debió de pensar ella cuando advirtió que yo no daba el salto mortal" [I am saying that it hurts to realize that everything that was true was a lie, but she must have thought the same thing when she noticed that I was not making the daring leap] (155).

The power of the confession is used against the instance that had required it as the narrator puts an end to her recollection of the story lived with her lover, admitting her initial incapacity to be "strong and brave," to support the weight of a true passion, but now admitting she is able to make "the daring leap," that is to say, to give herself completely to her lover. On the one hand, when the narrator loses contact with the world that surrounds her, the details displayed by the protagonist lose their legitimacy, suggesting that the "pardon" for the confession would be granted on the basis of improbable expositions, and raising doubt about the capacity of the power to reach the knowledge of the truth that it tried to discover. On the other hand, the admission that her error was indeed her inability to make the daring leap into a lesbian relationship destabilizes the heterosexual system on which the dominant discourse is based. The heteronorm, in order to grant the subject of the confession her innocence, to redeem her, to purify her, and to save her, will have to admit the prospect that a lesbian relationship is feasible, recognizing, "saying" the possibility of a plurality of sexualities, throwing away with that act the ballast of the ignorance that prevented it from accepting homosexuality as another acceptable expression of human sexuality.

Years later after his *History of Sexuality*, Foucault reelaborated his conception of the power of the confession, proposing that it does not seek the revelation of deep desires, but as Butler notices, the confession implies "an effort, through speech, to 'transform pure knowledge and simple consciousness in a real way of living" (Butler, *Undoing Gender*, 162). Thus, "[t]here are no desires that are muted by repressive rules, but, rather, only an operating by which the self constitutes itself in discourse with the assistance of another's presence and speech" (163). That is to say, then, that "[t]he point is not to ferret out desires and expose their truth in public, but rather to constitute a truth of oneself through the act of verbalization itself" (163). The protagonist of *Dame placer* knows that exposing the details of her confession is not going to change her situation, even though she underscores the control that prevails over her by doubting the capacity of her interlocutor to really be able to reach some useful conclusion ("Míreme a la cara. ¿Qué ve? Dígame, ¿qué puede ver a través de estos ojos, de estas arrugas, de esta boca y de estas canas? ¿Qué puede comprender usted de todo esto por unas cuantas palabras que salen de aquí y que ni siquiera anota, ni retiene? Subráyeme, hágame la letra pequeña, casi invisible, de su contrato feliz con la vida" [Look at me. What do you see? Tell me, what can you see in these eyes, in these wrinkles, this mouth and this grey hair? What can you understand of all this in a few words produced here and which you do not even write down, do not retain? Underline me, make me into the small font, almost invisible, of your happy contract with life] (69)). What the protagonist really takes advantage of is the opportunity that the surroundings of her confession give her "to say," to verbalize a repressed identity. Through her speech she declares that a lesbian sexuality exists indeed, one that can lead to the total enjoyment of the female body, that can lead her to identification with other women, to mutual recognition. Through the manipulation of the power of the confession, the protagonist finally loosens the ballast of the ignorance dragged by the heteronorm that ignored the possibility of a lesbian identity, allowing that the truth of that identity "suba hasta la superficie para hacerse visi-

254 INMACULADA PERTUSA-SEVA

ble flotando ante ojos capaces de reconocerla y, lo que es más importante aún, decirla" [to rise to the surface to become visible, floating before eyes capable of recognizing it and, what is more important still, of saying it.] (Company, "El pez austral").

MELALCOR: GENDER TROUBLE

While *Querida Nélida* and *Dame placer,* connected to lesbian identity and the expression of sexuality, initiate a process of destabilization of power strategies by means of the verbalization of sexualities repressed by the heteronormative discourse, in *Melalcor* we can recognize an alternative subversion of the hegemonic system that imposes sexual identities based on static gender constructions.

We can find the deconstructive strategy (allegorical) in which *Melalcor* is based in the formulation of a fictitious universe not so much different from our own. At the beginning of time, and in a very similar fashion to the biblical genesis that we are familiar with, the world of *Melalcor* began thanks to the "verbo divino" [divine verb], the Fuerza Creadora [the Creative Force], with everything created in black and white, as part of a harmonic, pure, and perfect order. "La pureza de los blancos y de los negros era el orgullo de la Fuerza Creadora del universo bicolor y, por esta razón, recomendó (ordenó) a sus habitantes que nunca se les pasara por la cabeza, bajo ningún concepto, mezclar el blanco y el negro, bajo amenaza de convertirlos en seres sin deseos, ni ilusiones, ni identidad" [The purity of the white ones and of the black ones was the pride of the Creative Force of the bicolor universe and, therefore, it recommended (it ordered) its inhabitants to never consider, under any circumstance, mixing blacks and whites, under the threat of turning them into beings without desires, illusions, or identity] (36). As expected, this bicolor universe is destroyed when its inhabitants "decidieron seguir su impulso y se mezclaron" [decided to follow their impulse and mixed] (37). The consequences were no less than foreseeable and the Fuerza Creadora, "vengativa, perfeccionista y obsesiva" [vindictive, perfectionist and obsessive] (37), was not satisfied with turning the insurgents, children of the Fuerza Destructiva [Destructive Force], gray, but also scattered the rest of the colors through the bicolor universe with the terrible curse of "[y]a no conoceréis la pureza y la perfección" [you will no longer know purity and perfection] (37). Subsequently, and under pressure from the original Gran Culpa [Great Original Fault], the descendants of the first inhabitants of the bicolor universe felt compelled to pair up with souls of the same color.

Following this arrangement, the anecdote that constructs the narrative frame of *Melalcor* develops another familiar argument: in their maturity, the two main characters, one of the narrative voices and Mel, childhood playmates, feel that their relationship goes beyond a mere friendship. Nevertheless they are individuals with souls of different colors, and even though everybody expected them to end up together, their union cannot be admitted within the system of the Fuerza Creadora which requires that souls of different colors are not to be mixed. In order to avoid greater problems, the father of the protagonist, Mr. Salvat, falsely promises to give her total control of the company if she breaks up with Mel. At the same time, both families encourage the protagonist to marry Mel's sister, and Mel to marry the protagonist's brother. In the classic line of a melodramatic novel, the protagonist agrees to run the family business, sacrificing the happiness that she could have had with Mel, thus rejecting Mel's proposal of fleeing the home town to go to the Ciudad (City) and live freely among people of many colors who are not under the prohibitive censorship of the Gran Culpa. From this moment on, the relationship between the protagonist and Mel becomes more and more distant, to the point that Mel does not want anything to do with her friend. Animated by a series of sexual encounters on the part of the narrator-protagonist, the plot arrives at its culminating point when, the day before Mel de Cor's wedding,[14] the protagonist admits her love for her, arriving unexpectedly at Mel's house to try to prevent her marriage to her hated brother. *Melalcor* concludes with a happy ending where the two lovers, after transgressing the social norm by mixing up their souls of different colors through the sexual act, flee to Paris with the millions stolen from Mr. Salvat to live happily ever after.

The subversive project that we need to recognize in *Melalcor* goes beyond the allegory of genesis and original sin. The subversion is developed in Company's novel from the text's implicit critique of the social institutions in which it is framed: church, family, the traditional couple, and marriage. There is no doubt that commentaries like "la familia es una institución caduca y demencial. Como la pareja" [family is an obsolete and idiotic institution. As is the traditional couple] (89), or "Yo creo que el amor no es sano, no es normal, no es ético, no es humano. Es una imposición cultural para obligarnos a ir a todos de dos en dos" [I believe that love is not healthy, it is not normal, it is not ethical, it is not human. It is a cultural imposition to force us to go two by two] (65), or even "No es nada fácil liberarse del miedo que produce la Gran Culpa" [It is not easy to free oneself from the fear produced by the Great Fault] (99) allude to a common feeling of uneasiness towards the society in which the characters live. Furthermore, *Melalcor* not only exposes the cracks of the moral and cultural framework in which its characters subsist but also points out the existence of a lesbian (alternative) sexual identity capable of developing its own desires and illusions in spite of the rigid normative margins delimited by the prevailing heteroideology.

In his *History of Sexuality*, Michel Foucault established that the concept of sexuality during the nineteenth century developed from the idea that "there exists something other than bodies, organs, somatic localizations, functions, anatomophysiological systems, sensations, and pleasures; something else and something more, with intrinsic properties and laws of its own: 'sex'" (152–53). In this context, and paraphrasing Butler, the body only acquires its sexual meaning in the moment that the power relationships of the dominant heterosexual discourse provide it with meaning by investing it with the "idea" of natural or essential sex.[15] As Butler notes,

[s]exuality is an historically specific organization of power, discourse, bodies, and affectivity. As such, sexuality is understood by Foucault to produce "sex" as an artificial concept which effectively extends and disguises the power relations responsible for its genesis (Butler, *Gender Trouble*, 92).

In *Melalcor* what places the subject at the margin of what is considered acceptable sexual behavior, condemning her transgression to a life "sin deseo, ni ilusiones, ni identidad" [without desire, illusions, or identity] (36), and in which "[y]a no conoce[rán] la pureza y la perfección" [they will not know purity and perfection] (37), is the criticism of this artificial cultural construction/imposition of the concept of sex and heterosexuality through the allegory of original sin. Therefore the cosmos represented in *Melalcor* does not attempt just to replace the terms of the problem (unacceptable relations between individuals of the same sex by condemning relationships between individuals with souls of different colors), but rather points out the weakness of the heterosexual construction of gender in which these relationships are considered perversions of the norm. The novel initiates the questioning of traditional institutions, by means of a defamiliarizing vision of sexuality and by articulating the representation of a fluid gender in trouble with the heteronorm. It is a vision that not only makes us "question what is real, and what 'must' be, but [it] also shows us how the norms that govern contemporary notions of reality can be questioned and how new modes of reality can become instituted" (Butler, *Undoing Gender*, 29), offering us an understanding of the body as something different that "makes us see how realities to which we thought we were confined are not written in stone" (Butler, *Undoing Gender*, 29).[16]

As Butler states when discussing the possibility of the female body locating itself outside the law of the father that relegates it to a position of submission and invisibility, "If subversion is possible, it will be a subversion from within the terms of the law, through the possibilities that emerge when the law turns against itself and spawns unexpected permutations of itself. The culturally constructed body will then be liberated, neither to its 'natural' past, nor to its original pleasures, but to an open future of cultural possibilities" (Butler, *Gender Trouble*, 93). In *Melalcor* the subversion that works inside the limits of the law is materialized in the story by means of the consummation of the sexual relationship between the main characters (the union of souls of different colors) and their consequent necessity to flee to Paris to be able to coexist with other individuals with the same affinities but who, like them, continue to be tied to the heterosystem that condemns their relationship; the sense of freedom reached by the protagonists acting against the rules of the Fuerza Creadora (the heteronorm) does not produce their return to the original paradise, but it provides them with the opportunity to learn new customs, new forms of life that respond to their physical (sexual) and emotional needs. Structurally, the subversion is expressed by the use of two different strategies: one through the use of a double narrative voice that challenges the sense of impartiality of the narrator, and another by the configuration of fluid bodies that oscillate between the masculine and the feminine (privileging the feminine) in order to dispute the heterobinomic conception that censures them.

The novel is divided into forty-eight sections or brief episodes that resemble those of a soap opera. Each section is identified by a title that, in a way, summarizes its contents. Within a narration characterized by fragmentation, the sections and titles serve as transmitters of the plot and as a useful and almost necessary guide to the reader who could get lost between the comings and goings of the story. If the first three sections are introduced by an omniscient narrator in the third person, from the fourth section on the narration begins alternating the narrative voice from the third to the first person, this being the voice of the anonymous protagonist. By studying the sections in which these changes take place, it is possible to say that there is no relation between the use of one narrative voice or the other and the referred events; what is more, we could even affirm that the ideology behind the thoughts of the omniscient narrator agrees with that of the narrator in the first person. This makes us think that we are exposed to the same narrative voice (the protagonist's) projected from two different points of view.

The effect of this double focalization of the narrative voice emphasizes the sexual ambiguity proposed in the text, in my opinion, by means of the fluctuation of the main characters' gender identity. At the same time as the oscillation between both narrators begins its alternation, the text exposes the protagonists' gender fluidity that will characterize the rest of the narration. Here are some examples:

> Encontraré a Mel más tarde—dice en voz baja—, en el Casino. Y jugaremos nuestra partida de cartas, y **la muy granuja** ganará porque hace trampas, y yo **la perdonaré** porque **es hermano mío,** no de sangre pero sí de hígado, porque lo que hemos **bebido juntas** no cabe ni en la bodega de la reina borracha (22) (emphasis added).

> [I will meet Mel later—she says quietly—, at the Casino. And we will play our card game, and **she,** so tricky, will win because **she** cheats, and I will forgive **her** because **he is my brother,** not of blood but of liver, because what **she** and I have drunk together does not fit even in the cellar of the drunken queen] (emphasis added).

> Yo, de Mel, quería tener un hijo; y que **ella hiciera de padre** y yo de madre; y que yo hiciera de madre y **él de padre.** ¿Por qué no? ¿Por qué? No se trata de preguntar por qué (140) (emphasis added).

> [I wanted to have a son with Mel; and I wanted **her to play the father** and I the mother; and that I would be the mother and **he the father.** Why not? Why? It is not about asking why] (emphasis added).

Although in the novel there are enough indications to establish that both main characters are women (as, for example, when the mother of the protagonist talks to her saying: "Es tu padre, y tiene razón . . . si fueras un hombre como él, lo entenderías. . . . Tu hermano piensa pedir la mano de Cor. Tu padre y yo estamos muy contentos, y suponemos que tú también te alegrarás. Será una buena esposa para tu hermano, una buena hija para nosotros y una adecuada hermana para ti" [He is your father, and he is right . . . if you were a man like him, you would understand. . . . Your brother is going to propose to Cor. Your father and I are very happy about it, and we suppose that you will also be glad. She will be a good wife for your brother, a good daughter for us, and a suitable sister for you] (104)), the arbitrary use of pronouns and adjectives that do not maintain gender agreement with the noun which they modify introduces the gender dispute that the novel promotes through the representation of unregulated gender performances by the protagonists. This phenomenon resembles the unexpected variations between the narrative voices that, as in the case of the masculine/feminine nominative exchange, physically force the reader to return to paragraphs already read to verify that it is indeed the text itself that is producing the dispute between the reference and the referee, and between a narrative voice and another, and not a careless reading. The result, in any case, is the destabilization on one hand of the traditional logocentric position that usually characterizes the narrative voice, and on the other, the imposed heteronormative gender identities.

In her discussion about gender normalization, and following Levi-Strauss's view of gender as "an index of the proscribed and prescribed sexual relations by which a subject is socially regulated and produced" (Butler, *Undoing Gender*, 47–48), Butler remarks on the impact of gender normalization on the individuals that it tries to regulate. While this North American philosopher accepts the possibility that gender norms are present in any social act, providing "a grid of legibility on the social and defining the parameter of what will and will not appear within the domain of the social" (42), she claims that to be outside the norm is to place oneself inside such a norm since it establishes the limit of itself because "if the norm renders the social field intelligible and normalizes that field for us, then being outside the norm is in some sense being defined still in relation to it" (42).

In another moment Butler points out the impossibility of destroying the restrictive space of the closet, given that in order *to be outside* a place, that place cannot stop existing as the reference *to being inside*.[17] Developing on this concept, when Butler analyzes the subversion sought by the representation of nonheterosexual bodies/behaviors, she also determines that social subjects cannot avoid living defined by the norm that they tried to disarticulate.[18] In order to detach the gender norm from the binary conception (man/woman, male/female, masculine/feminine), it is necessary to define oneself by what the norm regulates, offering an alternative performance beyond the heterobinomic coherence of masculinity and femininity, or as Butler says, beyond the restrictive gender discourse that "naturalizes the hegemonic instance and forecloses the thinkability of its disruption" (43).

As in the case of the confession, where the subject confessing her deviation from the norm has to overcome the series of impediments that had made her hide the truth about herself, thus reaching a certain level of liberation (purification, redemption, salvation), to be able to exhibit unregulated bodies and corporal functions, it is necessary to confront the obstacles created by that same norm that tries to naturalize such behavior in order to deny the subversive possibility they developed. In *Melalcor*, the representation of an alternative gender performance by the main characters fights against the effort of the restrictive discourse to naturalize them, finding explanations or solutions to what otherwise disputes the logic of its supremacy. In this way we can see that, although the protagonist's mother comments that Mel/Cor is pretending to be a man ("Cor está pasando un mal momento. Incluso dicen que se hace pasar por hombre y que en el estanco finge ser muda. ¡Pobre muchacha! [Cor is having a very bad time. They even say that she pretends to be a man and that at the cigarette store she also pretends to be mute. Poor girl!] (104)), this fact does not place her outside of the social regulation that identifies her as a woman since, according to the mother, when she assumes her biological feminine roles (to get married and have children with the first-born), she will be normalized by the very social rule that she threatens to destabilize with her peculiar behavior. As the mother explains: "Pero estoy segura que cuando comience a tener hijos se le pasarán todas esas manías. Las mujeres, cuando nos hacemos madres, somos otras. Si tú quisieras . . ." [But I am sure that when she begins having children all those odd habits will disappear. We women, when we become mothers, we are changed. If you wanted . . .] (104), confirming that her return to the gender and social functions attributed to her biological sex (to be woman, wife, mother) will free her from all those "odd habits" that dissociate her from the heteronorm.

Similarly, the change of sexual identity that Mel experiences is not perceived by her parents as a rebellion against the norm that she is visibly subverting with her sexual ambiguity, but it is justified as an individual reaction to an emotional situation that she is not able to assimilate, that is, her girlfriend's inability to admit her feelings for her. Apparently the narrator-protagonist seems to adjust to this process of normalizing Mel's "santa dualidad" [holy duality], as she calls it, by identifying it as a "ligero conflicto de personalidades" [slight conflict of personalities] when she explains that this conflict

> hizo que los progenitores de Mel o de Cor le pusieran un estanco. Los conocimientos de Mel en matemáticas hacen del estanco un buen negocio. La amabilidad lacónica de Cor atrae a los clientes. Por las mañanas, Cor está en el estanco. Por las tardes, Mel está en el casino (31).

> [resulted in Mel or Cor's parents opening a tobacco store for her. Mel's knowledge of mathematics contributes to the success of the store. Cor's laconic amiability attracts clients. In the mornings, Cor is at the store. In the afternoons, Mel is in the casino.]

More than to confirm that Mel's dual identity is a conflict of identities, and therefore accept the obstacle imposed by the heteronorm, the narrator insists on identifying both of her gender performances as part of a single individual, who is alternately man or woman, whether Mel wants to admit it or not:

> Cor o Mel se descubrió en una mesa arrinconada del casino y decidió ser la misma persona. Mel es la voz de Cor y Cor el cuerpo de Mel. . . . Cuando Cor es Mel, es un canalla. Cuando Mel es Cor, es una bellísima persona que, a veces, finge ser muda. . . . Alguna vez he intentado hablar con el uno del otro, pero aseguran que no se conocen (31).

> [Cor or Mel found herself in a corner table at the casino and decided to be the same person. Mel is the voice of Cor and Cor the body of Mel. . . . When Cor is Mel, he is a jerk. When Mel is Cor, she is a wonderful person who, sometimes, pretends to be mute . . . Sometimes I have tried to speak with one of them about the other, but they assure me that they do not know each other.]

By assigning masculine qualities to Cor and feminine ones to Mel, the protagonist-narrator justifies the duplicity in the mixture of masculine and feminine adjectives, articles, and pronouns when referring to her in the text, fighting against her parents' attempt to normalize Mel. When accepting, and consequently confirming her friend's gender fluidity, she debilitates the heterosexual norm, introducing the possibility of an alternative sexuality that operates within the very social and cultural margins that deny them.

Melalcor destabilizes the heterosexual concept of gender not only by developing Mel's manifestation of a fluid sexual identity but also by assigning to what turns out to be feminine bodies corporal acts associated socially and biologically with the masculine body. Without suggesting a hermaphrodite representation of the feminine body, the protagonist reproduces sexual gestures easily connected with the accepted concept of both normative feminine and masculine sexuality. The exchange/confusion of masculine and feminine generic markers, as well as Mel's changes of personalities throughout the novel, reinforces this effect. For example, we read:

> Decido ir caminando, aunque el sexo me molesta un poco. Lo tengo a punto de reventar. Necesito ponérselo en la boca y pasárselo por el culo. Viceversa después. . . . [quiero entrar] en el coche, bajarme los vaqueros y mostrarle cómo tengo el sexo. Ponérselo en las manos (131).

> [I decide to walk, although my sex bothers me a little. It is on the verge of bursting. I need to put it in her mouth and rub it on her ass. Vice versa later . . . [I want to get in] the car, pull down my pants and show her how my sex is. I want to put it in her hands.]

> Mientras subo, en el ascensor, me manoseo el sexo pensando en la boca y el culo de Alex. Cuando llego arriba, la puerta del piso está abierta. Voy directamente a la habitación. Me espera en la cama, a cuatro patas, sin una prenda de ropa. Genial. Tengo el sexo lleno de miel, tengo el corazón en el sexo. Necesito follar. Sin pensar. En absoluto (132).

> [While I go up in the elevator, I play with my sex thinking about Alex's mouth and ass. When I arrive, the apartment door is open. I go directly to the bedroom. Alex is waiting for me in the bed, on all fours, without any clothes on. Brilliant. My sex is full of honey, my heart is in my sex. I need to fuck. Without thinking. Not at all.]

The images summoned with the reference to her sex on the verge of bursting, or full of honey, respond to a description that could be considered as much that of the male organ at the moment before ejaculation as of the female organ in a state of sexual excitation before arriving at orgasm. The ambiguity of the biological sex of the protagonist's lovers (Alex can be the name of a woman or a man; and Meravin, the first sexual experience in the adult life of the protagonist, is never identified as man or woman) amplifies the effect of this alternative gender performance (neither masculine, nor feminine; masculine and feminine at the same time) introducing the possibility of sexual acts that are not limited to the ones accepted by the heteronorm.

The promiscuity characterized by the protagonist also refers to a sexuality that stands against the norm, that, as Butler remarks, operating outside the field of monogamy (and because of that outside the heteronorm), "may open us to a different sense of community, intensifying the question of where one finds enduring ties, and so become the condition for an attunement to losses that exceed a discretely private realm" (Butler, *Undoing Gender*, 26). What at a superficial level could be read in *Melalcor* as the protagonist's refusal to accept her feelings towards Mel (and by not doing so losing her relationship with her) should be seen as another subterfuge in the text to offer a valid perspective of lesbian relations in particular, and of relations that foment gender behaviors in dispute with the heteronorm in general. The protagonist's reflections towards the end of the novel as a result of the sexual encounters between Mel and Susan, the daughter of the Gran Puta, are directed towards the acceptance of alternative behaviors, which by their own manifestation produce a change in the way we see and accept our prevailing reality. The protagonist comments: "Sólo pasamos allí dos semanas, pero Mel tuvo tiempo de hacérselo como mínimo un par de veces con Susan. Es curioso hasta qué punto cambia la visión de la promiscuidad cuando queremos a alguien. Pero que cambie la visión no significa que cambien los actos" [We only spent two weeks there, but Mel had time to do it at least a couple of times with Susan. It is peculiar to what extent our view of promiscuity changes when we love somebody. But even if the view changes, it does not mean that the acts change] (244). After all, the point is to question the limits of the dominant discourse and destabilize its moral principles, its norms, offering possibilities that would be unthinkable within the established scope, since, as Butler indicates "when the unreal lays claim to reality, or enters into its domain, something other than a simple assimilation into prevailing norms can and does take place. The norms themselves can become rattled, display their instability, and become open to resignification" (*Undoing Gender*, 27–28).

The final break of the marriage between Mel de Cor and the first-born not only responds to the formula of a happy ending, with the protagonists running away, but it explains how the "unreal lays claim to reality, or enters into its domain," destabilizing the heteropatriarchal establishment that postulates marriage as the system by which gender/sexual conflicts are solved. The union between a man and a woman entails the supremacy of the social norm and solves the kinship problem (a family formed by a man, a woman, and their descendants). The main characters flee the day before the wedding and the appropriation of the wedding gown works again as a subversion of the norm within its own limits. ("Entonces, a medida que ella se lo quita, yo me pongo el vestido de novia encima del mío. Sé que quiere que lo haga. Me mira y sonríe toda desnuda" [Then, while she takes off her dress, I put it on over mine. I know that she wants me to do it. She looks at me and smiles, completely naked] (239)). The heteroideological system that requires the commitment of marriage to justify sexual relations and that tries to control the subject that has declared herself outside the norm is rejected (as in the case of Mel, who on the one hand showed a masculine identity when demanding to be treated as a man, and on the other insisted on maintaining a loving relationship with another person whose soul was of a different color). The protagonist's act of putting on the wedding gown over her clothes while Mel remains naked and pleased emphasizes the transgression of the heteronorm, introducing a heterogeneous conception of marriage where two souls of different colors can choose to complete symbolically the same union exclusively reserved to those of the same color.[19]

As we have seen, *Querida Nélida, Dame placer* and *Melalcor* are three novels that not only expose intensive lesbian relationships in dispute with the dominant heteronorms that repress them but also provide us with three models of representation of the lesbian subject: in *Querida Nélida*, via an intimate friendship between two woman that will allow each one to find herself in the other woman, thus reaching a sense of identity unknown for both of them until that moment; in *Dame placer*, through the recounting in confession style of an absolute passion between the female narrator and her lover, and that will be used to subvert the repressive power mechanism of the heteronorm; and in *Melalcor*, by the representation of a fluid gender identity that oscillates between the masculine and the feminine, at the same time privileging the lesbian identity, and in so doing, acknowledging its ability to exist as such. These novels allow us to understand not only how gender is instituted, naturalized, and established by hegemonic discourse, but also they lead us to challenge fixed gender categories by showing us that gender (desire and pleasure) is both flexible and unstable.

NOTES

1. Flavia Company, *Querida Nélida* (Barcelona: Montesinos Editor, S.A., 1987).
2. In an interview with Ana Alciana, Flavia Company explained how she met Miguel Riera, then director of *Quimera*, with the hope of finding a job at the magazine. During the meeting Riera asked her if she wrote fiction, and Company gave him, along with some poetry notebooks, a copy of the manuscript that ended up being called *Querida Nélida*. Fifteen days later, Riera called her to tell her that although he could not offer her a job at the magazine because at the moment there were no vacancies, he was interested in publishing the novel. Company accepted the offer without even changing a word in the original manuscript.
3. Flavia Company, *Dame placer* (Barcelona: Emecé Editores España, S.A., 1999).
4. Flavia Company, *Melalcor* (Barcelona: Edicions 62 S.A., 2000).
5. Meri Torras, "Addiciones y complicidades: placer, cuerpo y lenguaje o la osadía narrativa de Flavia Company," *Arbor* (Summer 2006): 625.
6. It is important to bear in mind the break from literary genres present in *Ni tu, ni jo ni ningú* (Barcelona: Península Ediciones 62, 1998), where we find what could be called a dramatic novel in which the characters/actors repeat the same actions, the same words, interchanging gender characteristics, clothing, and roles indiscriminately: or *Fuga y contrapuntos* (Barcelona: Montesinos Editor, S.A., 1989), where the narration evolves as if it were a musical composition inverted in time, and where the characters play their own roles as if they were the leads in a musical piece; or *La mitad sombría* (Barcelona: OVD Ediciones, 2006), Company's last novel, written in three voices gathering the experience of three different characters as each one fights to understand the reach of her own existence.
7. Ana Alciana, "Entrevista a Flavia Company," *Barcelona Review.* 22 (January–February 2001), http://www.barcelonareview.com/22/c_ent.htm.
8. It seems important to point out that the connection that we establish between *Querida Nélida, Dame placer*, and *Melalcor* does not correspond to a possible literary trilogy but, as we have indicated, to a thematic and ideological connection. Coincidently, according to the author, *Dame placer*, along with *Ni tú, ni jo ni ningú* and *Círculos de acíbar* (Barcelona: Montesinos Editor, S.A., 1992) constitute the trilogy of *the desire of the impossible*. As Company indicated: "Esta especie de trilogía, que no estaba premeditada, es un ciclo que

trata del deseo de lo imposible. Tomando como punto de partida las relaciones entre dos personas, el tema subyacente sería, en última instancia, el deseo de vivir para siempre. Una voluntad de intensidad absoluta que se basaría en el siempre y en el todo. Y eso significa no morirse nunca." [This trilogy, that was not premeditated, is a cycle that deals with the desire for the impossible. Taking the relationships between two people as a point of departure, the underlying theme would be the desire to live forever. An absolute intense will that would be based on the always and the whole. And that means to never die.] Interview by Lourdes Domínguez, *Avui*. Summer (August 21, 2001): 9, quoted in Torras, "Addiciones."

9. For a discussion of this aspect of the lesbian sexuality, see Inmaculada Pertusa *Lecturas desde la otra acera* (Gijón: Llibros del Pexe, SL, 2005).

10. Flavia Company, "*Lo de ella*, de Concha García." *Adamar: Revista de Creación* 6(21) (2005). http://www.adamar.org/numero_15/000018.company .htm.

11. Flavia Company, "El pez austral: Hallazgos," *Diario ABC* 2003. *El cultural.* http://cultural.abc.es/semanal/semana/fijas/libros/firmas_003.asp.

12. Michel Foucault, *The History of Sexuality*, Vol. 1, trans. Robert Hurley (New York: Pantheon Books, 1978), 61–62.

13. Judith Butler, *Undoing Gender* (Routledge: New York, 2004), 52.

14. Mel's character shows a double identity, or as the protagonist calls it a "santa dualidad" [holy duality], being sometimes Mel, and sometimes Cor. When the protagonist talks about her girlfriend in an affectionate way, she calls her Mel, and when she talks about the aspect of Mel that is going to get married to her brother, she calls her Cor. It is only the day before the wedding when she uses 'Mel de Cor' to refer to her, but using Mel again after they both flee to Paris to live together.

15. Judith Butler, *Gender Trouble: Feminism and The Subversion of Identity* (New York: Routledge, 1990), 92.

16. I disagree with Ricardo Senabre when he says that Melalcor shows "una mentalidad generacional que ha soñado la gran aventura de cambiar todo el orden de cosas recibido para acabar operando leves transformaciones superficiales después de descubrir que existen fenómenos perdurables y sentimientos contra los que resulta difícil erigir barreras ideológicas" [a generational mentality that has dreamed about changing all the imposed concepts to end up making only small changes after realizing that there are invariable facts and feelings against which it is difficult to build ideological barriers]. Ricardo Senabre, "Melalcor de Flavia Company," *El cultural* (January 20, 2001), http://www .elcultural.es/historico_articulo.asp?c = 1852). While I accept Company's disagreement with her social situation, I believe that the novel suggests deeper transformations than those mentioned by Senabre.

17. For an extended explanation of this paradox, see Judith Butler, "Imitation and Gender Insubordination" in *Inside/Out: Lesbian Theories, Gay Theories*, ed. Dianna Fuss, 13–31 (New York: Routledge, 1991).

18. In that respect, François Ewald indicates: "Normative individualization is not exterior. The abnormal does not have a nature which is different from that of the normal. The norm, or normative space, knows no outside. The norm integrates anything which might attempt to go beyond it—nothing, nobody, whatever difference it might display, can ever claim to be exterior, or claim to possess an otherness which would actually make it other" (cited in Butler, *Undoing Gender*, 2004, 51).

19. Even though the novel was published in 2000 (2001 in Spanish), and it was not until 2005 when the Spanish government approved the law that recognizes civil union between same-sex couples, we cannot but connect this scene, and our interpretation of it, to the discussions developed in Spain about the effect of gay marriage on Spanish social norms and to the discussions of the ultraconservative parties that see the union between same-sex couples as an appropriation of what is for them one of the most sacred rituals, reserved only to the union between a man and a woman.

REFERENCES

Alciana, Ana. "Entrevista a Flavia Company" *Barcelona Review.* 22 (January–February 2001), http://www.barcelonareview.com/22/c_ent.htm.

Butler, Judith. *Gender Trouble: Feminism and The Subversion of Identity.* New York: Routledge, 1990.

———. "Imitation and Gender Insubordination." In *Inside/Out: Lesbian Theories, Gay Theories,* edited by Dianna Fuss, 13–31. New York: Routledge, 1991.

———. *Undoing Gender.* New York: Routledge, 2004.

Company, Flavia. *Círculos en acíbar.* Barcelona: Montesinos Editor, S.A., 1992.

———. *Dame placer.* Barcelona: Emecé Editores España, S.A., 1999.

———. *Fuga y contrapuntos.* Barcelona: Montesinos Editor, S.A., 1989.

———. *La mitad sombría.* Barcelona: DVD Ediciones, 2006.

———. "*Lo de ella,* de Concha García." *Adamar: Revista de Creación* 6 (21) (2005) http://www.adamar.org/numero_15/000018.company.htm.

———. *Llum de gel.* Tarragona: El Mèdol, Edicions, 1996. (*Luz de hielo.* Vitoria: Bassarai Ediciones, 1998).

———. *Melalcor.* Barcelona: Edicions 62 S.A., 2000.

———. *Ni tu, ni jo, ni ningú.* Barcelona: Península. Edicions 62, 1998. (*Ni tu, ni yo, ni ninguno.* Barcelona: Península Ediciones 62, 1998).

———. "El pez austral: *Hallazgos.*" *Diario ABC* 2003. *El cultural.* http://cultural.abc.es/semanal/semana/fijas/libros/firmas_003.asp.

———. *Querida Nélida.* Barcelona: Montesinos Editor, S.A., 1987.

———. *Viatges subterranis.* Tarragona: El Mèdol, Edicions, 1993. (*Viajes subterráneos.* Vitoria: Bassarai Ediciones, 1997).

Foucault, Michel. *The History of Sexuality.* Vol. 1. Translated by Robert Hurley. New York: Pantheon Books, 1978.

Gutiérrez Pardina, Eva. *Cuatro caras de Hermes en la obra narrativa de Flavia Company.* PhD diss., Universitat Rovira i Virgili. 2006.

———. "*Género de punto* de Flavia Company." *Lateral: Revista de Cultura* 106 (October 2003). http://www.lateral-ed.es/revista/estanteria/106estanteria.html.

Larios Vendrell, Luis. "Flavia Company. *Melalcor.*" *Word Literature Today* 75:3/4 (Summer/Autumn 2001): 230.

Pertusa, Inmaculada. *Lecturas desde la otra acera.* Gijon: Llibros del Pexe, SL, 2005.

Senabre, Ricardo. "*Melalcor* de Flavia Company." *El cultural* (January 20, 2001). http://www.elcultural.es/historico_articulo.asp?c = 1852.

Torras, Meri. "Addiciones y complicidades: placer, cuerpo y lenguaje o la osadía narrativa de Flavia Company." *Arbor* (Summer 2006): 623–33.

Contributors

Jacky Collins is Senior Lecturer in Spanish Studies at Northumbria University, Newcastle upon Tyne, United Kingdom. Her main area of research is lesbian cultures in contemporary Spain. She is a contributor to *Contemporary Spanish Cultural Studies* (2000) by Barry Jordan and Rikki Morgan-Tamosunas, and *Women in Contemporary Culture: Roles and Identities in France and Spain* (2000) by Lesley Twomey. She is co-editor of *Mujeres Malas: Women's Detective Fiction from Spain* (2005), *Hispanic and Luso-Brazilian Detective Fiction: Essays on the Género Negro Tradition* (2006), and *Crime Scene Spain* (2009). She is currently working on the lesbian body in Spanish popular fiction and representations of lesbian motherhood in contemporary European cinema.

Maria DiFrancesco is Associate Professor of Spanish at Ithaca College in New York. A graduate of the University of Buffalo, Dr. DiFrancesco's research, presentations, publications, and teaching focus on the contemporary literature of Spain. She is the author of *Feminine Agency and Transgression in Post-Franco Spain* (Juan de la Cuesta–Hispanic Monographs) and is currently at work on another book-length manuscript on approaches to teaching about immigration, race, and ethnicity in Spanish literature, film, and other popular media.

Margaret G. Frohlich is Assistant Professor of the Department of Spanish and Portuguese at Dickinson College in Pennsylvania. She specializes in twentieth-century and contemporary narrative, with a focus on the construction of national and sexual identities. Her book, *Framing the Margin: Nationality and Sexuality across Borders* (2008), won the international competition for the Victoria Urbano Monograph Prize of the Asociación Internacional de Literatura y Cultura Femenina Hispánica.

Encarnación Hidalgo Tenorio works at the University of Granada, where she teaches English language and linguistics.

269

She is interested in the study of the relationship between language, gender, and ideology within the framework of Critical Discourse Analysis. Her recent research examines the linguistic representation of individuals and (minority) groups in the media and other socially relevant contexts. For some years, her research has been focused on metaphor in Irish politics and also the Spanish Parliament, the linguistic behavior of politicians, and the way they depict reality.

MARTA SOFÍA LÓPEZ RODRÍGUEZ is Senior Lecturer in the Department of Modern Languages at the University of León, Spain, where she teaches post-colonial and women's studies. She has published widely in those fields and has actively collaborated with local women's and queer associations in the organization of different cultural and political events.

INMACULADA PERTUSA-SEVA received her PhD from the University of Colorado at Boulder after completing her *licenciatura* in journalism at the Universidad Complutense in Madrid. She is currently Associate Professor of Spanish Literature at Western Kentucky University and previously taught at the University of Kentucky with the rank of Associate Professor. Her area of specialization is contemporary peninsular and Latin American literature in the field of gender and lesbian studies. Having authored a number of articles on Spanish women writers, She is co-editor of the book *Tortilleras: Hispanic and U.S. Latina Lesbian Expression* (2003), and is the author of *La salida del armario: Lecturas desde la otra acera* (2005), a book on the coming-out process in texts by Spanish writers Esther Tusquets, Carme Riera, Cristina Peri Rossi, and Sylvia Molloy. Together with Professor Nancy Vosburg, Dr. Pertusa has published an anthology of selected lesbian narratives by contemporary Spanish women writers in the past sixty years titled *Un deseo propio* (2009).

RAQUEL PLATERO is a political activist and researcher at the Universidad Complutense in Madrid, Spain. Her work relates to policy frames and entrance in the political agenda of LGBT issues in Spain: the inclusion/exclusion of sexual orientation in gender equality policies, the creation of public services for LGBT people, and lesbian feminist discourses and their impact on gender equality policies.

JILL ROBBINS is associate Professor of Spanish literature and culture at the University of Texas at Austin. She is the author of

Frames of Referents: The Postmodern Poetry of Guillermo Carnero (Bucknell University Press, 1997) and editor of *P/Herversions: Critical Studies of Ana Rossetti* (Bucknell University Press, 2004). With Roberta Johnson Dr. Robbins co-edited a special issue of *Studies in 20th/21st Century Literature* on "Rethinking Spain From Across the Seas" (Winter 2006). In addition, she has written several articles on contemporary Spanish authors, with particular emphasis on women, including María Victoria Atencia, Ana María Moix, Julia Uceda, Angela Figuera, Almudena Grandes, and others in the Spanish publishing business. Her most recent book, *Crossing Through Chueca: Lesbian Literary Identities in Queer Madrid*, which examines the mechanisms of lesbian cultural production in the capital with emphasis on the book business, is forthcoming.

YOLANDA SÁNCHEZ PAZ is owner and operator of the oldest lesbian and gay bar in León, Spain. She was one of the founding members of the local queer association, and her establishment is one of the main points of reference for the lesbian and gay community in León.

NANCY VOSBURG is Professor of Spanish and Chair, Modern Languages & Literatures at Stetson University, DeLand, Florida, where she teaches Spanish literature and culture. Her presentations and publications focus on twentieth-century Spanish women writers in exile, women's detective fiction in Spain, contemporary Spanish women writers, and Spanish popular fiction. Co-editor with Kathleen McNerney of *The Garden Across the Border: Mercè Rodoreda's Fiction*, and co-author, with Inmaculada Pertusa-Seva, of *Un deseo propio*, an anthology of selected lesbian narratives from Spain, she is currently editing a volume on Iberian peninsular crime fiction.

Index